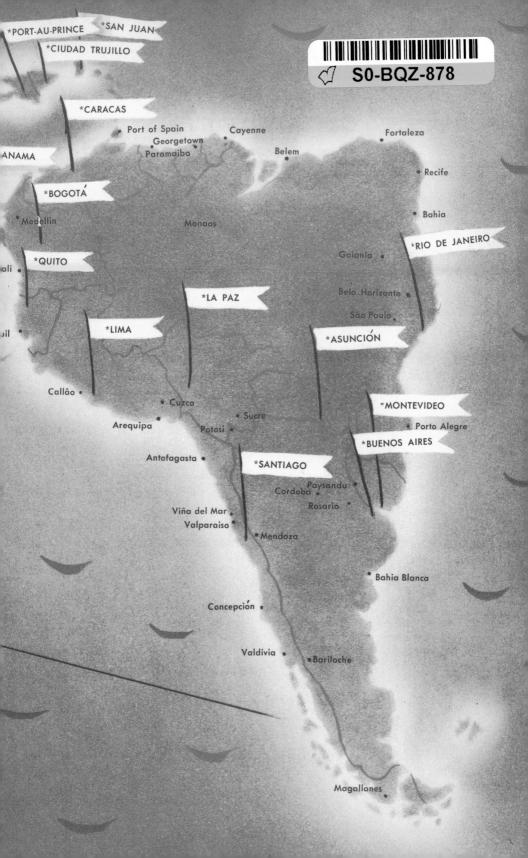

*PORT-AU-PRINCE   *SAN JUAN
*CIUDAD TRUJILLO

*CARACAS

Port of Spain   Cayenne   Fortaleza
Georgetown   Belem
Paramaibo   Recife

ANAMA

*BOGOTÁ
Medellin   Manaos   Bahia

*RIO DE JANEIRO

*QUITO   Goiania

ali   Belo Horizonte
*LA PAZ   São Paulo

*LIMA   *ASUNCIÓN

uil

Callâo   Cuzco
                                   Sucre   *MONTEVIDEO
Arequipa   Potosí   Porto Alegre
                                                *BUENOS AIRES
Antofagasta
                   *SANTIAGO
                                     Paysandu
                          Cordoba
Viña del Mar   Rosario
Valparaiso
              Mendoza

                                Bahia Blanca

Concepción

Valdivia   Bariloche

Magallanes

Cities of Latin America

Cities of Latin America

Housing and planning to the south

Francis Violich

REINHOLD PUBLISHING CORPORATION, N. Y.

NA
9159
V5

stacked 4-5

25573

To
My Mother and Phil,
who shared in this

CONTENTS

Introduction

This is more than a book about cities. This is a book about the effect of cities on the lives of human beings and about new forces that are pointing the way toward social advance in urban environment. It is based on the belief that no man in any country can longer afford to let the future of his city take care of itself, but that he must study his urban environment's pains, aches, and discomforts just as the doctor studies the human body, in order to guide the future form of the city so that it will function to suit his own well-being.

The purpose is to pass on certain knowledge and observations to all Americans, both North and South, who are interested in causes and effects of inhuman urban environments and in their removal through the application of intelligent human effort. The book is about Latin American cities because North Americans have too long thought of those cities as spots upon a map, spots without a vital past, present or future, rather than as urban centers inhabited by living, thinking individuals as highly concerned over their own welfare as are North Americans.

The material on which the volume is based was collected during a survey of urban problems and plans in ten Latin-American countries, chosen because they are relatively important and accessible. The survey began in Mexico and continued over a period of ten months and a distance of some 22,000 miles. The author made a brief stop in Guatemala, and longer visits in Colombia, Ecuador, Peru, and Bolivia. Even more time was spent in Chile and Argentina, Uruguay and Brazil. Venezuela and Paraguay, of the South American republics, and several countries in Central America and the Caribbean had to be omitted because of problems which arose under war conditions after the survey had begun.

The author followed a specific outline of desired information, got in touch with personnel of the professional fields of urban planning, architecture, and low-cost housing, and spoke with others informed on the social, economic, and political backgrounds of the cities of Latin America. Interviews were held with architects, engineers, government officials, and a few *alcaldes*, or mayors; valuable information and points of view were often obtained from informal conversations with people from all walks of life. Planning developments, slums, and housing projects were visited and photographed; a large amount of documentary material was collected in the form of maps, plans, reports, and books.

The survey itself was prompted by a need for a general picture of urban planning and housing practice in Latin America, in the interest of promoting closer professional relations with the technicians of those countries. The study was made possible through the Columbia Foundation of San Francisco, whose Executive Director, Marjorie de Young Elkus, showed an active interest from the beginning and encouraged the author to continue the project in spite of war-created difficulties.

In preparing the book, material has been organized by subjects rather than by countries in order to facilitate a rational discussion of the various phases of urban development. The reader interested in any single Latin American country or city is referred to the Index. No attempt has been made to present a comprehensive work covering all aspects of all cities of Latin America, but rather to provide in a readable form the first-hand knowledge gathered and the observations made.

Acknowledgments are gratefully expressed to many individuals in the planning and housing field in the United States, who offered helpful suggestions and support. Among them are Catherine Bauer, Lewis Mumford, Howard Moise, Vernon de Mars, Frederick Adams, Jack Kent, I. S. Shattuck, H. Leland Vaughan and Dr. J. C. Geiger. Many members of *Telesis* contributed indirectly toward the objectives and framework of the survey. I am grateful to Walter Blucher, of the *American Society of Planning Officials*, for his encouragement; and to Julien Bryan, whose films suggested the study.

I wish to thank Jeannette Gormley, Margaret Lyon, and Lucile Gay for assistance in preparing the material, John Ekin Dinwiddie for work space, and Walter Landor for his contributions toward format design.

Writing the book would have been impossible without the aid of two persons to whom I am especially indebted: Lucile M. Teague of the *University of California's Department of Landscape Design,* who typed endless drafts, and Dorothy Erskine of San Francisco, who contributed constructive editorial criticism.

Acknowledgments would be incomplete without praise of the generous and hospitable assistance offered by technicians in the planning, housing, and related fields in Latin America. Their expressions of cooperation seemed to be directed not to this individual technician alone, but to all members of planning and housing groups in the United States. No request was too great to be fulfilled. My apologies go to all those enthusiastic *simpáticos amigos* who were always most anxious that I spend more time in their particular country than my schedule permitted.

Such cooperation is a sincere indication of the common bonds that exist between professional and technical men and women of the Americas—and of common bonds among planning and housing people everywhere—which unite them in their desire to apply their ability to provide for all of us an improved, increasingly rational, twentieth-century environment.

FRANCIS VIOLICH

San Francisco, California
April, 1944

Not Fifth Avenue in New York City, but Diagonal Norte in Buenos Aires—with a subtle flavor of its own, yet how like the "main stem" of a North American city!

chapter 1

Differences can be bonds

1. We Take a Lot for Granted

We take a lot for granted here in the United States. That was the first thing I learned from the cities of Latin America. One way to find out something about the place in which one lives is to travel away from it for a while; I found that ten months among the Americans to the South is an excellent way to find out something about ourselves, Americans to the North.

On my return to the United States I became aware of how much we take for granted our cities and all that they contain: our high standard of living, our advanced technical skill, our radios, mechanical refrigerators, and cars—all the wealth of our industrial development—to say nothing of our social standards in regard to education, democracy, and opportunities to make the most of life. Our isolationist thinking even led us to take for granted our security in North America, and to build a mental Maginot Line around ourselves. We settled back to enjoy what we believed to be a satisfactorily full environment, until we were aroused by Pearl Harbor, or to a degree even earlier, by the threatened success of less self-satisfied national groups who had designs on our Latin American neighbors. We then realized how we had ignored the rest of the world, particularly those with whom we had most in common—the other republics of the New World. We knew far too little about them.

As students, our lack of schooling in the history, geography, and culture of the Latin-American republics has been nothing short of scandalous. As adults, our lack of accurate knowledge of the peoples, their politics, their economic and social problems, remains inexcusable.

In studying history, we are taught, in effect, that our Revolutionary leaders alone carried forward the principles of human freedom in this hemisphere; yet South America had San Martín, Bolívar, Bartolomé Mitre—men whose ideals of democracy equalled those of Washington, Jefferson and Abraham Lincoln. We are too often ignorant of these men who fought for the freedom of the southern half of the New World. We also fail in South American geography; confuse Paraguay and Uruguay; put Buenos Aires in Brazil; think of Chile as largely Indian; consider all South America hot and tropical. Thanks to Carmen Miranda, the Brazilian goodwill ambassador of song, we have nearly gotten over the mistaken belief that the people of Brazil speak Spanish. To point the moral in political terms, we think of the Latin-American countries more or less as states rather than as separate, distinct republics, each with its own characteristics. We call ourselves "Americans" and reserve the more accurate term "North Americans" for the Iroquois, the Apaches, and the Blackfeet. All residents of the New World, North or South, have equal claim to the name *Americans*.

We seem to believe ourselves the only people entitled to the products of modern technology—as a kind of reward for "right living" these past centuries. We have not considered the part played in our advance by the factors of geography and natural resources. We have gone blithely along heaping laurels upon ourselves, contemptuous of an inferior world.

Now, I found that Latin Americans are neither inclined to take so much for granted, nor to make such unsound assumptions. I found that although many of them have modern homes equipped with radios and electric refrigerators, and enjoy great wealth and high standards of education and democracy, these benefits of modern life simply do not exist to anything like the degree to which they do in the cities of the United States. They exist, of course, but inconsistently and in spotty patches. Latin Americans are aware of some very apparent differences between their environment and ours, and they are also conscious of the significance of some of these differences. Because they are avid to know what the rest of the world looks like and why, and because they have never luxuriated in isolationism, Latins know us far better than we know them.

Take my friend Eduardo, of São Paulo. I met Eduardo in the dining car of the jolting, crowded train on the way from São Paulo to Rio, one night before an important holiday. He sat opposite me talking Portuguese with Max from Santos, but when I got into difficulties ordering dinner, he broke into good English and came to my rescue. After dinner the train stopped and didn't budge again even after we had killed two bottles of Brazilian beer. It seemed to be waiting for something, so we got off to walk around in the cool, damp air. He asked me my name and I told him. He said,

2

"Mine's Eduardo, but you can call me Eddie." Then he proceeded to whistle a tune which I didn't know. I said, "What's that, a new Brazilian number?" "Brazilian, my foot! That's *Elmer's Tune*. It's being done to death all over the States. Don't you ever listen to short wave? You know this one?" And he broke into *Papacito*, otherwise known as *Daddy*. I said, "Sure, I know that one, only too well!" He grinned, "I'm sick of it too, but it's really O.K. for swing . . . so's *Chattanooga Choo-Choo* . . . you like swing?" I told him that I did and that I liked the Brazilian samba too.

So we started talking about "the States" and Eddie asked me if I knew the Radio City Music Hall. I said I did. "Well," he said, "You know the black glass lobby with the gold decoration, and inside—the way the ramps come down from the stage where the Rockettes sometimes give the audience a special treat?" Then he thoroughly covered the Waldorf-Astoria and its forty-seven stories; told me about the Park Avenue entrance and the murals in the Sert Room. Eddie went on to talk about the great bridges that span the East River and the Hudson, about our parkways that link the suburbs and the open country with the urban concentration of New York ". . . and out West," he said, "the Grand Canyon—that's a wonderful place but it does seem to me that Bryce Canyon is really more beautiful, maybe less dramatic. . . . Most dramatic of all is your Boulder Dam."

I said, "I'm from San Francisco—tell me something about my home town." And he described in detail our two great bridges, Telegraph Hill, the Coit Tower, Powell Street and the cable cars, the Ferry Building, and even the new subsurface garage four stories under Union Square. So finally I said, "Look here, Eddie, how much time did you spend in the States altogether?" And he said, "Who, me? Why, I've never been in the States."

I met many Eduardos, Guillermos, and Albertos, who liked to be called Eddie or Bill or Al, and who didn't have to travel in the United States in order to know that we have achieved a greater material progress than any other large nation in the world. Eddie kept his eyes open, learned English, and read everything on the United States that came his way. What didn't come his way he sent for—to our National Park offices, our city and state Chambers of Commerce, to young friends at school in New York, Chicago, and San Francisco.

Of course we can make very adequate excuses for ourselves and say that there is not yet enough information available on Latin America, or that traveling down there has been difficult or expensive, or that we just haven't the time. As a matter of fact, North Americans have traveled, extensively, but too often in luxury liners whose high-priced splendors have kept us from rubbing shoulders, either mentally or physically, with the good common people of other lands. We always had time for a Caribbean cruise or an all-expense jaunt to Hawaii, the escape paradise of the Pacific—until the shock of Pearl Harbor cut off our last means of escape and set us face to face with the real problems of our time.

For some while I had been curious about South America, especially since we undertook the good neighbor policy. I had worked as a technician in the fields of architecture, planning, and housing, with only a partial satisfaction in the effectiveness of those professions. My early school training had obscured my view of the southern half of our New World, even though it gave me a clear enough picture of the Old World of my father's origin. I went beyond my textbooks to rediscover that Old World, but soon my curiosity to know the remainder of the Americas got the best of me. I began to inquire about their cities as an expression of the people and the countries. I asked what they had done about housing and modern architecture, and what sort of planning *they* were doing and had done for the common man. I could find nothing in the United States about their work, although plenty of material on accomplishments in Europe had been published.

I decided to go down and see for myself. Through their cities I wanted to understand our neighbors, and to weigh the southern half of the New World against the northern half in which I happened to have been born. Here are some of the questions to which I wanted to find answers: How do the Americans of Latin America live? How do their cities compare with ours? To what degree of effectiveness is democracy operating in supplying the material needs of the citizens of the other American republics? What are their technicians, architects, and engineers doing about the living conditions of the common man? Are Latin Americans planning for the future of their cities, or is the future being allowed to take care of itself? And especially, *what can we learn from Latin Americans about building better cities for ourselves?*

2. The Background of Differences

As I traveled from one country to another, I found that even before I could begin to learn the answers to these questions, there was much of a general nature to be understood. I found that first I had to become aware of a certain background of differences, always startling because of their sharp, jolting contrast. In order to understand anything at all about the cities of Latin America, you, as well as I, must become more fully aware of these enormous contrasts and the complex reasons for them.

First, there are those numerous differences that exist between the United States and Latin America—differences that penetrate every phase of activity—political, social, and economic.

Second, the differences between the various Latin American countries themselves—historical and geographical, racial, and climatic.

Third, the differences that occur *within* each of the countries due to the influences of history, people, and geography.

Each of these differences must constantly be borne in mind when evaluating, in relation to any set of standards you choose, the work and problems of the Latins. Although many of them have been studied before, and written about much more completely by others, the fresh surprise which I experienced upon first-hand contact with them may serve to make my story more pointed.

3. Temperate Valleys vs. Andes and Jungle

First of all, we cannot overlook geography; geographical factors have greatly affected, in quite diverse ways, the development of the United States and that of Latin America. Compare the respective areas: Continental United States contains slightly more than 3,000,-000 square miles; while all of Latin America totals almost three times that amount of land area, 8,000,000 square miles. Natural barriers—the towering Andes, the sterile coastal desert of Atacama, the tangled jungles of Brazil, the heat and disease of the tropics, the enormous distances—all these have discouraged or prevented intercommunication, intermingling, and mutual understanding which might have occurred among Latin American peoples. The Incas in Peru realized this early in the development of their Empire, which they unified partly by means of a great system of roads. In the United States, easily navigable rivers, a temperate climate, passable mountain ranges, and resources easy to develop, encouraged early intercommunication between peoples and facilitated their political unification. In contrast, Ecuador and Peru, for example, situated in the most inaccessible portion of the west coast of South America, were virtually cut off from Europe until the opening of the Panama Canal; and progress in those two countries dates abruptly from that time. We in the United States certainly got the geographic plum of the rich Western Hemisphere basket, and although it is to our credit that we have put it to good use, we could hardly have avoided doing otherwise.

Geography in Latin America refuses to be tame, well-ordered, or to aid mankind in producing his necessities. An enormous variety of geographic and climatic conditions makes each country quite different from any other. These contrasting extremes can only be realized thoroughly when one has traveled in a few hours from the normal air pressure of sea level to the rarefied atmosphere of high mountain valleys in the Andes; or in a few weeks from the subtropic equatorial regions, hot and damp, to the temperate latitudes of Chile and Argentina.

People in the United States ask, "How was the climate down there—was it hot?" and you answer, "How is the climate in North

America?" The answer, of course, is that South America is hot, and cold, and rainy, and damp, and sunny, and foggy, and dry, and everything that is found in North America from Panama to Alaska. It is everything that tropic and temperate conditions permit, everything that sea level and 16,000-foot elevations produce. South America has every kind of climate to be found in any part of the world— all on one continent. Brazil no more resembles Chile than Oregon resembles Arizona. Our fixation on tropical South America is one delusion which we must get over quickly. Colombia has intense, damp heat and tropic living conditions in the lower elevations; there, people move about slowly in the few clothes that the tropics require. Higher up at Cali or Medellín, at what the Colombians call *Tierra Media,* you find warm, dry, southern-California climate and cool nights; while in Bogotá, the capital, black overcoats and heavy scarfs reinforce the populace against the cold winds and north-Europe temperatures.

In northern Chile, however, these same Andean heights look down on a burning sterile desert which hasn't been cooled by a drop of rain in forty years. You come down from the vacant heights of the Bolivian *altiplano*—plateau land—where, at 12,000 feet, Bolivia is bleak and cold, to sea level in northern Chile, and find this desert of Atacama—hot, dry, and completely devoid of vegetation. Almost 1,000 miles south at Santiago the capital of Chile, the climate is warm and dry, and the rich valleys, 2,000 feet above sea level, are full of green vegetation. The result is an abundance of fresh fruit—huge peaches, melons, grapes, "plenty of plenty," and it is a great relief to see healthy, well-fed people for a change. Traveling farther south through Chile is like going from southern California to Oregon and Washington. If you go far enough you find an Alaska-like climate, with deep fiords and glaciers. The only republics which are really tropic—and then only to a degree—are Colombia and Ecuador along the coast; northern Peru; Venezuela; and much of Brazil.

Topography as well as climate varies greatly. The West Coast is precipitous: the Andes soar up to 10,000-foot valleys, higher to many 20,000-foot, snow-capped peaks, and even to Mt. Aconcagua, highest point in the hemisphere, 23,080 feet above the sea. Such vertical geography contrasts sharply with the Texas-like flatness of Argentina, so effectively described by the horizontal line appearing in the background of every drawing of Molina Campos, the Argentine painter of the gaucho. Brazil undulates back from the sea in rolling hills, uplands, and small yet rugged mountains, the highest of which rises to only 9,462 feet.

What makes Latin America constantly interesting to the traveler, and often a problem to herself, are these sudden changes, which also take place *within* each of the countries. In all the West

Coast countries, differences in altitude separate and influence people as completely as do the thousands of miles of flat grazing land known in Argentina as the *pampa,* and the rolling pioneer country known to the Brazilians as their *sertão.* These geographic contrasts have caused contrasting degrees of human development.

And so one finds different types of people. In Colombia, the high, cold plateau on which Bogotá is located has had this effect: Bogotá is a cosmopolitan center, with a quiet, intellectual populace, while down in the warmer valleys of Antioquia where Medellín is located, the Antioqueño is an aggressive, industrially-minded man, who in turn is creating an evironment and way of life different from that of Bogotá. These changes in elevation are so strongly marked and have such a definite bearing on the lives of the people, that Colombians speak of them as regions marked by vertical bands of distinction. You can go from *Tierra Caliente*—anywhere in the tropical lowlands along the Caribbean and Pacific shores—to *Tierra Media*—half way up the Andes—and finally to *Tierra Fria,* the Andean highlands.

Medellín typifies the eternal spring of Tierra Media. The town lies in a beautiful valley some thirty miles wide and twice as long. Looking down from a plane, you see along the sloping sides of the valley the estates and country houses of the wealthier Antioqueños, with rolling lawns, swimming pools, tennis courts, and formal gardens. Down on the flatter land are the small farms, neatly cultivated and divided by long rows of tall waving bamboo trees which resemble the Lombardy poplars characteristic of the French countryside.

Flying up to Bogotá in an hour and a half is like traveling two thousand miles from southern France to a city in northern Russia or Poland—not the usual notion of South America. The snappy air of Bogotá brings to mind the ski country of New England or the High Sierras of California; and as you walk down the narrow streets to the Plaza Bolívar where 405 years ago Jimenez de Quesada built the first houses of Bogotá—today the site of the capitol and the cathedral—you see the men of the city well fortified against the cold with long black overcoats or heavy black ponchos. The few women you see on the streets of Bogotá are likewise warmly dressed. But Colombia is only one example—Ecuador, Peru, and Bolivia have similar vertical bands of separation, and as widely differing peoples.

In Chile one must travel by land the thousand miles from that strangely colored northern coastal desert of Atacama to the green-hued valleys near Santiago, to understand the hard, cold geographic facts that have caused many of the problems of that lovely country. Four distinctly differing geographic regions—the deserts of the north, the fertile valley areas of the central section, the green, timbered south, and the region of fiords and icebergs extending on to

Tierra del Fuego—have produced four uncoordinated spheres of economic and social activity. Such changes within each of the countries suggest reasons for some problems found in their cities.

4. Pilgrims vs. Conquistadores

If geographic factors have been basic in differentiating North and South America, so also have historic contrasts. From the very first, our United States and the countries of Latin America have had divergent backgrounds. In the early days, to Latin America came the Conquistador, an adventurer in search of the legendary Gilded Man of El Dorado, symbol of the mineral riches hidden in the newly discovered continent. The Conquistador cared little for exploration, settlement, or quiet agricultural security, much for plunder, power, and riches. In contrast, to New England's shores came groups of explorers and settlers in quest of freedom from the political and religious tyranny of European monarchs, and from the land-poverty of the Old World. Latin America's background has been based on exploitation by outsiders from the moment Pizarro put to a shameful death the Inca, Atahualpa, after receiving his ransom of a roomful of gold plate. The United States has known a development of resources based on home needs from the first Thanksgiving dinner of the Pilgrim Fathers.

Then, too, the first settling of Latin America took place during the early 16th century, not long after the Middle Ages; while the United States was first settled 100 years later when the seeds of the Reformation, with its philosophy of human freedom, were beginning to be sown throughout Europe. Not only was the pace of the early Latin settlers restrained by the heavy hand of European tradition; these settlers were also confronted by a highly organized Indian society whose well established habits of living conflicted with their own. It is estimated that sixteen to thirty-two million persons lived within the Inca Empire alone. In the United States, a comparatively small Indian population of about 900,000 had made a much less marked impression on the land and its resources. Our early settlers, once they had established their own security on the land, could begin from scratch to develop resources to meet their needs. Today in Latin America this problem of the Indian is as far from solution in West Coast countries as it was in the early days of colonization, 400 years ago. If anything, it has become more intense because descendants of Europeans deny the native populations full participation in the twentieth century world.

5. Assimilation vs. Heterogeneity

From a social point of view, while the United States has absorbed a great many immigrants from European sources, many parts of Latin America are still predominantly Indian or Negro. Of a total population of about 126,000,000 there are only some 25,000,000 who can be called white. Latin America is actually only one-fifth white, while the white population of the United States is roughly 118,000,000, or nine-tenths of its total 131,000,000. Our population in the United States has always been far more easy of assimilation, and as a result, we have a relatively homogeneous group with which to work in developing our cities. Because of this integrated social structure, we have been able more readily to make our citizens aware of their responsibility to cooperate in a democratic government. Our immigrant population broke more completely with Europe, while that of Latin America transplanted traditional patterns of living into the New World and attempted to superimpose them on the lives of the indigenous peoples.

Each republic has its own distinguishing racial strains. The populations of Peru and Bolivia, for example, contain some 80 percent Indian or mixed blood, while those of Argentina and Uruguay, with practically no Indian blood, are mostly of European immigrant stock. Chile's early settlers were largely from agricultural sections of the Iberian peninsula and included many Basques. In Colombia, on the other hand, early settlers, interested primarily in mineral wealth, came from urban sections and the wealthier class in Spain; Brazil, of course, was populated largely by Portuguese.

Even today many different languages betray these different backgrounds. A Yucatecan (native of Yucatán, Mexico) told me that there are 400,000 inhabitants of that great peninsula who speak Mayan almost exclusively, and that many of them know no Spanish at all. In all Mexico, he said, there are as many as 300 different dialects, and twenty-eight native languages as alive today as they were when the Aztecs ruled the great populace of pre-Cortez Mexico. In Ecuador, Peru, and Bolivia, I found it more profitable to learn a few words of *Quechua* or *Aymara,* the indigenous language, than to attempt to use Spanish with native groups. Spanish is as foreign a language to the mass of the indigenous populations of those countries as English is to the mass of the peoples of India.

More recent settlement has brought many other influences. German immigration and development in southern Chile and southern Brazil has marked those sections with the imprints of Munich and the cities of the Rhine. Large Yugoslav groups in northern Chile, and many English and Irish in Argentina, have left indelible signs of the energy and initiative of these peoples. Latin America is far from being consistently "Latin," just as the United States is certainly not 100 percent Anglo-Saxon.

Today these racial patterns remain evident in many Latin American countries. Let me take you to the two Perus I visited.

9

We land at Callao, the port of Lima, step from the modern customs building into a shiny new Ford taxi, and race into Lima over smooth concrete roads lined with trees and planned as boulevards for modern automobile traffic. We arrive in a city that is one of the most beautiful and livable in the world. The old heart of the city, founded by Pizarro, with its narrow streets and open plazas, its old churches and balconied palaces, is surrounded by the new city, spreading, Los Angeles-like, outward toward the sea. Boulevards and great parks, up-to-date suburban home districts, modern theaters and shops, grocery shelves laden with preserved delicacies and great quantities of fresh fruits, vegetables, baked ham and cold meats—these demonstrate the material, twentieth-century progress of the Peru that is Lima. This twentieth-century Peru is a result of the direct importation of Europeans with their initiative and ideas to the New World.

But a second Peru awaits. A few miles out of Lima, you climb sixteen thousand feet above the sea in a little over three hours. You leave modern Lima and enter the twelfth-century land of the Indian, the descendant of the great Incas.

The town is Cuarhuasi, high in the Andes, and we are standing on the balcony of the small lodging place, looking down into the courtyard and out over the moonlit roof-tops of the mud houses, to the white monolithic church dominating the square. The only light below comes from a wavering candle in a small room opening on the yard. In the dim interior sits an Indian woman, her black skirts spread on the earth floor, a large hat on her head and two thick braids reaching down her back to her waist. She drinks from a cup in silence. Another figure moves about the room slowly and aimlessly, casting deep shadows over the obscure walls. Without a word to the other this woman pads out and shuts the door without a sound. The courtyard is pitch dark now and she pulls up her skirts, squatting for a moment in the darkness before entering the next door off the cobbled pavement. A light flickers in the room and she prepares for bed.

Over the rooftops come the sounds of night. Dogs bark restlessly, a pipe plays over and over again a plaintive, minor tune that has come from Inca times; a young voice sings bits of the tune from the other side of the village; footsteps sound in the square outside the courtyard. The pipe plays on plaintively; the voice sings again; a cricket chirps; a dog barks; the pipe plays and the voice sings and you hear voices murmuring in the square. In the room where there is still a light, the woman talks with a man. The language is Quechua, not Spanish. They raise their voices heatedly and after a while there is silence and the light goes out. All the candles are out now and Cuarhuasi is like a town of the Middle Ages, dark and close to nature, covered with night and stars. There is only the moon making white and wonderful the massive church and the few houses which have been whitened. If it were day the others would be a deep red-brown, the color of good rich mud.

This is the second Peru: the Indian, the Inca music, the darkness, the great whitened adobe church dominating the square and the people of the village; a mournful serenade to quicken a love affair; the filth, the ignorance, and the miserable poverty. This and more is one Peru I saw in Cuarhuasi and in a hundred little towns and villages in the Andes. In them, life seems to have stopped long ago; those who have managed to exist have simply used the structures and facilities at hand as best they could, expending no creative thought on making them more usable, more efficient. There is an appallingly unbalanced distribution of the benefits of modern technology.

One of the most potent influences in maintaining this Medieval environment has been the Church itself, which, despite good intentions and Christian tenets, has far from solved many of the basic problems of health, education, shelter, food, and clothing of the indigenous peoples. Clerical influence varies a great deal from one country to another, but in general has a far stronger grip on Latin America than on the United States.

I remember one Andean mountain town with its church on the square. We walked in late one afternoon while brown-robed friars were preparing for Christmas Eve. This relic of Colonial splendor enclosed a huge, dark interior. A dozen urchins in dirty rags, with fine but dirty boy-faces, followed us in hope of receiving a "cut" on the fee for guide service—which was, as always, self-appointed. They wanted perhaps ten centavos, or twenty, for a *propina* (tip). That would be one-tenth or one-fifth part of the local monetary unit, and would amount to no more than two or three cents in the United States. But it would be big money to them. It was Christmas, and they could go into the market and buy a little miniature of something they never could own at full size in real life. (In parts of the Andes, this custom, held over from Inca times, is still practiced: it is believed that gifts made in miniature to a legendary character on his feast day will be returned in full size during the year.) Or perhaps they could buy a toy made in Japan, the profits from which have long ago been used to bomb out similar little urchins with dirty and fine Chinese boy-faces in Chungking.

In the darkness, we were led past chapel after chapel to the end of the nave where the darkened altar dimly suggested impressive size and grandeur. Suddenly, two huge electric floodlights were turned on, and this miracle of twentieth-century science lit up in a white blaze the sixteenth-century glory that had been made possible through the exploitation of the Indian in the name of Christianity. Of solid silver, the altar stood some forty feet high, some thirty feet wide, molded, embossed, and sculptured, a fortune in buying power—perhaps enough to educate, clothe, and house decently the entire town including the urchins who stood about us, some four hundred years after their forefathers' introduction to Christianity, gaping at this fantastic scene, waiting for their miserable *propina*.

Such differences as these have been basic factors in dividing some of the Latin American countries against themselves. Such differences have also been the cause of much of Latin America's economic grief, of which she has had plenty.

6. Industry vs. Agriculture

While our nation has been more or less economically independent, the Latin American republics have almost always depended on Europe or the United States to satisfy needs for whose satisfaction they have not, themselves, the resources, or have no developed resources. Early economic ties were closest with the mother country, Spain, just as the United States remained economically bound to England until our own independence. After we had broken free of England's political hold, that country saw the wisdom of aiding the colonies of Latin America to break with Spain in order to leave open a path for their own economic aggression. Consequently, with the independence of the colonies came a long period of close economic cooperation with England, which continues up to the present. However, the cultural tie with Spain, far from being completely broken, accounts for the strong feeling for and against the Franco government in Spain that one finds among "Latin" Latin Americans.

After the last war, trade relations with Germany increased gradually, and a new business exchange with Japan began. These new competitors for England's influence succeeded to an astonishing, alarming degree, and acquired unpleasant political implications in proportion, until the advent of World War II. Today these traders have largely been replaced by Uncle Sam.

But in spite of these foreign influences, and probably *because* of them, there has not yet been established in Latin America the sound economic basis on which twentieth-century communities and modern living facilities for the mass of the people can be planned, built, and maintained. Latin America is still operating under what is virtually an agricultural economy, still awaits a balanced form of industrialization. One Bolivian told me that his country is still a colony, although an economic one, and that her people still live culturally and economically as colonists.

South America's natural resources, in contrast to those of the United States, have been of a type which, for the most part, require the application of modern science and technology for effective development; and for that reason only large-scale, well-financed op-

Climate and geography in Latin America range to extremes even greater than are found in the United States, so that the question, "How is the weather down there?" becomes a little absurd. Above, the snow-covered Andes Mountains seen from Argentina; below, humid jungle near Buenaventura, Colombia (photos, top, Pan-American Airways; bottom, Grace Line.)

Geography:

Vertical

and

Horizontal

Vertical geography: Mt. Aconcagua, Chile, highest peak in the hemisphere, 23,080 feet above sea level (photo on facing page, Pan-American Airways.) Such verticality contrasts sharply with the Texas-like horizontality of much of Argentina (photo above, Moore-McCormack Lines); and between are the plateau regions in Chile or Colombia, the undulating hilly uplands of Brazil— in fact, areas of almost any geographic character you care to name.

Geography sometimes forces use of unusual types of transportation within cities. Valparaiso, Chile, has a lower city and an upper; a funicular railway links the two. In San Francisco, cable cars solve this problem.

On the facing page, top to bottom, are shown three radically different climatic and geographic regions, all in one country, Chile. Top, nitrate plant at Pedro de Valdivia on the burning, sterile plain in northern Chile; center, the fertile central region (photo Pan-American Airways); bottom, Negre Glacier near Tierra del Fuego, the fiord region (photo, Grace Line.)

There are at least two Perus: the Inca land and the contemporary. They exist side by side. At bottom of page is Lima, the capital city, with modern commercial and industrial development, broad thoroughfares, parks, proud buildings. Above them brood the men of the other Peru, inhabitants of the village of Pisac, high in the Andes near Cuzco.

Housing for copper miners at Rancagua, Chile, part of the Braden Copper Company's plant, typifies the elaborate preparations necessary in many instances to extract Latin America's resources. This difficulty has, in the past, retarded much national development. (Grace Line photo)

Copper ingots being loaded into a lighter at Autofogasta, Chile (photo above, Grace Line.) In spite of considerable investment of foreign capital, little wealth has stayed behind. Contrast the potential wealth above with the squatter's village, below, situated near Rio Mapocho, Santiago, Chile.

erators have succeeded. Extraction of the rich copper ore of the Peruvian Andes depended on dramatic engineering feats in highway and railroad building. The nitrates of Pedro De Valdivia and of other parts of the northern Chilean desert could not be taken out on any large scale without first bringing in water, developing transportation to bring in food to the sterile desert, and introducing refrigeration to keep the food fresh through the terrific heat. Modern housing would have been impossible without the technical skill required to provide all the necessary components. Development of the silver, the tin, the copper, the rubber, the many other resources of Latin America, required elaborate preparations.

But in the United States, rich mining areas have often been close to rich agricultural areas; thus California's gold-fevered population turned to agricultural pursuits when the gold rush was over. Pennsylvania steel has always had rich farm land nearby. In fact, from the point of view of natural resources, the United States has been a comparatively well balanced bread basket from the start, while Latin America has been a rich but inaccessible supply depot. Her extractive resources, located at great distances from her fertile agricultural areas, have been perforce slowly developed, have required careful study and planning of the many complicated factors, to the virtual exclusion of small-scale private initiative.

Many different stages of development are to be found. Argentina, Brazil, and Chile—the so-called A B C countries—plus small, progressive Uruguay, are the four most advanced. These republics present an enormous contrast to the less mature social and economic status of the northern West Coast countries. Yet while Ecuador is extremely backward in development, Colombia, right next door, is booming at a rapid rate. Peru, as I have indicated, seems well advanced in Lima but retarded elsewhere. Although standards of living are low in "high, cold, and hungry" Bolivia, and food for the masses is scarce, you find, after only a day by train, that northern Chile is well supplied with food which is transported easily by boat from the fertile south. Still later on, when you get around to Argentina, you find so much good food in such large quantity that you question your earlier impression of abundant food in Chile. In contrast, Chile seems to be an almost poverty-stricken California, while Argentina appears a wealthy and economically mature Texas. Then, in but a few hours' time, crossing the Rio de la Plata from Buenos Aires to Montevideo, you even find a difference between two countries so advanced as Uruguay and Argentina. Buenos Aires is rich, prosperous, but somewhat anarchic; Montevideo, less wealthy, is a good housekeeper; the city has a general air of order and civic discipline, and the Uruguayans are the most sophisticated, the most culturally mature of the Latin Americans. I shall speak later of the new industrial development that Brazil is experiencing

13

now during World War II, development which would never have been possible were it not for the war.

You cannot say, then, that all of South America is under-developed, all economically immature. Each country must be studied as a separate unit; but by and large, however, the West Coast countries have the most problems from an economic point of view, and are in the greatest need of planned development of resources.

7. One Democracy vs. Twenty

Politically, the essential difference between us and the Latins is that while the United States is one nation, composed of many states but coordinated by a basically centralized control, the "Latin" portion of the Americas is composed of twenty independent republics *without* coordination. We have a tendency to think of Latin America as something comparable to the United States in political structure, but in traveling south of the border you soon find that the Latin Americans do not think of themselves as Latin Americans. They think of themselves first as Chilenos, or Argentinos, or Brazileiros, or Uruguayos, and very seldom use the collective term, *Latin Americans,* which we so glibly throw over the enormous continent. We have seen how Eddie of São Paulo knew the United States. He thought of it as a single entity, but in relation to his own country, Brazil—not in relation to the continent of South America. Other Latins do the same. They think of their own countries as separate and highly individualized units in comparison with the United States or to Europe, *not of Latin America* in relation to the United States or the rest of the world. Each constantly emphasizes the many characteristics which differentiate it from its neighbor republics. I soon found it a mistake to talk about our relations with Latin America, and found it far more satisfactory in Chile, for example, or in Colombia, to speak of our relations with Chile or with Colombia. I was constantly asked, as I entered one country, how long I had spent in the previous one, and why I had stayed so long. After all, I would be told, there was far more of importance to see here in Ecuador, in Chile, in Brazil, or wherever I happened to be. Latin Americans simply couldn't understand that I had come down to make a study of Latin America—I was of course doing a study of Ecuador, of Chile, or of Brazil. After experiencing this in ten republics, I returned home thinking in terms of Ecuador, Chile, and Brazil with the same differentiation you have in mind when you speak of Rumania, France, and Italy.

These differences are quite well founded, and express themselves in a wide variety of political influences derived from different parts of the world. Various chronological stages of governmental development can be found, from socially democratic Uruguay to almost feudal Ecuador, coincidentally with periods of somewhat Russian

14

influence in Mexico and militaristic tendencies in Peru and Argentina.

Chile, perhaps, has the greatest degree of democracy in practice. I witnessed something there which indicated a way in which Chile is unlike any other country in South America: in freedom of expression. Just before the presidential election in February, 1942, the Rios supporters staged a tremendous torchlight parade and demonstration, with speeches, fireworks, and music in the main plaza of the Barrio Civico. From high above on one of the tall buildings, we saw people below moving toward the specially erected platform, very much like grains of iron being drawn to a magnet. When darkness fell, the various workers' unions had assembled and began marching with their torches, all yellow flame and black smoke, filling the air with the strong smell of burning oil. They sang *La Marseillaise* in Spanish, and the parade of torches could be seen for ten blocks along the beautiful Alameda. This peaceful yet virile expression of labor organization is something rarely seen in other South American countries, and this particular demonstration preceded an election which was marked by intense discussion—and was free of physical violence. It was as peaceful as the Roosevelt-Willkie election at home. But in spite of expressions of increasing democracy in government, Chile's lack of full political unity delayed for a long time the break with the Axis which I believe the Chilean people desired.

On the other hand, Argentina's *enforced* political unity is strong enough to prohibit free civilian expression. For that reason the desires of the majority of the Argentine people have not yet been realized, so she still remains the sole "neutral" in the Western Hemisphere.*

Such differences as these distinguish one Latin American country from another; but, in general, the last few years have seen a lessening of contrast, an increase in political stability. We have ceased thinking of Latin-American politics as a kind of a joke with power kicked from one dictator to another during endless revolutions. Latin America is fast growing up politically, and is definitely headed toward a democracy which can actually be reached only after providing for it a social and economic basis. But that is getting ahead of the story.

8. No Direct Comparisons

To sum up, then, natural advantages have given the U.S.A. a generous head start over Latin America, with the result that while most of the United States is living in the twentieth century or some-

---

* Author's note: Although Argentina eventually broke relations with Germany and Japan in January, 1944, while this book was being prepared for publication, the situation remained unclear for months.

thing close to it, only a small portion of Latin America does so. A greater portion lives in the eighteenth, in the sixteenth; and if you want to go further back, you will have no difficulty in finding the fourteenth and twelfth centuries going full blast. I had no difficulty. Where we in the United States have continued, and are constantly continuing, to grow up socially, economically, and in every other way, many of the Latin American republics are still quite immature. As a result, one finds side by side high degrees of culture and widespread illiteracy; fully advanced political thinking and feudal social relations; superbly luxurious housing conditions for the few, with run-down misery—housing for the masses—a stone's throw away. These broad gaps, between rich resources on the one hand and enormous social needs on the other, are in contrast to conditions in the United States, a divergence that must be well understood before we can embark on a sightseeing tour of Latin American cities, their past, present, and future.

Once you have well in mind this constraining network of differences that makes the words "United States" form quite a different picture in your mind from the words "Latin America"; that makes Chile mean the home of the Chileno and Brazil the home of the Brazileiro; and that makes you understand the difference between an Antioqueño and a Bogotano—then you will realize that you cannot make direct comparisons between the United States and the Latin American republics. Although we must constantly take into consideration Latin America's limitations, it was my strong impression while traveling down there that these background problems were never looked upon by Latin technicians as excuses for not having done more, but as very real problems to overcome.

Nor should these differences and limitations be looked upon as barriers to human betterment, but rather as stepping stones to real bonds of understanding that will develop as the sharp lines diminish and modern technology, used for human ends, makes possible an improved physical environment in all the Americas. The United States, too, has differences yet to be erased—poverty amid plenty, slums in even our finest cities, and racial discrimination in the midst of democracy. The mere fact that these differences exist gives us common ground over which to approach a better postwar world. Latin American technicians are already doing a valiant job of planning and housing, and as a consequence of the war, we in the United States are waking up to the possibilities of a new kind of foreign policy which will make us aware of these differences, and in time obliterate them.

The United States and Latin America already have in common many natural bonds with which to strengthen our reciprocal understanding. Our greatest natural bond is our mutual revolutionary past—the ideals for which the true leaders of our War of Independence fought are in no essential way different from those of José de San Martín and Simón Bolívar, the chief leaders of South America's revolt against Spain. Another bond is our common membership in the New World; when Columbus discovered it he presented us not only with the palm-groved shores of the sunny Caribbean, but with the rockbound coast of Maine and the deep fiords of Chile as well. We are all dwellers in the New World, partakers in the extension of that great discovery. Likewise do we hold in common —both the United States and the republics of Latin America—our existence as a refuge from European imperialism and royalism, which drove many of the fathers and mothers of Germans and Greeks, Italians and Poles, Irish and Yugoslavs to find new opportunities for themselves and their children in the New World. Whether they came to Antofagasta, Chile, or Watsonville, California, they came for essentially the same reason. These and other natural bonds, easily understood, can help unite the Americas.

But a lasting union depends not only on the recognition of those natural bonds, but also upon *our understanding the needs and problems of Latin America.* We must know each other well. As Eddie from São Paulo knew San Francisco and New York, we must know Santiago and Buenos Aires. We must be able to visit Brazil and say in Portuguese, "My name's Eddie . . . but you can call me Eduardo;" then whistle off Brazilian sambas like *Amelia* and *Se Vôce Soubesse* or *A Morena Que Eu Gósto* (the one about "the brunette I'm after who lives on Riachuelo Street and every time I call her up she answers the phone herself to say, *'Não, não está!'*— No, she's not in!") We must know such examples of Brazil's architecture as the new Ministry of Education and Health in Rio de Janeiro—an eighteen-story building, all glass and reinforced concrete, standing on columns thirty feet high. We must know why Montevideo has fewer slums than any other large capital; what the Chilean lakes are called and where they are; the distinction between Paraguay and Uruguay; how José de San Martín compared with George Washington and Bartolomé Mitre with Abe Lincoln. We must make friends with the *roto* of Chile and the *pelado* of Mexico, both half-forgotten men, the latter so well portrayed by Cantinflas, the great comedian and friend of the common man in Mexico. We must start learning the other "American" languages— Spanish and Portuguese—in grammar school, and grow up knowing the Eduardos, the Guillermos, and the Albertos as well as we know the Eddies, the Bills, and the Als at home.

Let us go far back into the past of Latin America's cities and explore some of the roots of her problems. Let us thoroughly understand these problems and these differences, and use them as common ground for approaching a better postwar hemisphere.

Contrast the development above, Rio de Janeiro's Copacabana Beach, a water-front park, with the entirely commercial and industrial development of water-fronts in most cities of the U.S.A. Copacabana is only one of several similar parks in Rio; and Rio de Janeiro is only one of several Latin American cities which have similar developments. Recently New York City opened the Henry Hudson Parkway along the upper reaches of Manhattan Island, but before that "Riverside" Drive in the same location overlooked railroad yards as well as the polluted Hudson River; and even now, the parkway is an express high-way, landscaped for the benefit of the high-speed motorist rather than those who might prefer to lounge in the sun.

chapter 2

400 years since Inca planning

1. Pearl Harbor and Macchu Picchu

Shortly after December 7, 1941, the dark day of Pearl Harbor, I found myself high in the Peruvian Andes in a remote corner of the ancient Inca Empire, where even before the Incas, a previous civilization had founded the majestically planned city of Macchu Picchu. The pre-Inca race built the city high on a peak in a vast amphitheatre of fantastic mountains, only to abandon it later to the jungle which soon overgrew the great stone walls and open plazas.

Many theories have been put forward to solve the enigma of the founding and abandoning of Macchu Picchu. One holds that a great society of cultured, civilized people was invaded and defeated by barbarous hordes from the plains of Patagonia and the jungles of Brazil. The great King was killed and his army defeated in a battle on the shore of Lake Titicaca. His followers took the body of the King and retreated far into the mountains to a peak which it would be impossible to attack. Here they planned and built an Ivory Tower, an Andean Shangri-La, in which to carry on their high standards of civilization. The extreme efforts which these people put forth in building their citadel of peace clearly show the importance they attached to preserving their way of life. Historians tell us that many generations later, the descendants of these people returned to the fertile valleys of their fathers with their culture intact to found the city of Cuzco, and establish the beginning of the excellently organized society of the Incas.

Today, some 1500 years since this crisis in the Incan Andes, history has come close to repeating itself in spite of a world-wide broadening of man's experience with what we call our civilization. Macchu Picchu and Pearl Harbor took on a related significance;

we, as well as they, have been aroused from our security and forced to move boldly to protect ourselves and our way of life. We had forgotten the importance of our past, taken for granted the comforts of the present, and, with no real motivation for the continuous protection of our society, had allowed ourselves to be dangerously assaulted.

The lesson to be learned from these men of the Andes is certainly not one of escape. For those times the Ivory Tower was the answer. Today we have science, education, and democracy to use as instruments for keeping our culture vigorous and dynamic. These are the weapons we must use to keep alive the revolutionary past of the Americas, the courageous, rebellious spirit of fight and freedom that in itself will make impossible a successful attack by any barbarous hordes at any Pearl Harbor in the hemisphere.

2. History and Tradition

It is no coincidence that history has placed such markers as Macchu Picchu along mankind's route. Those are the warnings which thinking men heed in order that they may better themselves. Other great markers in the Americas are those left by the revolutionary leaders of a more recent phase of Western Hemisphere history, and it is particularly true in South America that these signposts have not been forgotten.

History and tradition dominate in scores of ways the development of Latin American cities and the lives of their inhabitants. If the revolutionary past of the New World is the greatest potential bond between the Americas, North and South, that which differentiates the United States from Latin America more than anything else is the difference of age of human settlement. Every one of the major Latin American cities had been founded almost one hundred years when the Pilgrims first touched at Plymouth Rock in 1620. Traveling down the West Coast of Latin America in 1941 and 1942, I was told by citizens of most of the major capitals that the fourth centenary of the founding of their city had been celebrated some six to eight years before. Bogotá was founded in 1538, Lima in 1535, La Paz in 1539, and Santiago in 1541. These cities were already *one hundred and fifty years old* when the Padres founded Los Angeles and San Francisco on the West Coast of the United States.

In addition to being far older than those of the United States, Latin American cities have had quite a different history. Our cities today reflect no more than two marked periods of development: the colonial period as in New Orleans, Boston and other towns of the Eastern states, and the vigorous period of industrial expansion of the latter half of the last century—a period which built boom cities over night and filled them with new settlers from Europe.

20

But Latin American cities, on the other hand, have had as many as four principal periods of development. Pre-Columbian civilizations of the Mayas, Aztecs, and Incas built flourishing cities in Mexico and Peru long before the conquests of Cortez and Pizarro during the 1530's. After the coming of the Europeans, hundreds of new cities were laid out under the *Laws of the Indies* of Charles V, Emperor of the Holy Roman Empire, the first city planning legislation in the Hemisphere. This second period lasted almost three centuries—from about 1530 to 1820—when the wars of independence broke the grip of Spain. The Post-Revolutionary period, with its military influence, was vigorous and continued up to the turn of the century, which marks the beginning of a fourth period, one of industrial expansion and European immigration. The roots of many of Latin America's urban problems grew through four centuries of a turbulent history.

3. Pre-Columbian

The Incas were undoubtedly the best planners South America ever knew. Their planning of cities went beyond the physical layouts of streets and building location to the broader background of planning for the best economic uses of the resources of the Empire within the technical limitations of the times. They used economic strategy in aiming at a high level of social development.

The Inca Empire extended from what is today northern Ecuador as far south as central Chile, and east and west from the Pacific to the tops of the Andes. The realm even reached over the Andean ridge to the tropical valleys where the Amazon waters begin to collect in a thousand torrential streams. A strong but benevolent central control, coordinating an almost Marxian social structure, bound together a diversified Empire in which the profit motive was as unknown as the use of the wheel.

Three factors made the Inca Empire a success: 1) a complete system of communication throughout the country by means of well planned roads, bridges, and stopping places for travelers; 2) an emphasis on the importance of the general welfare of the community over that of any one individual or group of individuals; 3) the planned development of the resources of the Empire in the interests of the general welfare. All land was owned by the State and loaned out for productive use for specific periods in accordance with the good behavior of the user. Production was maintained at such a constant peak that idleness was punishable as a social crime, while industry was publicly commended and stimulated by rewards. The use of the land was dictated by national needs according to a plan carefully studied to meet the economic requirements of the people. For example, if there had been an over-production of corn in one year, the land would be turned over to some other agricultural use the following year. Because of such intensified and consciously planned use of the land and its resultant production, the West Coast of South America sustained a population which, according to authorities, was considerably larger than it is today. It is estimated that the population of the Inca Empire reached a minimum of 16,000,000 while today no more than 13,000,000 persons inhabit the republics of Ecuador, Peru and Bolivia. It must be remembered that this population maintained itself according to high standards under the most primitive conditions in a mountainous region and without the contact with the outside world that is available today. Records of production were kept by a complicated system of knotted, colored strings known as *quipus*, the only method of recording which the Incas ever developed.

Prescott throws light upon the planning of resources by the Incas in giving the observations of Garcilasso, an early chronicler: "At certain intervals, a general survey of the country was made, exhibiting a complete view of the character of the soil, its fertility, the nature of its products, both agricultural and mineral—in short, of all that constituted the physical resources of the empire. Furnished with these statistical details (a register was also kept of all the births and deaths throughout the country, and population changes taken each year) it was easy for the government, after determining the amount of requisitions, to distribute the work among the respective provinces best qualified to execute it."

The Incas were the first in the Western Hemisphere to practice economic planning in the interests of the general welfare, and this they did one thousand years before the AAA and the New Deal. Great terraces for intensified agriculture lined the Andean canyon walls. According to historians, poverty was unknown; freedom from want was attained. Under the rule of the Incas, regions like Ecuador were rich and fertile, where today there are dust-bowl areas, populated with poverty-stricken Andean "Okies."

The planning of the city of Cuzco, capital of the Inca Empire, and other cities, was of such a high standard that the Spaniards needed only to build on the identical plan laid down by the Incas. Long before there had been any knowledge of the existence of Europeans, broad avenues entered the cities of Quito and Cuzco. In fact, during my visit in Quito, the municipal authorities showed me one of these broad Inca avenues which had been narrowed down, and told me that today it has become necessary to buy back fifty feet of right-of-way in order to satisfy demands of modern traffic. The first Spanish planners had shown so little vision in establishing property lines that they cut in half the generous width allowed by the Incas for this important roadway.

What makes Cuzco one of the most interesting of all historic towns of South America is this contrasting fusion of the stern, solid planning and building of the Incas with the more imaginative, if chaotic, work of the Spaniards. In the work of the Incas, however, basic principles of planning correspond to similar laws of Spanish, Roman and even Greek urban designing. The gridiron plan of streets was used; a differentiation of width for more important avenues was practiced; the main plaza was planned in the center of the city as a focal point for social activities while minor plazas were located elsewhere; public buildings were located on the plazas or on the main avenues. Naturally, we must disregard the possibility of the same origin, but we can give credit to the correspondingly high degree of culture that was reached, and the fine sense of order which motivated such planning. Today, in spite of four hundred years of European domination and almost complete rebuilding under the Laws of the Indies, the urban spirit of the Incas still pervades Cuzco and many smaller towns in the region.

Inca culture focussed upon Cuzco, the capital of the Empire. The main plaza in early times was the meeting place for the populace, while today the same broad plaza provides a spacious setting for the great cathedral and an open, planted area where descendants of the Incas sit on green park benches to listen to contemporary music broadcasted through loud speakers. Such "contemporary music" may include anything from boogie woogie to *Tales from the Vienna Woods*. Although the life of Cuzco is marked with such incongruities, its people are still Incan; its plazas, streets and many of its walls and foundations are those of the original inhabitants.

The founding of Cuzco is lost in history, but its site selection is explained in legend by the story of Manco Copac who, it is believed, instigated the curious abandoning of Macchu Picchu and the return to more fertile lands, of which I spoke earlier in this chapter. In selecting the site, undoubtedly more than divine instruction led Manco Copac to plant in the soil the rod of gold given him by his father, the Sun God. Manco Copac was more likely a level-headed fellow who took a good look at the fertile lands, the supply of water, the excellent drainage of the valley of Cuzco, before he admitted divine guidance. Those who planned the city divided it into four sections representing the subdivision of the Empire into four great regions, separated by the four main roads which extended to the limits of Inca domination. In each section of the city lived the people of the race of the corresponding quadrant, and the title of The Inca, *Tahuantisuyu,* or "Lord of the Four Corners of the Earth" carried out this same concept. Earth and sand were brought from all the provinces of the Empire to cover the principal plaza at the junction of the four main roads. The plaza had two functional divisions: one for the priests and for ceremonies, the other for the people and for popular festivals.

Other smaller plazas from Inca time still remain in exactly the same form today and many of the streets still carry either the original Inca name, or a Spanish translation of it. One of these is *Intipampa*, or *Llanura del Sol*, meaning the "Plain of the Sun." Private property, as we know it, did not exist. Each city block was an allotment for one family; its distance from the center of the city depended upon the degree of relationship to the Inca ruler. Each block contained only one opening in the wall surrounding it, indicating that life turned inward to the family unit.

One of the greatest achievements of the builders of Cuzco is the fortress of Saccsayhuaman which stands on the hill overlooking the city. This is believed to have been built long before the coming of the Spanish at a time when danger of invasion from as yet unsubdued tribes was imminent. Stones measuring thirty feet in height by fifteen in width and ten feet thick have been put together with dry masonry to form this fortress in which the Incas long withstood the siege of the Spaniards. From one of these great stones the Inca general, Cahuide, leaped rather than submit to capture by the men of Pizarro, the ruthless, un-Christian Conquistador.

The Inca culture and way of life sprang from close contact with nature and deep reverence for the Sun, the Moon, and the Stars. In selecting sites for the public works of the times, the Incas were deeply influenced by these natural phenomena and deliberately chose settings of topographical distinction. Thus, their forts, temples, and palaces always fit beautifully into the landscape. One day I stood on the green slopes of the mountain where Khencco, the remains of a theatrical or ceremonial center, looks majestically out over the valley of Cuzco, and I wondered why we, with all of our technical skill in building, so seldom fitted our cities to the natural character of the sites we had selected. To the nature-respecting Incas, man's use of the land seemed a sacred privilege, requiring careful evaluation and consideration for every scar or mark made upon it. That, in essence, is planning.

The entire Cuzco region is full of smaller towns—some in ruins, many in use—which demonstrate the ability of the Incas as city planners. Ollantaytambu (*tambu* in the language of the Incas refers to the inn or post established along their highways) is the home of many twentieth-century Incas who live very much as their predecessors did five hundred years ago. Pisac is another. These towns reflect the sense of organization of the Incas, their organic philosophy of symmetry, order, regularity, and precision. It is a sad commentary on the white man's influence, but nevertheless true, that the farther one goes from towns inhabited by whites or *mestizos* (those of mixed blood), the cleaner and more sanitary become the villages and the more like those of Inca times. Paucartambu is one of these; it is less perfect in symmetrical layout but probably older and the result of gradual evolution of form, as are the medieval cities of Europe. So perfectly did Inca planning suit Spanish needs that today these towns follow the exact plan of Inca times.

Many towns in the Andes are still almost purely Inca in character. I spent an afternoon on the shores of Lake Titicaca exploring Chucuito, a village typical of many which dotted the shores of that lake during pre-Spanish times. According to old chronicles, Chucuito had sacred significance to the Incas as a religious center. Today, on the site of each ancient temple stands a colonial church built by the Spaniards who made the town the capital of the province. Some of the finest remains of colonial architecture, with warped adobe towers and arcaded walls, are to be found here.

Today Chucuito (like most towns in the region) is inhabited by Aymaras, some of whom are of pure Indian blood, others of mixed blood. The town as laid out by the Incas displays a clearly conceived plan and a high degree of civic form. An upper and lower plaza, each with a large church facing the paved space, dominate the plan. From the main plaza in front of the most imposing church, a cross-town street takes you to a *mirador*, a circle open to the sky and enclosed by a thick adobe wall pierced with arched openings. From this you look out over the strange, age-worn landscape and the blue expanse of Lake Titicaca. Down the center of all streets of the village lies a stone channel, dating from Inca times, which supplies clean, constantly running water from the spring above for cooking and washing. Canals of running water kept the Inca cities clean and hygenic. On the other side of town, opposite the mirador, the walled-in swimming pool which may have come from Inca times, is the center for picnics and *chicha* parties. (*Chicha* is a potent popular brew beloved by all Incas.) Two roads, one on each side of the town, ascend the hill and meet at a smaller plaza above the village. This plaza is used once each year, before Christmas, for the special fiesta in which a custom of the Incas is kept alive. Here a replica of the village below is built in miniature, completely equipped with houses, furnishings and domestic animals, all of which are then sold—for buttons instead of money!

Higher on a rocky hill above the town is another mirador looking out far over the lake. Here the townspeople of Chucuito go each year on a special feast day to sacrifice a vicuña, the prized animal of the high Andes, closely related to the llama. Ordinarily, baking and roasting are done communally in the town oven; all agriculture is also carried on communally by special family or clan units. These activities are all part of the strong community life which originated in Inca times and still expresses itself in the city plan. Chucuito's plan shows a very close relationship between its physical features and the social life of the village. It has that quality of conscious design in relation to community needs which modern planners of—

let us say—Greenbelt, Maryland, or Welwyn Garden City in England, to name two examples of consciously planned communities, have achieved, but which we have more generally missed in building our cities of the twentieth century.

According to Harry and Marian Tschopik, Harvard anthropologists studying in Chucuito, the earliest settlers in this area are supposed to have been a tribe brought from the north by the Incas as a part of their plan for intermingling peoples in the interests of national racial unity. (Where have we heard similar ideas recently?) The present settlers of Chucuito, who came in only within recent years to re-settle the old town, had been forced through questionable land ownership transactions either to leave land back of the lake where they had lived for generations, or to remain to work for the new "owners" at exploitation wages. They chose to move to Chucuito and live independently.

Before leaving this pre-Columbian period in the development of Latin American cities, I should like to discuss in greater detail Macchu Picchu, since it is the high spot in pre-Spanish city building. Most intact of all Andean remains, these pre-Inca ruins lay hidden to the world until uncovered by Bingham's expedition from Yale University in 1912, although they had been known for many years by the people of the locality. Even though it lay only eighty miles north of Cuzco in the Urubamba Valley, the center of pre-Inca culture, Macchu Picchu was never mentioned in the legends of the Incas nor was its existence discovered by the Spaniards. The builders of Macchu Picchu had selected a perfectly isolated site, and the jungle had done the remaining work of camouflage. Even the highest words of praise for Macchu Picchu as a work of city building will remain a gross understatement. It is certainly the engineering, architectural, and city planning high spot of the West Coast of South America. Traveling down the narrow and wildly verdant valley of the Urubamba River, you see Inca and pre-Inca ruins studding the heights above the canyon-sides which had been terraced for the purpose of intensifying agricultural production and then watered by an elaborate system of irrigation canals. These terraces, beautifully built, are so solid that many of them are in use today. Over one thousand years ago the Incas practiced the same contour planting and terracing that today our own U.S. Department of Agriculture endeavors to encourage in the United States. As the valley narrows down, the terraces can be seen higher and higher up the side of the canyon, which becomes more rugged and more tropically overgrown.

After an hour's climb on horseback from the bottom of the river canyon, up the steep sides of the canyon wall, you look out over a fantastic landscape where all lines are vertical instead of horizontal and where clouds drift down below instead of above. On the shoulder of a ridge two thousand feet above the river are silhouetted the dramatic remains of the city of Macchu Picchu, gray-green against a porcelain sky. A series of stepped plazas separate a community of stone houses, now roofless, covering the knoll on one side from a group of larger houses and courts where a series of steps lead to the high point of the city—the Temple of the Sun and the stone sundial. The plan of the city is curiously modern, amazingly well-organized.

This is the city that was built by an ancient people some 1500 years ago when their Pearl Harbor forced them to withdraw to the mountain tops and practice four hundred years of isolationism in order to preserve their culture. I have described at the beginning of this chapter how, some five hundred years after the founding of Macchu Picchu, Manco Copac, the king, wandered away in the direction of the rising sun to found the city of Cuzco and the beginnings of the Inca empire. During the 400 years that followed, up to the coming of the Spaniards, the descendants of Manco Copac developed the unique and powerful Inca civilization.

This story, patched together from old chronicles, seems to be the most credible explanation of Macchu Picchu. But there are others. New discoveries of the Cedrobamba ruins by the Wenner-Gren Expedition suggest that perhaps Macchu Picchu was only an intellectual center or ceremonial nucleus for a great chain of mountain cities. Among these Cedrobamba ruins, three miles of narrow, graded roadway with retaining walls and tunnels indicate missing links in the story of Macchu Picchu.

Most impressive about Macchu Picchu is the effect of space—both solid and vacant space—from the great masonry walls, marking off rooms, decorated with niches, to the mountains 3000 feet high, marking off huge canyons, lightly furnished with clouds and double rainbows. At times, this scale of the Andes has a way of putting you in your place as an insignificant creature and at other times, of inspiring you with the dignity of man's position on earth. But at all times, whether threatened or inspired by the Andes, you cannot escape being dominated by them. It is no wonder that all the great Indian civilizations which have come and gone among these mountains have left some great enduring work behind to speak for the things they have learned from the forceful Andes.

With the inspiration and the challenge of the Andes behind them, the Incas built a great and prosperous civilization, rich in art and high social standards, in a little more than 400 years. In the same amount of time—400 years—our European culture has humiliated man before these mountains and lowered the descendants of the Incas to a condition scarcely better than that of its native animals. There is much to be learned and much to accomplish before we can justify bringing the benefits of our civilization to the Incas.

Even down along the dry desert coast of Peru the remains of Chan Chan and other pre-Inca towns indicate the high civilization of peoples who lived thousands of years ago. The most significant fact to consider in studying these cities is that, completely lacking our technical development, they were able to plan and provide for living facilities of a high order, and for a remarkable use of natural resources. They planned and provided in the interest of the community. Such accomplishments put us on the spot: if they were able to achieve a fairly high standard of living with their limited means, we, today, with miraculous techniques on every hand, are left without a single excuse for poverty, bad housing, or poorly equipped cities, whether in South America or in North America.

4. Colonial

When the Conquistadores had conquered and the spilled blood of the trusting owners of the land was dried on the streets of Cuzco and Mexico City, when the gold plate from Atahualpa's ransom room had been greedily removed to increase the royal wealth of Europe, then the colonizing began. Charles V, Emperor of the Holy Roman Empire and self-appointed ruler of Spain, sent missionaries, settlers and engineers to lay out cities for the New World under the famous *Laws of the Indies*. First written in 1523, but revised many times, these included the first planning legislation of the Western Hemisphere. They were actually based on colonial building laws of Greek and Roman times and, like them, took into account the quality of soil, availability of water, suitability for defense, and other factors essential to site selection. The laws established consistent standards of design: size and form of the main plaza, width of streets, orientation of gates and walls, location of public buildings, and subdivision of land into lots. The Laws of the Indies looked ahead to future development only by requiring a quadrangular street layout "in order to extend and expand the city."

As a result of these standard laws, such distant cities as Bogotá, Colombia and Concepción, Chile, and practically every city between, have exactly the same size of block, the same width of street, the same general urban pattern. Few modern cities in Latin America have escaped being marked for their period of foundation by the regularity of the gridiron plan of the Laws of the Indies. A uniformity of city layout has been rubber-stamped all over the face of the continent no matter what the site, hill or dale, valley or pampa. The Spanish block which formed the basis of the colonial plan was 112 meters (about 336 feet) square, with a street width of thirteen meters (about 39 feet). The entire block was originally laid out for the use of a single family as a kind of family compound, and contained living facilities for large numbers of family mem-

Cuzco, Peru, once the capital of the ancient Inca Empire, as seen from above Saccsayhuaman, the ruined fortress in the foreground.

Street in Quito, Ecuador: in foreground, ample width as laid out by Incas; in background, as narrowed by Spaniards.

Canals in the centers of the streets kept Inca cities clean; street in Chucuito, Peru, with Lake Titicaca in background.

Panorama of Macchu Picchu, pre-Inca city 80 miles from Cuzco, to which tradition claims that a highly civilized early race, defeated in battle, retired to preserve their culture. Wild canyons, raging rivers protected them while they

The plan of Cuzco as it existed in Inca times bears strong resemblance to that of the Aztec plan of Tenochtitlan in Mexico. There

maintained their city on the peak. Its plan, clearly discernible, and the tremendous difficulties which beset its creators, make it the most exciting example of city planning on the West Coast of South America.

are the same central plaza in each, the same four roads leading to the four points of the compass and quartering the towns.

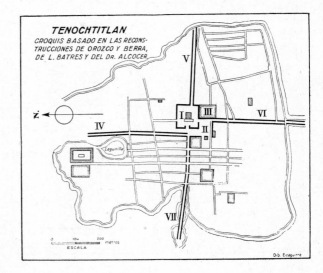

TENOCHTITLAN

CROQUIS BASADO EN LAS RECONS-
TRUCCIONES DE OROZCO Y BERRA,
DE L. BATRES Y DEL Dr. ALCOCER.

COLONIAL PLAN-
NING: At right, the
cathedral at Puno,
Peru, dominates the
central square as it
does in every Latin
American community.
Below is a plan of
Mexico City in early
colonial times.

At top of facing page
is a map of the forti-
fied colonial town of
Callâo. The two lower
illustrations are of
Lima, Peru. Colonial
Lima, shown in the
map, appears in the
air view of the modern
city as the congested
darkish mass at the
bend of the river.

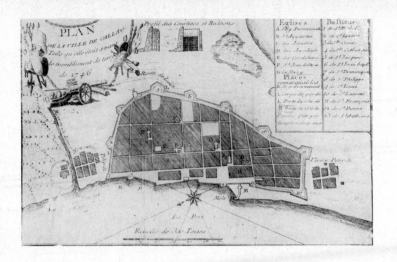

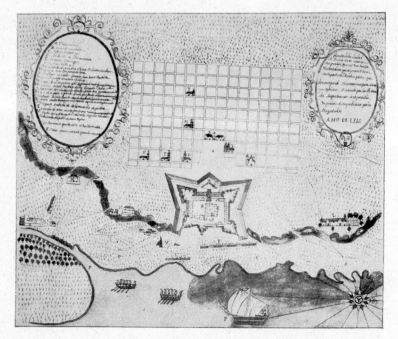

Buenos Aires, above, in colonial times; and below, as it was built
up in successive stages to the imposing, uncontrolled urban giant
of today. Compare the rigid adherence to a formula, however
faulty, in the earliest days, with the more recent "development"
that is continually nibbling at the city's remaining amenities.

ZONAS EDIFICADAS EN LA CAPITAL, EN DISTINTAS EPOCAS

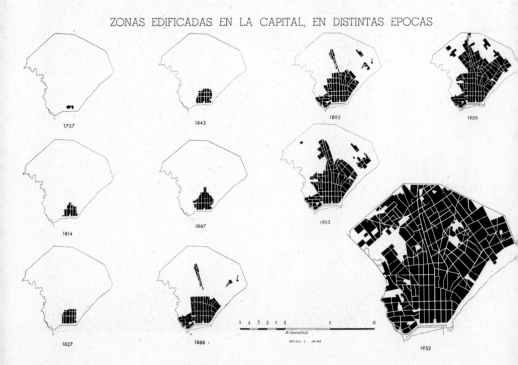

Three typical scenes in Buenos Aires: Avenido de Mayo, the central axis of the city.

Diagonal Norte, opened in recent years.

Plaza de Mayo, overlooked by the Old Cabildo.

Above, panorama of Rio de Janeiro and its beautiful harbor, from the air.
The waterfront is spectacular; its well developed parks are only one example
of human advantages derived from the natural surroundings. Below, at left,
Avenida Rio Branco, tree-lined, fronted with elegant structures, looking toward the waterfront. At right, looking inland away from the bay, the city
begins to wander confusedly, if picturesquely, up neighboring hills and valleys.
(Photo by Brazil D. I. P.)

bers, servants' quarters, and accommodations for visiting travelers. In Lima today, this family compound system accounts for the street names which progress block by block according to the old family names of colonial days. Later on, of course, these blocks were divided into smaller properties—generally eight lots, each 28 by 56 meters. The street which carried the front entrances of these became the principal street. Later, space was rented on the side street which came to be known as the *calle atravesado,* or equivalent of our term "back street," used to brand socially those who lived there.

The foundation of the cities of Latin America followed the route of the Conquistadores. The new towns were no more than vantage points for the ambitious and ruthless Spanish captains to use while robbing the native population of their former freedom and security in the name of Christianity. Hernán Cortés founded Vera Cruz, on the Gulf of Mexico, and Mexico City on the ruins of the Aztec capital, Tenochtitlan. He converted Aztec cities into sites for Spanish settlement, and the sacred city of Anahuac became Cholula, city of many churches.

Francisco Pizarro and his captains left a trail of blood and newly founded cities down the West Coast of South America from Panama to Valparaiso. Bogotá was laid out from scratch on a vacant site by Jiminez de Quesada in 1538 at exactly the point where the main plaza of the city now stands. Popayán, Quito, Lima, Cuzco, Arequipa, Tacna, and Copiapó were scattered down the West Coast as the seeds of urban Spain—either under Pizarro's initiative or that of Almagro, his general and chief competitor in conquest.

When the Laws of the Indies were found to be inadequate, the new cities dictated their own new laws. Lima, in 1553, required the walling-in of all properties under the penalty of confiscation, planted trees, cleaned streets, required the washing of animals and clothes at a restricted section of the Rimac. The Indians were put into special settlements called *Las Reducciones,* consisting of smaller blocks and narrower streets than those of the Spanish settlement, and amounting to little better than concentration camps. The walls of Lima were built in 1683 by the Duke of Palata to protect the city from the pirate Clerk, although they had been planned as early as 1625 by Manuel Escobar, one of the well-known architects of the time, who did many of the fine churches of wealthy Lima, the rich Capital of the viceroy.

Other cities were founded as colonization began less for their strategic defense location as in the case of Lima than for richness of natural resources. Thus Pedro de Valdivia founded Santiago in one of the fertile valleys of central Chile, where before the coming of the Spaniards no tradition of city building of any kind existed. The indigenous people, the Araucanians, lived in an agricultural

29

economy and had not advanced to the degree of culture and social organization of the more northerly Incas and Aymaras. Santiago was laid out in 1541 under the Laws of the Indies, and consisted of no more than some twenty-five square blocks surrounding the present Plaza de las Armas, now in the heart of a metropolitan area of over fifty square miles.

Discovery of mineral wealth in Bolivia led to the founding of La Paz, named in honor of the peace agreed upon between Pizarro and Almagro. Potosí developed as a rich silver mining center. First settlement of La Paz took place on the present plaza of Alonzo de Mendoza adjoining the broad new Avenida America. Later on when the city was officially laid out by law, the Plaza Murillo, now the center of the city, became the central plaza and the surrounding gridiron plan was laid out in defiance of the rugged topography. For a large urban capital, the site of La Paz is poorly chosen, but as a small colonial center, its location was excellent from the point of view of defense. Barricades once stood where two present-day streets—Calles Loayza and Coroico—and the river formed three sides of a triangle defending the enclosed settlement from Indian attack.

With the flow of silver from the mines of Potosí near La Paz carried down the east slope of the Andes by mules especially bred for the purpose, down to the rivers and to that great mother of rivers, the Rio de la Plata—whose name was derived from samples of Inca silver seen by early explorers—it became necessary to build a stronghold at the mouth of the river near the Atlantic, and Juan de Garay founded the port of Santa Maria de los Buenos Aires in 1570. Restrictions enforced by the Council of the Indies made this the favored route for smuggling the precious metals of Peru and Bolivia rather than the older one by ship from Lima, stronghold of Imperial Spain, to Panama, point of embarkation for Europe. The site of Buenos Aires was chosen because there was deep water at the junction of the Riachuelo River and the Rio de la Plata, today the picturesque ship-building quarter known as La Boca. Thus the greatest city in Latin America was founded. Garay divided the town into 232 blocks and gave one block to each family of settlers. The central block, that nearest the river, was used as a site for the fortress, and the Cabildo (Town Hall), church, and other public buildings took their places around the open square before the fortress. This square is today the site of well-known landmarks, such as the Casa Rosada, the Cathedral, and the Old Cabildo, which surround the verdant Plaza de Mayo and stand in the midst of Buenos Aires' rushing traffic and roaring subways.

Meanwhile, the Portuguese had been exploring Brazil, and had founded Bahia, Rio de Janeiro, São Paulo—all without benefit of planning standards such as those established by the Laws of the

Indies. Unlike the cities of Spanish origin, these evolved as did those of the Middle Ages in Europe, at times less systematically than those of Charles V, but more functionally. Rio de Janeiro's first streets, like those of Boston, followed the paths of the cows as they wandered across the marshes. The original town was built for defense on the Morro de Castelo; later another settlement grew on the smaller hill of São Bento. The first main street of the future city grew out of the road which crossed the swampy intervening land to connect these two settlements. All other streets were laid out more or less at right angles to this one, and the basic pattern for the future city was established. Some of these narrow streets, only eighteen feet wide between buildings, are today pedestrian shopping streets like Rua Ouvidor and Rua Buenos Aires. Avenida Rio Branco, Rio's main artery, was not to be opened until more recent times.

Brazil's second city, São Paulo, was founded in 1555, but unlike most of the larger Latin American cities, remained quite unimportant until the turn of the last century. Defense motivated its location on a small hilltop, which was walled in, forming a triangular nucleus, now the three-sided downtown shopping and business center. The chief incentive in founding São Paulo was the Christianizing of the Indians; no El Dorado, symbol of ready-made wealth, attracted early settlers, nor did any one dream of the hard-earned wealth to come with the enormous immigration and industrialization which, less than 400 years hence, were to make this a bustling metropolis of a million and a half people.

5. Post-Revolutionary

For almost three hundred years—from about 1530 to 1820—these cities of the New World remained small colonial towns completely under the domination of Europe. But the restraining influence of the mother country, Spain, became intolerable for the creole descendants of first settlers, who wanted economic and political freedom to develop the land of their birth as they saw fit. In a few years' time, Simón Bolívar, José de San Martín and a host of other revolutionists broke the grasp of Spain, and Latin America embarked upon a third period in her history. The close of the revolutionary decades saw an early form of postwar planning on a large scale. When Simón Bolívar retired and José de San Martín withdrew quietly to Boulogne-sur-Mer in France, the liberty for which these great leaders fought had been achieved and the new republics set about the task of national development.

It was natural that these new, young nations, in an attempt to vie with the impressiveness of the European capitals, should turn to expanding their own young capitals. Small colonial towns were replanned as great capitals in the Haussmann tradition. The enormous amount of work which was accomplished during those years today makes the Latin American capitals generally more attractive and yet urban in character than the colossal centers of the United States. Our chief motivation in city building has been the desire to profit materially by the arbitrary subdivision of land, giving commerce and industry first choice in its use, while the mainspring of the Latins was the desire to express their new-found freedom and unleashed nationalism in city planning works representing a community spirit.

Even today one realizes how their revolutionary past is kept alive as one learns the names of the important streets and plazas of Latin American cities like Buenos Aires and Rio de Janeiro—or even the smallest villages of the Andes. To learn these names is to learn the outstanding dates in the wars of independence and the names of military leaders who fought them; it is to learn the heroes of the wars and those who took part in the planning of the peacetime cities.

Young *porteños* in Buenos Aires (a *porteño* is a native of Buenos Aires) grow up knowing that it is not mere accident that Avenida de Mayo, the avenue of their day of Independence, links the Casa Rosada (the White House of Argentina), where the city was originally founded in 1536, with the Congreso, the symbol of the republican form of government which was the outcome of the rebellion against European domination. University students in Santiago need no history books to tell them that Bernardo O'Higgins, Chilean grandson of an Irish tenant-farmer, was their first post-revolution planner, that after he led the fight against Spain along with José de San Martín, he planned the great avenue that today bears his name. Simón Bolívar is remembered daily in Lima and in Bogotá when friends plan to meet at the Plaza Bolívar in either of these cities. Nor are North American heroes excluded, for the Latin American sees beyond his own national heroes. There is more than one Calle *Jorge* Washington in Latin America; there is the Praça Monroe in Rio de Janeiro, the Avenida Wilson in Lima (at the moment I cannot recall a Joseph San Martin Street, a Bartholomew Mitre Square, or a Bernard O'Higgins Boulevard in New York, Chicago, or any other of our cities).

In the years to come, then, as one of twenty-one democratic nations of a democratic Hemisphere of nations, we might learn from the Latin Americans and keep alive in postwar city building those names of great men of all the Americas. The cities of Latin America suggest this effective way to keep before us the significance of our revolutionary past.

However, those who fought the wars of revolution committed one great error when the peace began. These postwar planners failed to fight to gain economic independence, and in spite of their new political freedom, the Latin American republics remained economic colonies of the European powers. Instead of standing firm on a policy of development of resources for the use of the people themselves, they allowed foreign, private interests to begin the 100-year period of economic exploitation that increased both riches and poverty simultaneously, side by side. This lesson applies today to World War II as it did then: to win the war is only the beginning; the greatest task is to win the economic peace that follows and to strike at the core of war-causing conditions.

However, in return for exploitation, foreign interests left behind many great works of public planning and environmental improvement.

In Mexico City, Maximilian of Austria built the Paseo de la Reforma, copied after the Champs Elysée of Paris, from the old Aztec center of the city out to Chapultepec, which was his palace during the 1860s and is now a popular park for the people. Mexican planners appreciate the inheritance of such works and claim that the worst errors in the planning of their city were made during the period of individualized commercialism that came later, after the turn of the century.

With political independence in Bolivia, development of the tin and silver mines expanded and the real growth of La Paz took place. The Prado, or Avenida 16 de Julio, the city's central boulevard, was developed as a setting for the finest homes of the wealthy mine owners, and the area south of the river was built up. Sopocachi, Miraflores, and Villa Obrajes began to develop but it was not until very recent years—after the close of the war with Paraguay —that these sections were built up.

The patriots themselves used their vision and imagination to plan impressively in an effort to make up for their economic servitude. One military leader who became a peacetime planner was Bernardo O'Higgins who, under the direction of the Argentine liberator, José San Martín, had led the Chilean troops in their fight for freedom. At the close of the war, over one hundred years ago, inspired by the freedom he had helped to win for Chile, he left a mark on the city and set the standard for future development by building the great boulevard which bears his name, Avenida Bernardo O'Higgins. The site of the Alameda, as it is also called, was an arm of the River Mapocho; filled in and planted with poplars or *álamos*, it was given the name "Alameda." The álamos were later taken out and replaced with the present broad, leafy sycamores. Another Chilean patriot of the last century, Vicuña MacKenna, gave the city the Cerro Santa Lucia development, one of the most delightful urban parks in South America.

One similar example of civic planning promoted by a North American patriot comes to mind: the imagination shown by General Washington in envisioning a planned capital on the Potomac. Later leaders in the United States, stirred less by national pride and patriotism and more by an urge for financial betterment, expressed their freedom by exploitation of the land for private interest rather than in lasting works for the future public good. South American public leaders, in general, have made a greater effort to leave behind public works and to take an active part in planning the physical development of their cities than have those of the United States. We have, too often, left our urban land in the hands of the private operators to carve up in the manner most suited to their interests, while a more democratic and public-minded policy would have been to look upon urban land as a community resource to be most carefully apportioned for individual use. Only within the last two decades have we realized our errors and been forced to take steps toward their correction, by zoning, other city planning control measures, and expenditures of large sums of public money.

But to get back to South Amerca: Other public leaders have left an imprint on the pattern of today's cities. General Nicolas de Pierola, who was President of Peru from 1895 to 1899, built splendid avenues for his capital, Lima: the Paseo Colón, Avenida Brazil, and the Colmena. Argentina, the first of the republics to declare independence from Spain, was also the first to profit by the new political freedom and to begin to establish a basis of production and trade through which to gain economic freedom as well. The early arrival of railroads and European immigrants brought development to Buenos Aires. In 1889, the engineer, Juan Buschiazzo, built Buenos Aires' axial boulevard, the Avenida de Mayo, the central core of the city linking the Plaza de Mayo (at which the city was founded) with the Congreso, symbol of the republican form of government. With new wealth and improved transportation, suburbs like Abrogue developed. Few of Buenos Aires' suburbs have the charm of that town patterned deliberately after the style of some of the smaller centers near Paris. Abrogue has been given much of that charm—in spite of a flat, uninteresting landscape—through the public-spirited efforts of the owner, after whom the town has been named, and by application of carefully considered principles of over-all planning.

Montevideo had a briefer colonial period than most of the larger South American cities, since it was founded a great deal later—in 1726. In 1829, a sea-wall was built for defense; the sturdy stone battlements remain today as a part of the *Rambla* waterfront development. Part of the defense plan included a "greenbelt" one kilometer in width at the neck of the peninsula—a zone in which no building was permitted and where cannon could be fired without obstruction. Defense remained an issue in Montevideo for such a

34

long period after independence that this area remained unbuilt upon until about 1870, when warfare was no longer imminent. As a matter of fact, from 1843 to 1851 there were two Uruguays, during the civil war in which rebels founded a small town nearby, built a new port and besieged Montevideo for some eight years. In 1829, a visiting Spanish doctor with some ideas of city planning for health purposes proposed maintaining the defense greenbelt as a permanent defense against overbuilding and congestion. Today, Montevideo's planners regret that his advice was not heeded.

6. Turn of the Century

Although many of the grandiose schemes of the city-building of the post-revolutionary period began without sound economic development of the republics, they did serve as the basis for some of the expansion which took place at the turn of the 20th century. Two factors were responsible for the new growth. First, a vigorous and widened industrialization of natural resources, and second, an enormous influx of European immigrants. The old gridiron pattern of the colonial towns, built under the laws of Charles V, shrank to mere spots in the hearts of the spreading cities. New urban growth spread out like slow-moving lava over quiet, rural areas, to distant limits. Today, unlike most of our cities in the United States and more like those of Europe, Latin American cities show marked rings of growth, the largest of which results from her fourth period, which began toward the end of the last century.

While in the United States our cities embarked upon expansion without an established nucleus, without a sense of civic form or dignity inherited from history, most Latin American cities had such a pattern for future growth. Not in every case did Latin cities follow the old traditions of planning in the grand manner, but a general comparison today between our cities and theirs indicates a greater planlessness in the development of our urban environment. The early established civic discipline of Latin America has served to endow their cities with a better feeling of form and urban character, which goes far to counteract some of the weaknesses in other respects (which will be discussed in following chapters). Where the basic patterns of Chicago, San Francisco, and Omaha were determined in one fell swoop by a single surveyor of the last century, South American cities grew slowly over centuries from well-established colonial settlements to expanding centers for export of nearby resources. Where the factors of history and economic development varied, the plans of the cities themselves varied. This last period has the greatest bearing on present problems and future improvement of the cities of Latin America, and deserves more detailed discussion.

The turn of the century saw the beginnings of the first conscious effort to cope with the problems that had developed in the cities. This took place through a more or less comprehensive program of city planning conceived as beautification, but it was the start of a series of steps leading toward the evolution of a mature science of urbanism, as effective in solving the problems of cities as the study of medicine in relation to ills of the human body.

Twentieth century planning in Santiago received its first real stimulus after the earthquake in 1906, when the Plan for the Transformation of Santiago was made. However, even before that, as early as 1890, comprehensive and enforced plans for widening the old colonial streets were begun. The year 1900 saw new park development in Santiago. The lovely Parque Forestal along the channelized Rio Mapocho was planned and built by the French architect, Dubois. The old-fashioned 19th-century quality of this park still makes it a charming place for a *paseo*, the favorite pastime of the Latins. Little boys in ruffled rompers, under the eyes of nurses, roll hoops, and bonneted little girls in pinafores play on the grass. Dirty, barefooted urchins tear about the well kept paths and make the upper-class children green with envy. The Parque Forestal is like this on a Sunday, or any day around six or seven o'clock—the great hour of the *paseo*, the fine Latin American institution of relaxation which may be a walk, a drive, or a two weeks' vacation.

The cities of Argentina, easily accessible from Europe, underwent the most phenomenal growth. Buenos Aires, the capital, grew from a town of three hundred thousand to a metropolitan center of almost four million people in the fifty years from 1875 to 1925. Rosario, in 1853, housed some three thousand people; at the turn of the century thirty-three times that many; and by 1940 the population had reached six hundred thousand. Resources, ranging from wool and hides to meats and grain, began to be developed and put to use.

Montevideo's twentieth century growth developed with the meat-packing industries, and has expanded even more in the last 25 years when the beaches were discovered to be one of the city's greatest assets. Up to 1910, beaches were never used, but with the reform of recreational customs, the acceptance of brief swimming clothes, and the mixing of men and women on beaches, came a greatly increased development and use of the magnificent beach areas of Uruguay. Now two hundred thousand tourists come into Montevideo each summer simply because of this one feature. *Turismo* is Uruguay's most highly developed and profitable industry.

The fantastic natural advantages of the location of Rio de Janeiro, the spectacular capital of Brazil, were recognized. Swampy areas, gradually filled in or drained, became healthy and habitable. The tangle of narrow streets which had developed without plan required nothing less than a bold stroke, and in 1903, Avenida Rio Branco was cut through about 100 feet wide by engineer Pereiro Passos, who was the Mayor of Rio under the administration of President Rodrigues Alves. Between 1905 and 1910, Passos and the famous Paulo de Frontin did many of the public works along the waterfront—Flamengo and Botafogo—which have proven to be fully justified in following years. In 1922, the Morro do Castelo was removed and the six million cubic meters of earth was used to fill in the bay for what is today the splendid Santos Dumont Airfield. The remaining area was at first used for an exposition, but is now proving valuable ground for needed expansion of government and business buildings.

Two hundred miles to the south, in São Paulo, the earliest roads were located purely through usage. The functional radial street system leading from the city out to the countryside is the pattern that was established in colonial times. The central triangle, formerly marked by the city wall, is now paralleled with two more circumferentials which are being improved and are an important part of the new plan for the city. São Paulo began its urban growth with the coffee industry, which was typical of the single-standard industrial development in most Latin American cities. But today, São Paulo is shifting from an agricultural base to one composed of many diversified industries made possible by waves of European immigrants and by the development of electrical power. São Paulo's growth has been phenomenal. Her population, 35,000 in 1883, increased to 239,000 by 1900, to 579,000 by 1920. Today it is almost 1,500,000.

The effect of World War II on the cities of Latin America is penetrating. In fact, therein lies the high point of our story, but in order to understand fully the potentialities, the reader should become more familiar with the weaknesses and strong points of these cities. I shall reserve a later chapter in which to tell you how World War II is causing the cities of Latin America to embark upon a fifth period of development.

7. The Challenge of Historic Contrasts

After four hundred turbulent years, Latin American cities find themselves with many more historic remains than do our comparatively young cities of North America. These influences have had a very definite effect; in some cases have acted to advantage; in others, to very decided disadvantage.

Latin American cities have inherited some excellent examples of civic equipment. North American tourists looking for Old World charm well realize how the plazas, parks, and old architecture have contributed a quality quite lacking in our own matter-of-fact Main Streets. Bogotá's Plaza Bolívar is typical of many which serve to provide a focal center, a starting point, for the twentieth-century city. Even today life centers about the small colonial plaza at which the city originated. This is true of Buenos Aires, Santiago, La Paz, Mexico City, and many smaller towns such as Cuernavaca and Puebla in Mexico, Ayacucho or Andahuailes in Peru. Later history has given almost every large South American city a good-sized park near the downtown area which serves an excellent purpose today. When the central plaza was no longer adequate, larger parks were frequently located near the downtown area as the city began to emerge from its colonial period. In Mexico, the Alameda was laid out adjoining Bellas Artes, the opera house. In Santiago, we know the Avenida Bernardo O'Higgins and in Buenos Aires, the Parque Palermo. In São Paulo there is the Jardim da Luz and in Rio, the waterfront parks of Flamengo and Botafogo.

Old architecture in the form of churches and other public buildings emphasizes the age and permanence of the old plaza as a focal center of the city, and marks it as a nucleus of growth, giving integrity to the city plan. These historical remains are one of Latin America's greatest attractions—a very definite resource to be developed. This is particularly true of Quito, Ecuador, where planning for the future of the city must consider the need for preserving these features. From this point of view, Quito has unused possibilities as a tourist and recreational center, because it has scenic and historic resources. The churches of Quito are the best preserved that exist in the New World and the purest in design taken out of the Old World. One church still standing in Quito was built in 1535, two months after the founding of the city, two hundred and forty-one years before the building of the first mission in California.

At least one North American made some contributions to the historical growth of a Latin American capital. About 1851 Henry Meiggs built Fisherman's Wharf in San Francisco, was later chased out of California for forgery in the lumber industry and went to Peru in 1864. There he lived as Sr. Don Enrique Meiggs until his death in 1879. He built the highest railway in the world to Cerro de Pasco, 15,865 feet in the Andes above Lima, and later undertook the job of tearing down the great walls of Lima that had been built in medieval fashion 150 years before to protect the city from the ravages of pirates. In place of these walls, Meiggs built two great avenues—Alfonso Ugarte and Avenida Grau—as well as a third, Avenida Republica Argentina leading to Callao, which has a width of 300 feet. His boulevard planning included spacious plazas such as Plaza Union and Plaza 2 de Mayo, which today act as focal points for orientation and movement of modern traffic.

He did well financially and earned himself a two-way, scandalous reputation: for pocketing other people's money, and for planning streets at ridiculous widths. But today, he is looked upon as a planner of vision and some of the great street widths which he laid down, and which were later cut down by others to thirty feet, are being re-established by the city at considerable expense.

Argentina, in 1850, passed a law affecting Buenos Aires and La Plata, placing a street 150 feet wide around the city's perimeter in order to mark the capital from the surrounding area. This was later used for the development of a perimetral parkway by acquiring additional land.

Such works as these, handed down from history, have helped to make many Latin American cities thoroughly delightful, yet dignified, but other remains from history have acted to the disadvantage of the development of many cities, have hampered growth and strangled normal functioning. Narrow streets are the worst offenders; they complicate traffic enormously and require very careful planning and control. In Mexico City, traffic is kept in one direction on the more important streets, but a width of some forty feet between buildings is hardly enough to provide for two lanes of moving cars, one lane of parked cars, and the steady flow of pedestrians. On Buenos Aires' Calle Florida, the most important shopping street, all automobile traffic is restricted during shopping hours and the street is used entirely by pedestrians. On Rua Ouvidor in Rio de Janeiro, automobiles are *never* permitted; thus, the utility of the narrow street for shopping is greatly increased.

The narrow streets of the older sections of cities like Bogotá and La Paz are inadequate for efficient traffic movement to such an extent that a gradual migration has taken place to newer sections where more ample street widths have been provided.

The old "Spanish blocks," 336 feet square, required under the Laws of the Indies, were well laid out for their original use as family compounds, but today are an awkward shape for efficient commercial development. The interior of the blocks is nearly always wasted or put to inefficient use, and many schemes (such as Carl Brunner's plan for Santiago, Chile, which included a method of utilizing these wasted centers) have been suggested. Some cities have opened walkways within the blocks for shopping, which function quite well in Santiago and Rio de Janeiro.

The psychological effect of extensive historic remains cannot be overlooked. One Uruguayan city planner told me how townspeople in the smaller, urban centers want to group *all* public buildings—school, hotel, town hall, library, police, post office, etc.—around the main plaza because that is the established tradition. In one town he proposed locating the new school away from the crowded center in a spacious site just two blocks from the plaza overlooking a park; in another case, putting the new hotel on the bank of a river overlooking a grove of fine old trees; but in both cases it was of no avail—tradition and custom won out.

Contrasting conditions of inadequate colonial streets and broad, more recent boulevards, are found to exist side by side. In Lima, because of this contrast, one knows precisely when one leaves the old city and enters the new sections. In rebuilding the earthquake areas of Chile, the old and new widths stand together on the same street, where new buildings have been placed on the newly established street line, and old, partly destroyed buildings have not yet been removed.

The Zocalo in Mexico City, once the center of the bizarre life and culture of the Aztecs, holds exactly the same function in the plan of twentieth-century Mexico City. Today, for this ancient square of the Aztecs, plans are being discussed for an underground garage for some 1200 cars, air-conditioned, with facilities for emergency use as a bomb shelter. A competition was recently held for the scheme, which includes redevelopment of the entire area around the square to meet present needs.

Buenos Aires has had a definite tradition of planning since its earliest day. There is the historic Plaza de Mayo at the focal center of the city, with its Casa Rosada, the White House of Argentina; there is the Avenida de Mayo, the central axis of the city leading from the Casa Rosada to the Congreso with its spacious Plaza. But these and other evidences of good planning in the past are in sharp contrast with glaring problems growing out of the urban growth which took place at the turn of the century with the wave of immigration that likewise exploded New York into its suburbs.

Perhaps it is because such sharp contrasts as these exist today that South American planners and technicians are so conscious of the needs of the modern city, while we in the United States, with our more uniform technical standards, are unable to look either backward over the development of the city or forward to the use of new and broader standards.

At the foot of Rio de Janeiro's main downtown street, Avenida Rio Branco, is one of the most interesting of the city's developments. The tall buildings at the left, including the glass-walled Ministry of Education and Health, occupy the site of Morro Castello, the hill which was removed to form Santos Dumont airfield, visible at far right, and the Praça Paris, in the foreground.

Chicago

Buenos Aires

chapter 3

Latin cities have their problems

1. Our Cities and Theirs

We have seen how thousands of years of pre-Columbian settlement and over four centuries of European development have left behind a good deal of useful urban equipment and some that fits in nowhere. How does this equipment differ from the technological advancement of our cities in the United States? What are some of the more critical urban problems with which Latin Americans must cope?

Basically, these cities to the south of us are both older and younger than ours: older in the physical sense, but far younger economically. From the point of view of physical development, Latin American cities today are making a leap to the twentieth century from stages of development of the nineteenth, eighteenth, seventeenth, and in some cases the fourteenth centuries. I found Quito, Ecuador, delightful because only occasionally is it twentieth-century—more frequently, eighteenth-century. Yet a few hours away, Otavalo goes back to the fourteenth century with cobbled streets and harmonious buildings of white-washed adobe and red tile roofs. The handsome, richly-arrayed Indians are of the fourteenth century, with their bright pink shawls, their beads and rings, their great round hats and characteristic loads of bundles and babies on their backs, their graceful walk and courteous "Buenas tardes," their rich-hued ponchos and flashing smiles of good humor. The cities of the United States have known nothing earlier than the seventeenth century, and few urban centers have remains or influences even from that period. Our cities, then, are products of the late nineteenth and early twentieth centuries and reflect much of the lawlessness of that period of rugged individualism, and yet

41

at the same time contain the most widespread distribution of physical comforts and the highest standard of living that any large nation has developed.

For this high standard of living and advanced urban development, we have to thank our economic and technological *maturity*. In Latin American cities economic and technological *immaturity* accounts for many of their problems. Economically, we have already experienced "boom" periods of real estate speculation and know well the folly of inflation and the damaging costs, which follow. Mexico, in recent years, has been going through these growing pains, with over-building and over-subdivision of land, with the result that property values have increased enormously all over Mexico City. Newer, more modern buildings will be in demand, and rents and values of old buildings will go down, resulting in useless, blighted areas near the center of the city—just as we find in most of our cities in the United States. The problem is to provide planned, economic guidance in order to prevent unsound, towering property values. In the United States, the economic structure of urban land has already been "built-in"; in most Latin American cities such land values are only now being formed. For this reason, Mexico City and many others may profit by our errors.

From the point of view of technological immaturity, here is another very essential difference: The cities of the United States have been made possible by a tremendous industrialization of natural resources *to meet the needs of the people*, while Latin American cities have developed, for the most part, concurrently with partial industrialization which has been extractive in the sense that resources have been developed only for exportation *to meet the needs of world markets*. The maintenance of a low wage and low standard of living, as we shall see, has made this both profitable and possible. Latin America has carried all her economic eggs in one technological basket, and it is only within the last decade that really diversified productive industry has begun. This simply means that Latin American cities are in just about the position in which our cities were some fifty years ago, insofar as technology has been applied to human needs. Where foreign capital has generally developed the resources of Latin America in the interests of exploitation, the resources of the United States were developed locally and directed toward local consumption. The result of our more widespread industrialization has been the development of more and larger cities and a higher percentage of urban dwellers. About 29 percent of the total population of the United States lives in cities with populations over 100,000, while in Latin America only about 14 percent of the population lives in cities of that size. Five cities in the United States have over 1,000,000 inhabitants and in them live about 16,000,000 people, or 12 percent of the total population of the country; in Latin America there are four such cities, but with only 6,800,000 dwellers or about 5½ percent of the total population of 126,000,000. Including cities upwards from 500,000 population, in the United States there are 16 such cities with about 22,-000,000 persons or 17 percent of the total; in Latin America there are ten cities of that group with 9,900,000 inhabitants or about 8 percent in the group of countries. Lowering the population grouping to cities of 100,000 and over, we find that in the United States there is a total of 93 such urban centers with 38,000,000 dwellers or 29 percent of the total population; while in Latin America there is just about half that number, or 45 cities, housing 16,500,000 inhabitants or about 14 percent of the population.

But these conditions are changing with the rapid advancement of an industrialized economy in many countries. The diversified industrialization that has begun in Latin America is causing economic changes resulting in the expansion and development of cities to a degree that echoes the boom days of the twenties in our own country. Latin America's most dramatic example of sudden industrialization is Eddie's home town of São Paulo, Brazil, which has a story reading like that of Chicago in its boom days, full of bustling industrial activity, new building, and promising future. I have already described how São Paulo is shifting from an agricultural economic basis to one of diversified industry, made possible by European immigration and development of electrical power. Two dams nearby back up some thirty miles of streams forming two huge lakes—Guarapiranga and Reservoir Rio Grande. Turbines located at the foot of a 2,160-foot drop, near Santos, can generate, I was told, one million horsepower, three times the present consumption. Spinning and weaving, tanning, machinery, lumber, ceramics, clothing, footwear, building, and construction materials are some of the industries and products which are removing São Paulo's former dependence on coffee production. In 1937 there were 9,051 factories, employing 245,715 workers. Industrial power consumption increased twenty percent in 1941, eleven percent the year before. The government has under way a million-and-a-half-dollar industrial trade school to help provide future trained personnel for her growing industry.

Closely related to the recent increase in industrial and technological development is another significant way in which our cities differ from theirs. A single-standard economy in Latin America has produced cities which have quite a different relation to national life, where population is concentrated in the national capitals or in a few of the larger centers. For example, one-fifth of the population of Argentina lives in Buenos Aires; one-quarter of the population of Uruguay lives in Montevideo. Until the potential resources of entire Latin American countries have been developed, there can be no rational distribution of population such as there is in the United States. Nor has transportation been developed enough to disperse normal patterns of urbanization.

In some countries, there has been a recent movement of population from rural areas into the smaller urban centers, rather than to the capitals, in search of better living conditions and new opportunities. Colombia, once a one-city country like most of Latin America, is developing a pattern of urban and industrial distribution more normal than any other in South America. Cali, one of these thriving centers, has doubled its population since 1920 when it held 50,000 inhabitants and today is growing rapidly beyond the 110,000 mark. Located in a fertile valley at 3,000 feet elevation, it is a comfortable, healthy place in which to live. Cali's share of the new industrial activity is only a part of that which is developing other towns like Manizales and Medellín of the Tierra Media region. Small industries and intensified agricultural uses have brought new population to these towns and new residential districts are springing up rapidly. The architecture, climate, and hills of many of these pleasant valleys remind one of southern California.

Latin American cities are the expression of the warped national economy of the republics, an economy which calls for correction through over-all guidance and rational planning of the development of resources.

Latin American cities differ essentially from those of the United States in yet another way: they show an astonishing amount of direct influence from Europe in architecture, physical form, and way of living. Although recent skyscrapers have made São Paulo somewhat North American in character and although Buenos Aires is said to resemble Chicago at times, it is generally true that all Latin cities resemble those of Europe far more than they do those of the United States. To a North American visitor, this fact is often startling, particularly because it underlines in no uncertain terms our own lack of contact and our lack of technical cooperation with the builders of the cities of Latin America.

Buenos Aires, particularly in those parts built during the late '90s and early '00s, recalls Europe, especially France. In fact, some streets seem lifted bodily out of Paris and, like Paris, every street in Buenos Aires has a personality. Avenida de Mayo, the central axis of the city, is one which very agreeably takes you back to Paris for its gray French buildings, the trees in the downtown streets, and sidewalk cafes where people sit at all hours to take coffee, wine, or an ice cream. Beneath the surface, well-designed *subterráneos* suggest the Parisian Metro subway system. At right angles to Avenida de Mayo runs Calle Florida, the main shopping street which houses most of the shops and department stores, and brings to mind the Rue de la Paix in Paris. Between twelve and

44

two, and between four and seven in the afternoon, automobiles are prohibited the length of the street and crowds of people cover its entire width, strolling, shopping, or just window-shopping.

Another street with a French personality is Avenida 25 de Mayo, where the sailors' bars are located. More like Marseilles than Paris, this international galaxy of small cafes includes the Norden Bar, Bar Texas, Balalaika Bar, American Bar Broadway, Suisse Bar, Bar Singapore, Bar Hawaii, and a dozen others, in one of which every foreigner should be able to find a spot in which to drink and speak in his own language.

Avenida Alvear, at some distance from the center of the city, is not unlike the Champs Elysée in Paris for its apartment houses, automobile showrooms and smart shops, its trees and nearby parks. In many ways Buenos Aires is international and cosmopolitan like the cities of Europe, but at the same time it is quite North American for its vitality and material progress. For its industry and meat packing (one section near the slaughter house section is called Nueva Chicago) it resembles Chicago. For its spread-out, one-story suburbs, it resembles Los Angeles; for its saw-toothed downtown skyline of apartments and skyscrapers, it resembles New York. But for its sidewalk cafes and tree-lined downtown streets, and for an intangible spirit throughout the city, it resembles Paris.

These are the essential ways in which Latin American cities differ from ours: in their age since settlement, in their economic youth and unbalanced industrial development, in the concentration of population, and in the strong influence from Europe.

2. Problems in Physical Terms

Now let us look at some of the critical urban problems as they express themselves in social, economic, and physical terms—the scars that have been left by four hundred years of stormy evolution. In talking with Latin American technicians who work with the problems of cities, I found that these clear-thinking men and women are as well aware of their weakest points as our own technicians are in the United States; that generally they were more than anxious to discuss their problems frankly with me (in fact, they seemed to prefer this to boasting of past accomplishments) ; and finally, I found that Latin American technicians are earnest in their desire to solve these problems within the not-too-distant future. Although these problems are at times of different origin and call for a different solution than do those of the cities of the United States, they nevertheless require the same careful, scientific study which must be applied to urban problems anywhere. In speaking of "planning" problems I refer to those obstacles of a physical, social, economic, and political nature which stand in the way of providing a twentieth-century environment for the average man.

The special problem of housing is important enough to warrant special treatment.

Many physical problems, the result of uncontrolled growth that has been in some cases too sudden and in others too slow, confront the Latin American urban technicians. Some of these are: inadequate sites, poor sanitation, inefficient use of land, over-congestion of population, traffic and transportation problems, and a desperate need for adequate housing.

Sites which were well selected for small colonial towns have become inadequate for modern cities. Take, for example, the site of La Paz, one of the strangest cities in the world. You travel over the flat, 13,000-foot *altiplano* or high plateau, devoid of habitation, seemingly on top of the world; suddenly the ground drops away below you outside the train window and you look down into one of the biggest holes in the world—three miles wide and 1,400 feet deep! Down in the bottom and struggling up the sides lies the city of La Paz, a metropolis built of concrete, steel, and adobe in a miniature Grand Canyon of Arizona. The train descends on loops of steel track over slopes of bare earth of bizarre colors, washed away here and there leaving precipices and pinnacles of purple and red. Beyond the old adobe buildings whose gray corrugated iron roofs were until recently of red tile, stand the modern office buildings and apartment houses built within the last few years. From this vantage point just below the edge of the altiplano the city looks like a model by Norman Bel Geddes in which four-story buildings appear no higher than four inches. But at last, down in the heart of the city itself, you look up the steep, narrow streets, reminiscent of San Francisco, to the strange cliffs of red earth and far above you see the edge of the altiplano against a deep blue sky—blue as though you were looking up from the bottom of a well.

Dramatic as the site may be, it has cramped the growth of the city as effectively as the binding of Chinese women's feet. Some of La Paz' capable planners told me how difficult the city's growth has been. A past tendency to build on a miniature scale made possible a full use of the cramped space, but now under twentieth-century building standards with greater requirements for space, there is a desperate need for building area. Almost all available residential land is now in use; industrial expansion is thwarted by the limited area and the hilly character of the terrain.

From the regional point of view, the location of La Paz is poor because there is available nearby too little usable land which might serve to widen the economic basis for the population living at close range. In colonial days the site served well for a small urban population which required but little agricultural development. But today, with strong regional and international influences, new growth and a greater demand for more diversified production—both agricultural and industrial—La Paz needs space. Because of her location far off the natural center of gravity of the country, and lacking a well-developed highway and rail system, La Paz finds it difficult to contact the rich Yungas Valley—a potentially great source of fruits and vegetables—to reach the Rio Abajo area where production of grapes and wines can be promoted, and to maintain close relations with other cities like Potosí, Sucre, Cochabamba, and even Arica, her Chilean seaport. At present, all of these regions center on La Paz through an involved system of incomplete rail and highway connections, and Bolivians with whom I talked felt the need for a more rational distribution of sub-centers with stronger spheres of local influences.

It is true that an attempt was once made to move the capital to a more central location at Sucre, but even though that city is today the official capital, it fails to function as such because of inadequate internal communications.

Another city struggling with acute physical problems because of its site is Rio de Janeiro, capital of Brazil. This spectacular city of two million has grown over almost all of the buildable land which lies between the fantastic granite peaks. Like Manhattan Island, the new tendency has been toward vertical growth in the form of skyscraper apartments, calling for greater ingenuity on the part of Brazilian planners to provide arteries and other facilities for transporting the ever increasing population through congested areas to more distant, undeveloped points.

Health and sanitation problems are generally uppermost in need of solution in Latin American cities. Sanitation systems, so frequently taken for granted in the cities of the United States, have yet to be fully developed in many of the cities south of our borders. The lack of adequate drainage and sewerage disposal is the source of unhealthful living conditions frequently to be found, particularly in tropical and semi-tropical regions. City planning programs in Latin America frequently spring from a need to erase a condition of sanitation which has adversely affected the health of the community. In this way, the capital of the Brazilian State of Paraná, Curityba, with its 150,000 population, had to call in a firm of planning engineers from Rio de Janeiro to cope with the spread of typhus, the result of an unchannelized river flowing through the city. A comprehensive planning program grew from the channelizing of the river to the development of parallel riverside parkways and a complete zoning and highway plan for the city.

Bad conditions of health and sanitation are the factors which lead to the filth of forgotten corners of some of the Latin American cities. These always exist in proportion to the economic well-being of the particular country. Such superficial conditions are naturally more apparent when travelling than are the actual average conditions of community health.

I remember vividly my entrance into tropical Guayaquil, the Pacific port of Ecuador. The dock was filled with an assortment of peddlers seeking earnestly to make a living through hawking a wide variety of merchandise: boats carved of balsa wood, shrunken heads, Ecuadorian money, and telephone numbers of girl friends who spoke English. On the way to the hotel along a main street close to the splendid Simón Bolívar Drive which runs some six to eight blocks along the river, doorsteps were filled with sleeping men and all odd corners smelt strongly of urine. On minor streets where I later found my way, the sights and odors cannot be described with decency. Individual sanitary discipline is, of necessity, as primitive for the majority as sanitary facilities are scarce. A common sight is that of a man turning his back to stand against a wall in the absence of other facilities. On one of the main streets near the market, two small boys didn't bother to turn against a wall, but held a contest in the middle of the street to see who could reach nearest the curb. Smaller tots, squatting in corners, stared into space, adding more filth to that of many predecessors. In the markets nearby, food is sold directly off the pavements. The houses of these unfortunate people are unworthy of twentieth-century dwellers of the "New" world.

Up in Quito, 9,500 feet in the Andes, water ran for only a few hours in the morning in my hotel and for a few hours at night, and then only a dribble. The water level in the city's small reservoir followed closely the current rainfall. In addition, a slight earthquake which occurred while I was there damaged the pipeline, taking off some of the precious water supply. Young Quiteños, small boys and girls and servants, constantly carried buckets of water up the hills and it was a standing joke that one could always bathe in two bottles of *Guittig*, the bottled mineral water—the only water safe to drink.

Although extreme conditions such as these exist in many sections of Latin American cities, they are by no means to be found everywhere. Urban cleanliness goes directly with economic and political stability. In fact, it would be difficult to duplicate the order and cleanliness of the streets of, let us say, Guatemala City and Buenos Aires, to take two diverse examples, even in the cities of the United States. Nor are such conditions limited to Latin America. These problems are certainly not less tolerable than those to be found in the small towns of our deep South or in the shacktowns of the Southwest. In this day of technological progress, the people of all cities, whether in South or North America, must have, at a minimum, a sanitary and healthful environment.

The larger cities of Latin America have their traffic and transportation problems just as those of the United States, but these are confined largely to the capitals where population and automobile ownership are concentrated. Buenos Aires, for example, is concerned with the problem of moving its four million people about its seventy-one-square-mile metropolitan area. An increasing automobile ownership rate made possible by greater wealth and facilities has increased the traffic problem of Buenos Aires until it is comparable to that of any large North American city.

In many cities such as Bogotá, Colombia or Santiago, Chile, where automobile ownership cannot be compared to that in the United States, the narrow streets of colonial dimensions in the business centers have complicated the problem to such a degree that even more drastic steps have to be taken than are necessary in our cities. This is complicated further by the problem of mass transportation which, in the absence of widespread individual car ownership, must be depended upon to a considerable extent. Street car systems installed around the turn of the century by foreign-owned utility companies are in need of renewing, and in many cases have been supplemented by locally-owned bus lines. Buenos Aires, Santiago, and Rio de Janeiro operate excellent bus service along the many boulevards and avenues left from the days of city-beautiful planning. Once free of the narrow streets of Old Lima, the ride out to the San Isidro residential section takes one along spacious tree-planted boulevards. From crowded downtown Rio de Janeiro, the eight-mile drive to Copacabana is made in fifteen minutes over the finest waterfront boulevards in the world.

On the outskirts of the cities themselves one finds roads in sharp contrast with the highways of the United States. In general, highways, as we know them, are virtually non-existent in Latin America. If they are to be found—as in the Lima region or in and about Buenos Aires and other larger cities—they almost always cease to exist outside the fringe of the urban area. Of all the Latin American countries, Argentina has the most fully developed highway system, while Mexico follows a close second. Yet out of a total of 250,000 miles of highway in Argentina, only some 2,200 miles are paved according to our better state highway standards.

Chile has a total of about 27,900 miles of highway with only 212 miles paved. At least 10,000 miles of existing highway are in real need of paving. The building of a modern highway system would have direct effect on Chile's economic well-being and would vitalize the movement of goods and materials. However, since there are only 40,000 cars in the country (most of these in Santiago), there is not enough revenue from gasoline tax to build a road system, and the number of cars cannot increase until the high tariff on imported automobiles and the low income of the working and middle classes are adjusted to make more widespread ownership possible.

Rapid population growth, in recent years, has been an important factor in further complicating contemporary urban problems, particularly with respect to housing. Not only has increased economic activity in the capitals and larger cities brought in many from the rural areas, but this has been added to by a large influx of European refugees since the war.

The population of La Paz, Bolivia, for example, is today about 270,000, but increased by 100,000 between 1931 and 1941, most of this growth taking place in the six years since the end of the war with Paraguay. Twelve thousand of that number are European refugees who have come in during the last two or three years. La Paz cannot build housing fast enough for its present population.

European refugees have flooded into other cities of Latin America, with similar results. Ecuador has absorbed a great many who have helped to bring urban facilities up to date by starting small industries, taking over hotels and restaurants, and in general contributing toward the enlivening of a backward economic life.

Lima, Peru, has increased at a rate of 5.5 percent per year since 1933. Following are the amazing figures of growth for the Lima urban area since 1919:

```
1919........140,000 ⎫
1923........209,000 ⎬ Lima only
1931........280,000 ⎪
1940........450,000 ⎭
```

1940........660,000—Total Lima urban area

In the official agencies, there was general agreement that one of the chief obstacles to an adequate solution through planning was lack of information about the cities. Basic data concerning such matters as population distribution, housing conditions, amount of traffic, and so on, is difficult to obtain, frequently does not exist. Argentina has had no complete census since 1914. This need for basic data became apparent after the great earthquake in Chile in 1938, which devastated a 200-mile-long strip south of Santiago. So little data was available concerning the towns of the region to be rebuilt that special maps had to be drawn and information had to be hurriedly collected before the work of rebuilding could begin.

If the future of the cities of Latin America is to be secured through intelligent planning, a much more complete compilation of information about these various problems of a physical nature must first be made. Full knowledge of the extent and scope of a problem is the first step toward its solution.

3. Problems in Economic Terms

During the last decade, Latin American cities have been undergoing a tremendous amount of new economic activity, marking what might actually become the beginning of a fifth period in their history. In addition, World War II (to be discussed later) is perhaps the most significant event since their wars of independence.

This new economic activity is partially indicated by building booms, the biggest of which I observed in Mexico City, Bogotá, and La Paz. These are typical of the kind of activity which is taking place in other Latin American cities to a smaller degree. This new construction, bringing forth many urban planning problems, is the result of interesting and complicated causes.

One of the reasons for Mexico City's building boom was the fact that a great amount of money from abroad had found its way back to Mexico because of the international situation and was being invested in land and building. In addition, unsettled political and labor conditions in past years had encouraged investment in real estate rather than industrial or agricultural development. This resulted in a skyrocketing of property values and a great intensification of land use without time for proper planning control. Mexico City was full of mushroom building activity, from the Zocalo where an underground parking area was being planned, to Chapultepec Park, where new subdivisions nearby were filling with homes. Unfortunately, most of this investment has been speculative and based on "minute thinking" rather than on actual quantitative needs. We in the United States know that the result of such unplanned building is sure to be an over-supply of certain types of buildings and blighted values of less desirable types, together with lowered tax income for the city. Mexico City's building boom recalls the period of real estate inflation through which our cities in the United States have already passed to the detriment of the general urban economic stability. It is unfortunate that Mexico is not profiting by our experience.

The second big boom I found was in Bogotá, Colombia. The reasons for this spurt in building activity are similar to those in Mexico City, but, in addition, the conservative Bogotanos have a strong tendency to carry out the old Spanish tradition of investing in land rather than in business or industry. The result has been increasingly high land costs in the center of the city: up to 650 pesos per square meter or around thirty dollars per square foot. During my visit in November 1941, there was not a single business street without several eight- or ten-story buildings under way. A reliable source gave $50,000,000. as the amount spent in construction in 1940. At the outset of the war, just before Pearl Harbor, one architectural construction firm alone had $1,500,000.-worth of signed contracts held up and was expecting to lay off about three to four thousand men if steel was not forthcoming. Since construction is the major industry in industry-poor Bogotá, the whole economy of the city could have been upset, opening the door to social violence and giving a definite advantage to latent anti-democratic Nazi-sympathetic forces. That situation has since been recognized, but the example points out the dangers of a narrow economy. Here in the United States we take for granted our WPA, relief, savings, and unemployment insurance. The somber-faced, black-coated man in Bogotá is less inclined to question our good will when his bread-basket is full than when it is empty.

Progressive Bogotanos, who are for the most part very friendly toward the United States, want a program of balanced industrial planning to give them more economic independence. To do this, they told me, they must have technicians and men to organize and direct, and assistance in studying a diversified pattern of industrial development. Such a pattern might develop Medellín, Barranquilla, and Cali as industrial centers, while Bogotá would remain the financial and cultural center. The most economically progressive town in Colombia is Medellín, in the year-round spring climate of Tierra Media. Here is one of the liveliest and finest cities on the entire West Coast. The people of this region, known all over Colombia for their progressiveness and industry, have made Medellín a city with an economic future.

The third major building boom I found was in La Paz, Bolivia. In spite of its difficult location and lack of space, the city was bristling with new construction. The reasons follow those of Mexico City and Bogotá, with the addition of one more. Enormous wealth in silver and copper had been drained out of Bolivia for hundreds of years since the coming of the Spaniards. But it was only six years ago that, for the first time in its history, the Bolivian government passed laws requiring that a portion (in this case about forty-five percent) of the value of exported ore remain in the banks of La Paz. The result has been extensive investment in building and increased commercial activity. All new construction dates from the passage of that ruling. Because this new activity provides opportunities for employment, it is in turn partly responsible for the influx of population into La Paz during the five or six years since the close of the wasteful war with Paraguay.

These three countries, Mexico, Colombia, and Bolivia, lead in building activity. Others are undergoing building activity but only insofar as new economic life permits. Ecuador, for example, is practically dormant in contrast to the activity in Colombia. High prices in the United States and the low value of the sucre in the international market make it impossible for Ecuador to buy United States' products, building materials, and machinery for industrialists. It follows that there can be no real physical planning until economic development of the country gets under way. Ecuador is an agricultural nation and cannot compete in the international market without using machinery and industrializing agriculture.

She cannot get farm machinery without adjusting the value of the sucre and, in turn, cannot put machinery to work without providing alternate employment for the Indian. Ecuador's agricultural economy in the mountain regions is tied to the Indian and the almost feudal *huasipango*, a small parcel of land given the Indian in exchange for services rendered on the hacienda. This important aspect of Ecuador's basic economy is described in the novels of the Ecuadorean writer, Jorge Icaza.

New industrialization in Chile, which has taken place in some of the larger cities during the last ten years, has caused some new building. But this industrialization is of a diversified nature, not to be confused with the investment of foreign capital in the nitrate and copper mines which have been Chile's economic lifeline for one hundred years. Judging from the poverty and squalor of certain parts of Chilean cities, such huge investments as the thirty-five, million dollar nitrate refining plant at Pedro de Valdivia have done little to help raise the average income or the standard of living of the mass of the Chilean people. Diversified industry got off to a good start up to the time of the earthquake of 1939, which actually did more economic than physical damage. All the country's resources had to be used to rebuild the devastated area; there just were not enough funds, workmen, or materials to do the needed replanning and rebuilding. But as a result the spotlight was placed on the desperate need for a more self-sufficient industrial basis.

To stimulate building in Santiago back in 1932, the city went so far as to pass a law making all new construction tax-free for a period of several years. Then, when the earthquake occurred, there was a rush of capital to Santiago, away from the area which had caused such psychological terror.

According to many people there, the tax income of Chilean cities is so low in proportion to that of the federal government that her cities' financial well-being is always questionable. In general terms, I found that most Latin American cities suffer from too small an income from taxes. Valparaiso, for example, with its 200,000 people, has an income of only about $100,000 per year. Federal taxes in South America are generally high in proportion to municipal taxes. One important source of taxation—most important in the United States—is comparatively small in many Latin American countries: I refer to the income to be derived from large-scale native industry. One planner in Chile suggested the possibility of direct loans to cities in Chile for needed public works, to be spent only in accordance with United States' specification as to standards of planning.

In Argentina, the financial situation seems to be quite the reverse. One Argentine who knows the situation pretty well told me that Argentina has *too much* money—too much lying idle in the banks; money that could be put to work against the Axis by the young men of the country. He said Argentina's wealth needs the direction of its young men to reorganize, replan, and remanage.

Greater Buenos Aires, with close to 4,000,000 people residing within the metropolitan region, definitely the leading urban center of South America, has all the earmarks of a North American city: uncontrolled uses of land, over-building, traffic mazes, too-small park areas, bad housing. Preston James * describes these problems: "Associated with this rapid growth of Buenos Aires have come all those social and economic phenomena which are characteristics of modern Occidental cities: the rapid rise of land values in the center; the development of "blighted areas" in the old residence zone near the center, and in the suburbs; the rapid expansion of the city along the lines of travel, including the establishment of detached suburbs and satellite towns; and the over-rapid subdivision of land into small residence lots in the scramble for profits by land speculators." Buenos Aires has a strong sense of property rights like most cities of the United States, intensified by the fact that property was originally sold in small pieces, then re-subdivided.

One economic problem in Uruguay is to secure a sounder economic basis than agriculture and the tourist program which, up to the present war, has been one of the country's biggest industries.

Programs of national planning, for better use of resources, dovetailed with plans for a more rational distribution of urban population, can begin to iron out some of the social, economic, and physical problems facing these fast-maturing South American cities.

4. Problems in Social Terms

In social as well as in economic terms, Latin American cities are replete with problems which, in comparison, make the United States look like a paradise for city planners. Two basic conditions must be changed: (1) the generally low income of the mass of the people must be elevated in order to provide a sound economic basis on which to plan; (2) the prevailing level of education must be raised considerably higher before the process of planning an improved environment can become a democratic, cooperative effort.

Of these two problems, the matter of income is most striking. Wages in Latin America are unbelievable low. One Latin American gave me the following standard of comparison of wages in relation to buying power. In order to buy one kilo (2.2 pounds) of bread in the United States, a laborer must work about twelve minutes; in Uruguay, fifteen minutes; and in Chile, sixty minutes. Gerard Swope † has figured out what a kilowatt of electricity and a news-

---

* Preston James, *Latin America*, Lothrop, Lee, and Shepard, 1942.

† *The Cost of Living in South America*, Gerard Swope; *Atlantic Monthly*, June, 1940.

paper means to a Latin American worker in terms of work time. He says that in the United States a laborer must work 4.5 minutes in order to pay for one kilowatt, while in Brazil a laborer must work 30 minutes; in Argentina, 31 minutes; in Uruguay, 36; and in Chile, 37. As for newspapers, a worker in the United States can buy one with three minutes of his time; in Argentina, with twelve minutes of his time spent in similar employment; in Brazil, twenty-four minutes; and in Chile, sixteen. A worker in Bogotá, where wages are comparatively high, gets from thirty to forty pesos a day, or about $1.20 to $1.85, which in buying power would be the equivalent of about $2.50 per day in the United States, or $75 per month. How long could a worker in Gary, Indiana, maintain even a minimum version of the "American" standard of living on $75 a month? How could a laborer in Concepción, Chile, while working for such wages, maintain a tile-bathroomed home, educate his children, contribute sufficient taxes to the city, and speaking of his economic well-being, live as does his fellow-worker in Gary, Indiana? The highest wages in relation to buying power are in Argentina and Uruguay, but even there, only in the large cities. As a result, these two countries are the most progressive from a material point of view and have the largest middle class.

The resultant poverty expresses itself in many ways. For example, the Peruvians sometimes call the Ecuadoreans *monitos*— little monkeys—and make fun of them. Now, this is easy to understand. Members of poorer classes in Ecuador and all Latin countries do make a rather poor impression. They often appear unhealthy and round-shouldered, sleepy and shabbily dressed. But a little social analysis may explain this condition. They are unhealthy because they lack good food, proper diet, and medical care. They are round-shouldered because coupled with under-nourishment they seldom have exercise other than back-breaking labor. They are sleepy because they have no decent homes in which to get a night's rest and they are poorly dressed because in their country there is little manufacturing of the things they need. The value of money, the sucre, is so low on the international market that Ecuador cannot afford to buy foreign-made products. And this is true of other countries.

Here is another result of economic exploitation: a lack of buying power and the existence of low incomes explain why the Indians and mestizos of Ecuador, Peru, and Bolivia chew the coca leaf, from which cocaine is obtained. Because coca deadens the sense of feeling they use it to relieve pains of hunger; to them it is inconsequential that they go undernourished. A Bolivian miner earning fifteen cents a day does not look far beyond the coca leaf. He also believes it to be a kind of cure-all, to cure the toothache or any minor pain. None of these countries has taken steps to break the practice, which is firmly established because the people have become so habituated to use of the drug and the authorities, to the revenue derived from its sale.

Against the background of the low economic level of the inhabitants of Latin American cities we must place the second basic condition in need of change: the shockingly high level of illiteracy. Compare the percentage of illiteracy of South America's largest country, Brazil, with that of the United States: Brazil's population is about seventy percent illiterate; the United States', less than four and one-half percent illiterate! The populations of Bolivia, Paraguay, and Ecuador range between seventy-three and eighty-three percent illiterate; Cuba, sixty percent; Colombia, fifty percent; Mexico, forty-five percent; Chile, twenty-four percent; Uruguay, twenty percent; Argentina, twelve percent.*

Increase of wages alone will not necessarily bring a more equalized standard of living. In Mexico I was told of a case which illustrates the necessity for advancing mass education along with an increase in wages. In an agricultural section, a substantial raise was made to all workers in the community, but each pay day, the moment the checks arrived, the money was spent for unnecessary, extravagant wares of traveling salesmen. Poverty reigned again until the next pay day. My informant suspected a deal between the employer and the salesman.

It is obvious, then, that poverty cannot be erased by higher wages alone, but must be accompanied by a program of education and encouragement of savings, perhaps through social security. Real wages in the form of social necessities such as housing, health protection, and education can go far toward improving the standard of living and laying the foundation for planning better communities.

Along with low income, the general lack of education was pointed to over and over by Latin American planning and housing technicians as the chief cause of many social problems, making impossible the kind of planning and housing program they would like to see. These men and women realize, and made clear to me, that the only reason we in the United States had been able to develop a planning process to the extent we have, is because, generally, our people and officials are geared to it by education and general enlightenment. The degree of public enlightenment in Latin America varies a great deal from one country to another, but generally there is a reluctance to accept new methods. This lack of understanding of what modern methods of planning and housing can do was dramatically demonstrated in the earthquake of 1939 in Chile, where in one town alone—Chillan—ten thousand houses were razed in less than five

---

* These figures are from Luis Quintanilla's *A Latin American Speaks*, Macmillan Co., 1943.

minutes. After the quake there were only five hundred houses left standing and only twenty of these had roofs on them. Forty-three thousand houses were destroyed altogether in the region; all roads were cut off by destroyed bridges; wires were down and railroads cut off. The planning organization set up to handle the rebuilding according to a better plan found that the populace just could not make the sudden jump from the complete absence of planning to a full understanding of the new standards provided in the Master Plan, nor to comprehension of the benefits to be derived. Education of the public is a gradual process, but a very essential one if democracy is to survive.

This problem of social education is particularly necessary in housing work. I remember visiting a new housing project in Rio de Janeiro which replaced a very miserable *favella* or shack town. As I approached the gate, I saw a small boy, screaming at the top of his voice, being pulled out from behind a wall by the ear. The gatekeeper was giving him the beating of his life. He had caught him urinating against the wall. To the smiles of adults standing nearby and the terror of the youngsters, he was being made an object lesson in sanitary discipline. This boy had never known the use of plumbing fixtures. Without social education housing, as well as planning, is a waste of time and energy.

Many technicians spoke of a Latin indifference to new ideas, to changing the old ways of doing things. Those who complained were usually individuals who had traveled or studied in the United States or in Europe, and had taken on a fresh, progressive point of view. One native of Rio de Janeiro who had worked two years in the United States had come back to Brazil with the idea in mind of beginning a profession of landscape architecture patterned after that of the United States, but found an enormous inertia to be overcome. Another, a planner, studied four years at Harvard, in the planning school, and on his return to Rio met with tremendous opposition in his efforts to apply modern design standards to subdivision work. He was dubbed "the North American engineer," and although he did an excellent job in planning several large subdivisions, non-acceptance of these "new" ideas was too hard to overcome and he has given up trying.

Another very definite obstacle in the way of good housing and planning is the lack of trained technicians, from plumbers to hydraulic engineers. In a country as backward as Ecuador, for example, it is no simple matter to have a door fixed. A friend of mine in Quito had a new door cut through the adobe walls of his house and called in a carpenter to hang the door and put on a frame around the opening. The framing had to be done over three times with three different carpenters and three pieces of wood before the joints worked out as they should. On the larger scale, planners in

Brazil, Ecuador, Chile, and Colombia discussed the need for trained personnel in engineering, research, planning, housing, and related specialized fields.

But still more is needed than public education. Underlying changes must take place in the social and economic structure, like those which took place in America, giving a new philosophy to those children of immigrants who have come from the Old World. São Paulo in Brazil is showing this kind of awakening; a new acceptance of changes because a new economic life is replacing the old. The shift from an agricultural to an industrial basis means that people are seeing new things, thinking out new ways of solving old problems. In contrast, other Brazilian cities like Baía or Rio de Janeiro are going along quite in the old pattern of social thought. Donald Pierson, the North American sociologist in São Paulo, pointed out that Brazil's most socially advanced people are the Paulistas because basic economic changes are taking place in that city.

5. Problems in Political Terms

Standing shoulder to shoulder with the social and economic obstacles to good planning and housing in Latin America are the enormous difficulties of a political nature that come from the immaturity of these democracies. Our own political unity in the United States and our long, steady evolution toward effective democracy are other things which we take too much for granted. However, in spite of this comparative harmony, even we suffer from a lack of coordinated control, particularly in city government. The case is far worse in Latin American cities where there is much less municipal independence. Since most of the countries are one-city countries, and this one city is the capital, the federal government has a good deal to say about that city's development.

I was told in Buenos Aires that a major political obstacle to more rational planning was governmental ignorance of planned coordination of public expenditures. The conservative, compact group which ran the government for twenty years up to the *coup d'état* of June, 1943, maintained a complicated system of independent, over-lapping departments—federal, provincial, and municipal—with resultant waste of expenditures. Eight different governmental agencies authorized to plan public buildings operated without any coordination. For example, the new building of the Ministry of War, under construction during my visit, caused considerable comment on the part of the public and technicians because of its location. Totally unrelated to other public buildings like the adjacent Casa Rosada, the scale of the New Ministry was such that it dwarfed everything around it. Engineers with whom I spoke voiced a need to centralize and coordinate these various agencies into one or several centers, with more opportunity given to the younger men of the country.

The lack of political stability, long periods of unenlightened governmental administration, and a restrained citizenry are some of the causes of uncoordinated, lop-sided development of resources and the still unsolved problems of the physical environment. Mexico and Brazil are two examples. Mexico at times has had a very enlightened policy toward housing and planning, particularly during the administration of Mayor Saenz of Mexico City during the early thirties, but this policy ceased with a change of administration.

Today, Brazil has many of the advantages of a strong, unified government, but few of these advantages have been put to work to provide better housing and planning. President Getulio Vargas' centralized control offers a splendid opportunity to establish a coordinated, far-reaching program of planning and housing, but the degree to which this has been done is small. In Brazil's capital, many praised the present administration while others complained of an involved bureaucracy, full of red tape and personal favoritism, a bureaucracy which makes no distinction between politics and administration. A complex maze of laws and ordinances confuses building practice. Rio de Janeiro, I was told, has had numerous mayors in some ten years since the beginning of the Vargas regime; each new man appoints his own staff of technicians who must make a fresh start on the involved urban problems of that capital. Many capable men, knowing such limitations, stay out of public work; their talents, so necessary in a growing country, go unused. However, Brazil *is* progressing as never before under the Vargas administration in spite of the underlying political obstacles.

Personal politics, one of the toughest obstacles in the way of rational development and the application of progressive technical standards, is probably the greatest weakness of the Latin American governments. This was stressed to me in many places—Peru, Colombia, Chile. In most Latin American cities, mayors and other city officials are generally appointed rather than elected, as they are in the United States, with the one exception of Montevideo. Many technicians expressed a desire to see a Civil Service set standards for public office in order to replace those political appointees who hold technical positions without training, background, or integrity. Along these lines, our own experience in government in the United States should prove helpful to Latin Americans.

Political reform is essential to the planning of a more balanced economy and a full, wise development of resources. Many clear-thinking technicians with whom I spoke look for leadership to the younger generation in seeking solutions to some of the problems. They said the break will come naturally through the young people, as they receive more education and come more into contact with the

United States. In doing so, they are building up a force of ideals so great that solutions to problems will break through the restraining mesh of arbitrary, artificial limits set by governments.

Considering the limitations with which Latin American planners have to cope, and the obstacles that have grown up during the years, it is a wonder that anything has been done at all. But actually these technicians have done plenty; so much so, that Latin American cities in many respects actually have qualities which make them more attractive and livable than the cities of the United States. Before turning to the story of the outstanding accomplishments of the Latins, their ability and imagination, let us paint the picture a little blacker and look at the special problem of housing.

Contrast between the old and the new in building: at right, old adobe building beside a modern structure of reinforced concrete in La Paz, Bolivia. Below, left, portion of a new avenue in La Paz, built over the channel of a river which has had to submit to technological advance; the barefoot Indian is no more incongruous beneath the neon sign than the adobe buildings which are being torn down to make way for concrete. At right center, milk delivery by ox-cart in Concepción, Chile; bottom right, new construction in Concepción after the 1939 earthquake is set back from the old building line in preparation for street widening.

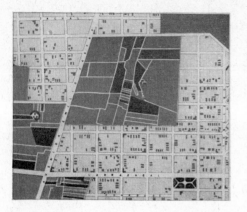 

Buenos Aires, subject to almost uncontrolled speculative building, has suffered severely during its modern period of expansion. The three small maps above show the reduction of open space within the city in one small area along the Avenida Emilio Castro: left, 1916; center, 1925; right, 1932. Below, suburbs creep over the surrounding open country. Aerial view on facing page shows the congestion of the modern city and (below) a closer view of downtown Buenos Aires.

Products of overbuilding during boom times clog Latin American cities too. Upper left, downtown Buenos Aires; skyscraper is Edificio Cavanagh, tallest in Latin America. Upper right, the heart of São Paulo; Praça da Republica in foreground, Parque Dom Pedro II in distance, both to be linked by a circumferential boulevard now being built. Lower left, maze of governmental and commercial buildings in downtown Rio de Janeiro; many buildings, such as the Ministry of Education and Health at extreme right, are individually admirable. Lower right, central Montevideo, Uruguay, has its share of competing building, in which, too, individual buildings have much merit.

Three building booms: *At right, new construction in Mexico City, Mexico; below, center, La Paz, Bolivia, where it has been necessary to channelize a river to aid the building program.*

Below, new construction, Bogotá, Colombia. Site conditions, not of the best in all three cases, are particularly constrictive in La Paz, where the city is hemmed in by precipitous canyon walls.

Foreign ownership and exploitation of resources has brought little material or cultural improvement to the common man of Latin America. Above, nitrate plant at Pedro de Valdivia, Chile; below, typical "conventillo" in Santiago, Chile, the type of slum in which many Chileans still live despite increased efforts to provide decent housing.

In some ways, Latin American city governments and people display more common sense than do we in the United States. For instance, faced with the problem of a narrow street favored as a shopping thoroughfare customarily thronged with thousands of people, and with doubtful value in any program of street widening for this particular thoroughfare, Buenos Aires has arbitrarily forbidden vehicular traffic on Calle Florida in the afternoon (photo at left). Rio de Janeiro, with a similar problem, has the same solution for Rua Ouvidor (right; both photos Moore-McCormack Lines).

chapter 4

Two-thirds of Latin America

1. Neighbors without Houses

In the early days of the New Deal, housing surveys brought forth the startling news that in the United States, *"one-third* of the nation is *ill-housed,* ill-clothed, ill-fed." Today in Latin America, housing conditions are more like the converse: only *one-third* of the people of Latin American republics is *well-housed.* We can safely say in general terms that *two-thirds* of Latin America is *ill-housed,* and it follows without emphasis that this two-thirds is equally ill-clothed and ill-fed. This fact I found to be true from the moment I crossed the border into Mexico until I flew back into the U.S.A. at Miami, after passing through some fifteen republics, visiting and studying conditions in ten of them.

Luis Quintanilla, Mexico's Ambassador to the Soviet Union, substantiates these conclusions in his excellent portrayal of Latin America.* He says, "The naked truth is that of the one hundred twenty-six million Latin Americans certainly *no fewer than eighty-five million* are actually starving. *They have no houses, no beds,* no shoes. . . . Roughly, the per capita number of beds in Mexico is equivalent to that of automobiles in the United States, about one to every four people. Of the 3,884,600 houses in all Mexico, fewer than 265,000, sheltering some 2,500,000 people, have drinking and running water. Even in Mexico's stately capital, with 1,-700,000 inhabitants, 500,000 lack those conveniences. And Mexico is one of the most advanced of the Hemisphere republics, certainly the leader in labor legislation. . . . In Chile, children fourteen years old earn less than three cents American money a day. It is not unusual to see nine people living in a single room."

---

* *A Latin American Speaks,* Macmillan Co., 1943.

This is not going to be a "pretty" chapter. I am going to talk about the worst of housing conditions under which significantly large groups live. I am going to tell you what I saw and what was told me about the enormous, tremendously vital problem of housing for two thirds of our Good Neighbors who live in the other half of this hemisphere neighborhood.

Like the North Americans, and like any people anywhere who are proud of their achievements, our Latin neighbors are not too anxious to air the extent of bad housing and the need for its improvement in their particular country. But because of a desire on my part to understand constructively the problems to be overcome, Latin American technicians assisted me in inspecting slum areas and learning of bad housing conditions. I tell of them here only that a fuller knowledge of these conditions and their significance will lead to a better understanding of the needs of the Latins, and help to indicate methods by which we may be able to make more broadly effective our program of inter-American cooperation.

I hardly need point out to Latin American readers that removing the extensive slums of New York and Chicago is no less important than remedying similar conditions in Santiago and Buenos Aires. In spite of the penthouse version of the United States portrayed in many of our motion pictures, Latins are aware that we have slums in our largest and wealthiest cities. I was told many times that "everyone knows that people in 'Norte America' do not all live as one sees in the movies." Many were fascinated by *The Grapes of Wrath* and considered it one of the finest pictures to come out of Hollywood. *Tobacco Road* was another which they liked for subject matter, although some criticized the treatment. Existence of slums, whether in North or South America, indicates a social weakness, a disease which needs immediate diagnosis for treatment and cure.

An examination of Latin America's housing conditions in large urban sections particularly, though in the rural areas as well, will lead to the uncovering of many other social and economic problems and will indeed make more urgent the solution of those problems. For, after all, is not the object of a democratic government and an effective economy betterment of the home? Stuart Chase in his *Goals for America* * lists as the "Big Five" (essentials for a decent environment) : Shelter, Food, Clothing, Health and Education. But all of these center upon the family dwelling and are, in fact, the components of a home itself. A few years of business prosperity or a rising stock market, a new high in tin production in Bolivia or a flood of Good Will to Latin America—all these are void of meaning in a democratic world if at least one object is not the attainment of decent housing for all.

Housing for all peoples is so closely related to the economic pic-

---

* 20th Century Fund, New York, N.Y., 1942.

ture that you need only to take a look at the way the majority of the people of a country live to find out how effectively its economy is working. At the same time, a lively program of housing, whether public or private, is one of the soundest ways of activating a dormant or stagnant national economy. For that reason, the housing problem in Latin America is particularly significant. Solve this one problem and you solve a host of others.

In order to understand these broader problems, the whole, not the partial picture of housing must be understood. In order to understand what the Latins have done to solve this problem and to compare that work with ours in the United States, it is necessary, first, to wade knee-deep or further into the quagmire of a dozen Latin American slum types and see for yourself. I am going to take you from Mexico on south to Chile, over to Argentina and up to Brazil, through the various kinds of slums—the *rancho* of Colombia; the *conventillo* of Chile and Argentina; the *cortiço* and the *favella* of Brazil. A full picture of Latin America must speak of these housing variations, the conditions and extent of the slums, the effect on the people, and some of the economic and political aspects.

2. Excursion through Slum Types

The slums of Mexico City are surprisingly extensive. One conservative estimate gave 300,000 persons out of the 1,500,000 in Mexico City as living in sub-standard dwellings. (Compare this with Quintanilla's figures, p. 61.) According to United States standards, this estimate should be tripled. One of the worst areas I saw is known as "Colonia Buenos Aires," ironically translated as "good air," near the brick manufacturing section on the south side of the city. At the time of my visit this slum community covered an area of a good half dozen square blocks. Its hovels of brick, wood, metal and cardboard brought to mind our shack towns and Hoovervilles of the depression, and contrasted sharply with Mexico City's splendid new sections. "Colonia Buenos Aires" was formerly a grazing field for a large hacienda opened during the revolution as a temporary camping ground for refugees coming in from the suburbs for protection. Later, the area developed into a more permanent camping ground for refugees in need of economic protection.

Since my visit "Colonia Buenos Aires" has been removed, but more of these squatters' camps are scattered around the very fringe of the built-up area and conditions of health and sanitation in them are intolerable. No surveys have been made of the exact numbers of families living in these shacktowns, but one figure given me by a member of the *Comision Nacional de la Habitacion,* an agency beginning a study of the problem, estimated that there were 80,000 such ramshackle dwellings.

The more highly congested slum areas, consisting of older, permanent dwellings, are those near the center of the city where, for example, the newly widened Calle Lopez cuts through what was formerly the Calle de Las Pajaritas (Street of the Little Birds), the quaint name for the old-time red-light district. The "Little Birds" have been moved into fancier quarters but whole families are now crowded into the remaining one- and two-room hovels of adobe that surround the little courtyards. The new street widening will provide new building sites for middle-class apartments, but the low income families will probably have to move out to some "Buenos Aires" shack town.

The social and economic effects of such slums cannot be underestimated. Money that could be used to fulfill the need for housing and raise the general standard of shelter in Mexico City is going into high-priced apartments for the well-to-do minority. This would be more wisely invested, both socially and economically, if directed into at least a proportional number of low-cost housing projects, but during my visit in October, 1941, no housing program was under way. There seemed to be the same unfortunate attitude on the part of land owners once held in the United States, that slums, and likewise poverty, are a permanent institution. Such poverty is subsidized by the upperclass Mexicans, who are generous to the beggar on the street and who (at least the land owners) profit well from the rents paid by the residents of the acres and acres of hovels which make up slum areas like Colonia Buenos Aires. The value of a steady flow of income with a minimum amount of overhead expense has become of more importance than the human value of re-housing slum dwellers under decent standards. Mexico's true monument to the Revolution still remains to be built: housing for the masses of her urban population. Until that work is accomplished great architectural attempts at monumentality, like the costly Monument to the Revolution which towers above the old Paseo de la Reforma, remain static and meaningless—mocking the objectives for which the Revolution was fought.

My study did not include Panamá, but while passing through the Canal Zone, I did have an opportunity to spend some time in Panamá City and Colón. The slums of these towns (along with housing in our own possession, Puerto Rico and within our borders, in the deep South) stand a challenge to our wealth, technological ability, and concept of democracy. The special type of slum dwelling of Panamá City consists of two- and three-story wooden tenements with windowless and lightless two-room apartments opening on the street or balcony. One such apartment may be used by a family of six or eight persons. As much as ten dollars per room is what the poorer people pay for one of these apartments, at street level. Second and third floors are somewhat higher in rent. Rooms are no more than ten feet wide; and, passing by on the narrow sidewalk, you see the interior crowded with cheap, ornate furniture, and the dark, windowless room beyond. This low-income standard extends without variation throughout Panamá City.

Two years before my visit, a major fire in Colón on the Atlantic end of the Canal had burned out four or five square blocks of tenements of this type. As a temporary expedient, army tents were put up throughout the central parking strip of the main street, and also in a huge vacant area nearby. The spaciousness of the tents, and their suitability to the climate over that of the standard ten-foot-room of the tenements, created a great demand for them and all filled up very well. Two years had passed and the temporary canvas tents were dilapidated from the tropic rain and sun, patched with cardboard, tin, rags and what-have-you, but crowded with families. That the expected filth, dirt, and depressing squalor of the tent village is kept to a minimum is proven by the brown little boys who have their showers by running naked in the warm rain, drying off in the sudden warm sun, and by their mothers who stroll majestically carrying on their heads huge bundles of wash. A look inside one of the tents shows the same attempt at acquisition of furnishings that one sees in the permanent wooden buildings—the cheap bureaus and beds, crowded together, streaked and stained with the rain that is no stranger to these interiors.

Much of this land in Colón, I was told, is owned by the Panamá Railroad Company, which in turn is owned by the Panamá Canal, which in turn belongs to us. That is why such conditions remain more a challenge to our government than to that of Panamá. In Panamá City, most of this land is owned by land-poor Panamanians. There is practically no home ownership by the masses of the population, which would suggest the need for providing an adequate economic basis before good housing for all can be practicable. Here in the Canal Zone, as in Puerto Rico where housing conditions and poverty are even worse, our Latin American policy is on the spot. What we do in these two places has a lot to do with the attitude of the rest of Latin America toward us. Part of our program of military fortification of the Canal area and Puerto Rico should go toward *social fortification* to take the steam out of all disbelievers in our intentions in Latin America. In the long run, housing must be an integral part of public works wherever we invest public funds, whether in Vallejo, California or Panamá. Such a policy should keep us above reproach.

Slums in Latin American cities are generally built on the hillsides rather than on flat land, as they are in the cities of the United States. Bogotá, Colombia, has cleaned off many of the slum dwellings or *ranchos* which formerly covered the slopes of Monserrate above the city, but a great many still remain. Warned against the dangers of going into the section, I went anyway, and found unhealthful and depressing conditions, rather than the expected threats to my personal safety. These sections, built on steep slopes overlooking the city, are well-drained by the frequent torrents of the Andes; at the same time, waste waters pass right down into the city itself, threatening public health. The land was sold to the people of the ranchos some thirty years ago on a rather vague business basis—a flat rate was charged of about ten cents (U.S. money) per day for a specified number of years, with no deed given to show for the transaction. From a legal point of view, the "owners" are today really no more than squatters, but that at least facilitates their removal from the site and into better dwellings, as the city has done to a good extent. An unfortunately more permanent section is called La Perseverancia. Here streets were laid out and paved by the original owner and the community is said to house about 15,000 people. Tiny lots, some ten feet wide by thirty feet deep, were sold; and in this case each family has a deed for its own lot and house. The result is that clearance or improvement is next to impossible. Impressed with the supposed security of ownership of his postage-stamp of land, each owner pays no heed to the overcrowding, the bad sanitation, and depressing environment. Each lot is covered entirely with building; there is no garden area, front or back.

Arriving at Guayaquil, Ecuador, I was impressed by an elaborate waterfront development, Simón Bolívar Drive, where parks and large public buildings overlook the river. This park and others in the city are laden with pompous monuments of costly bronze and marble brought from Europe. But only a few blocks away, behind this extravagantly planned front, lie poverty and sub-standard housing conditions. One example tells the story quite well: I walked along the river, just beyond the end of the park area, where half-grown boys as sleek and as unencumbered by clothes as eels were diving into the brown water. Amid the filth that dots such forgotten corners I saw a three-story, concrete-frame apartment house, in the best of the "modernistic" tradition, standing unfinished and without side walls. Smoke was ascending slowly in the damp air from all the floors; and, looking closer, I found that some thirty or forty very-low-income families had simply moved in and set up housekeeping. Ceaseless cooking was going on in brasiers on the concrete floors, and partitions of split bamboo or burlap had been put up in an attempt to achieve privacy. Looking back at this section along the river where I was standing, I realized that this little corner adjoining the boys' swimming hole and the public food market, was the community privy.

Because Quito, the capital, 9,500 feet in the Andes, remains fairly well back in the 19th century from a standpoint of development, she is as yet relatively free of the evils of congestion that come from urbanization without planned development. Although a definite need for modern housing exists, no particularly large areas of over-congested sub-standard houses have collected.

In Lima, Peru, slum demolition has been practically automatic; frequent earthquakes shake down those buildings which are most poorly built. How these have been replaced by well-built projects will be covered later. However, communities of shacks and shanties still exist on the outskirts of the city. One of these, Barrio Leticia, is located on Cerro San Cristobal, a hill topped by a huge cross. The Barrio consists of a collection of mud streets with adobe houses and corrugated iron roofs. Living conditions there differ little from those of the first settlers of Old Lima 400 years ago. The foot of the Cerro is washed by the Rimac in which the friendly ragamuffins of the slum sections keep clean and cool.

Although extensive areas of completely sub-standard housing in Lima are rare, authorities told me that the congested housing in the center of the old city is one of the causes of the high tuberculosis death rate. This is indirectly the cause of a large portion of the 24.4 deaths per 1,000 per year. (Compare this with the death rate in the United States—11.6 persons per thousand.) 78.3 percent of the old portion of the city consists of one-story buildings, which means high coverage of land, lack of open space for sunlight and air, and high density of population. (The prevalence of one-story buildings is common to many Latin American cities.) This, of course, is true only of the city of Lima itself. The suburbs such as San Isidro and Miraflores could not be more healthful nor lovelier for their spacious lot sizes, gardens, boulevards and parks.

In La Paz, Bolivia, the standard form of socially inadequate housing is built around a series of connected patios of the Spanish type, designed for the tropics but hardly adapted to the high, cold climate of La Paz, 12,000 feet above the sea. Such structures as these cover much of the south section of the city below the Prado, the fashionable boulevard, and Avenida Santa Cruz. Originally intended for one or several families, *one family to a patio,* they have since been re-subdivided; dwellers are packed in at the rate of *one family per room.* As many as thirty families share one building. Three small courtyards, one behind the other, lead to the back of the property. Water and sanitation facilities consist of a single water spout in the middle of each courtyard, and in the back of the third patio is a single privy for the use of all families in the three linked courtyards. The rent for one room in patio No. 1 is about 200 bolivianos ($4.00 U.S.) per month; in patio No. 2, 100 bls. ($2.00 U.S.) ; and in patio No. 3, 50 bls. ($1.00 U.S.) per month. You may take your choice. There are no baths at all. This is typical housing for the "two-thirds" of the people, not only in La Paz but in many of the other cities of Bolivia.

It is easy to understand the problem of providing cheap, good housing for workers in Bolivia when you compare wages with living costs. A worker in La Paz, I was told, earns about 500 bolivianos ($10.00 U.S.) per month, while the cost of a small five-room house and lot in La Paz is about 200,000 bolivianos ($4,000 U.S.)

Outside the cities in Bolivia, the housing problem in the vast mining regions is even more difficult. Although much excellent, though minimum-standard, housing has been built by the tin mining companies, much, indeed, remains to be done. Since a very large percentage of the workers in Bolivia are miners, a very special kind of housing problem exists, and is being given a good deal of study by the Bolivian Ministry of Labor and Social Welfare. In spite of improvements made, it would seem unlikely that the 1943 Bolivian tin strikes would have occurred on such a large scale had the miners been working under fairly decent conditions as to wages, housing, and other social necessities. Vicente Lombardo Toledano, President of the Confederation of Latin American Workers, who recently inspected conditions in Bolivian tin mines, stated on his return: "Living conditions of the Bolivian miners are miserable to the extreme"; and told of wages of 10 and 15 cents for a 12-hour day, for work under most primitive, unsafe mining conditions at an elevation of 13,000 feet. Toledano also spoke of the widespread use of coca leaves provided by the employers to make existence possible for the workers.

To give some idea of the housing problem among these miners, I translate from *El Problema Social en Bolivia* * by two Bolivian sociologists, Remberto R. Capriles and Gastón Arduz Eguía: "Condition of housing among the miners varies appreciably from one camp to another. In some camps—very few—housing fulfils the elementary standards for healthful living: ventilation, space, electric light, and community facilities such as running water and sanitation. But what is more likely is to find the house cramped for space, miserable, sordid, and provided with none of the minimum standards of hygiene. If the house is not a crude and miserable cabin—through whose half-demolished walls enter the cold and the wind of the *puna* (high plateau)—it may be a dwelling which has no windows or other method of ventilation at all, no flooring, electric light, drinkable water, beds, or sanitary facilities. In the majority of cases, the worker gets along with a single room. . . . The confusion and lack of privacy is appalling because within this single room—storage space for odds and ends of rubbish and refuse—live together the worker, his wife, and his children, besides the domestic animals. This is the condition which exists when such a single room serves for one family. Sometimes it serves for two or more families."

* Editorial Fenix, La Paz, 1941.

68

Is it any wonder that the strikes occurred in spite of Hemisphere solidarity against the Axis? The Century of the Common Man must indeed appear a remote objective and an ironical motivation for these members of the United Nations who live under such conditions. From a social point of view, or even as a matter of pure political realism, it would seem more desirable to apply the benefits of increased tin production due to the war and recent legislation, to improving housing conditions for the working class of Bolivia.

The Chilean slum type is called the *conventillo*, home of the *roto chileno*, the forgotten man of Chile. Translated literally conventillo means "little convent," but according to Appleton's New Spanish Dictionary, the word is translated and defined as a "tenement inhabited by persons of ill repute." Actually, this is far from the case. The people who inhabit the conventillos of Santiago, Valparaiso, and other Chilean cities are no more of ill repute than those who inhabit the Old Law tenements of the East Side of New York.

The conventillo consists of a long narrow courtyard, sometimes no more than an alley, leading off the street, with one- or two-room cubicles down both sides. If there are any sanitary facilities, they are located at the end of the court. Wash tubs with running water may stand in the middle of the courtyard. In a typical case, I found thirty families living in one conventillo that took up an area of about fifty by one hundred feet. A family with whom I spoke paid forty-eight pesos per month for one room (about $1.50 U.S.) with cooking facilities outside the door of their single room in the courtyard. A few wash tubs with running water stood in the center; one bath marked *Baño* and two toilets for all fifty families stood uninvitingly at the end of the courtyard.

Chile's liberal and deeply democratic people are concerned over the importance of the housing problem. Several of the newspapers of Santiago have carried on campaigns to lead public opinion toward increased government action. Through these articles, my own observations, and other sources, I received a general idea of the conventillos and shocking figures on the conditions therein. Statements by various public health officials indicate a general recognition of the fact that the greatest number of cases of sickness and death are found in the areas of the conventillos; for example, eighty percent of the existing cases of tuberculosis were found to exist in them. One public health authority pointed out that such an environment makes completely impossible the teaching of healthful living habits. He tells of the futility of preaching high standards of personal hygiene in the absence of modern facilities such as wash basins, showers, sanitary toilets, ventilation, and structurally sound houses, free of rodents. It was pointed out that, while the present condition of health in these areas is bad enough, much worse is the incipient danger of epidemics. These two dangers of sickness and death are added to by a third, their influence upon the morality of the people of the conventillos, through what one authority described as, "crowding together persons of different ages and sexes, creating an unwholesome condition which leads toward vice and corruption."

My own visits to the conventillos gave me the opportunity to verify cases described in articles on the subject in various Santiago newspapers. In the following case I found none of the conditions to be exaggerated: "This building has 18 rooms; all flooring, stairs, and roofing are in a wretched state of repair. One hundred and forty persons live in the building; fifty of them are children under fifteen years of age. For these one hundred and forty, there are two toilets and two baths; two faucets with running water used primarily for washing clothes—the means of livelihood for most of the women. Entering one dwelling place, the room seemed to be on fire, but was actually full of smoke from the cooking facilities. The family consists of the husband and wife and five children, from thirteen down to two years of age. The income for the family, between the wife's washing and the husband's job, is 800 pesos per month (or about $27.00 U.S.) for the support of a family of seven."

When I returned to my own dwelling place after visiting that conventillo, I felt as though I were entering a palace. I was paying just about that same sum per month in a pension of simple, North American standards, for a clean, sunny room, three good meals a day, modern bath facilities and maid service, and the use of a garden and terrace.

On one excursion my companion was a friend from Chicago who was also interested in the problem. Attracted by her red hair and by my camera, little crowds of urchins followed us about from one conventillo to another as self-appointed guides. We found that both the children and their parents were always courteous and polite to us when we explained our interest in knowing something of conditions in order to help toward their betterment; these people went out of their way to be informative. We also found that on the whole they were industrious—that most of the residents were too busy with cooking, washing, etc., to pay much attention to us—but, then, who other than the most industrious could survive under such conditions as these? Ninety percent of the women who live in the conventillos live by washing clothes in the narrow yards along with the playing and the crying of the youngsters. The ironing is done inside the single room on a table or bed.

Another case reported in the Santiago press which I re-investigated was found on Calle Roberto Espinosa: The conventillo consisted of 14 rooms and was owned, according to the reporter, "by a Doña X who lives adjoining the Parque Forestal and who is also owner of a luxurious streamlined automobile, has central heating and all kinds of comforts." The reporter writes that: "one hundred persons are living in the fourteen rooms (8 persons per room), for whom there is one shower and one toilet. A shoemaker occupies one of the better dwelling units with his wife and *eight children from 21 years down to three,* and the entire family lives in a single room some twelve feet long and ten feet wide, facing on the street. There are two beds; all cooking is done in this room, and the father also carries on his shoemaking trade in a little shop in one corner. Rather than risk the dirt and danger of the distant 'sanitary' unit, the family must use improvised toilet facilities in the room." The father of the family reported that by working all day, every day in the month, he was able to earn thirty pesos ($1.00 U.S.) a day. His rent was about 100 pesos ($3.50 U.S.) per month.

Overcrowding and intermingling are grave problems in the conventillo. In frequent cases many persons of different ages and sexes must sleep in the same bed. One writer cited the case of six persons, mother and father both forty years old, one son of twenty-three and three daughters, seventeen, fifteen and ten years of age, all of whom occupy the single bed which the family owns. It is not sheer coincidence that thirty percent of all births in Chile are illegitimate and that out of every thousand children borne alive, 284 die within the first year. Chile's child death rate is the highest in the world next to that of China.

The Second Inter-American Congress of Municipalities held in Santiago in 1941, attended by officials of cities throughout the hemisphere, presented some interesting material on the extent of the housing problem in Santiago. A paper by members of that city's Department of Statistics claims there are 3,000 conventillos in the city of Santiago, and that these are inhabited by 250,000 persons out of the city's total population of 540,000, excluding surrounding municipalities like Los Leones, Las Condes, etc. These statistics show that Santiago's average density is about 127 inhabitants per hectare (51 per acre), which is normal for a city becoming as rapidly industrialized as Santiago. But in those sections where conventillos are crowded together, the density is as high as 500 persons to the hectare or 208 inhabitants per acre. These sections comprise about 34 percent of the total area of the city. Taking 160 persons per hectare (66 per acre) as a maximum standard of density for healthful urban conditions, the density of upwards from 250 persons per hectare (104 per acre) in the conventillo districts signifies a dangerous over-crowding, particularly at a building height of one story. The Department of Statistics paper points out that the abnormally high mortality rate which throws out of balance all other statistics in Chile—an average of 26.7 deaths per 1,000 (see following paragraph for comparison with other countries), is provoked primarily by unhealthful housing conditions. This paper sums up the housing needs for Chile by saying that "of the 750,000 dwellings in Chile, it is totally necessary to reconstruct seventy percent of them, or approximately 500,000 dwellings, in order that the population of the country may live in at least minimum conditions of hygiene and comfort in accordance with the most elementary principles reached by the degree of advancement of urbanism and civilization in our times."

Oscar Alvarez Andrews, Chilean lawyer, makes some significant comparisons of living conditions in Chile with those of other countries. For each room in Chile, he says, there are on the average 5.6 persons who must live together in that single room, while in the United States, the average is three persons per room; in Germany 3.5; in Spain 4.6 persons. Consider the relation of such over-crowding to the death rates in those countries: Andrews gives a death rate of 26.4 persons per thousand per year in Chile, while in the United States an average of only 11.6 persons die each year out of every thousand—in Germany 12.6, and in Spain, 18 persons. (Between 1930 and 1935, deaths per thousand persons in cities over 100,000 population in the U.S.A. ranged between a low of 7.5 persons and a high of 16.8. This high figure occurred in many cities in the deep South where housing and living conditions are particularly unworthy of our United States.)

The crux of the problem lies in the average monthly rents paid in the conventillos—a minimum of twenty pesos to a maximum of one hundred and fifty (.60¢ to $5.00 U.S.)—so one Chilean journalist says—who adds that this is a problem which must be studied with care and made public so that the citizens of Chile may see that effective action is taken. He tells of several cases investigated by Don Eduardo Hamilton, Professor of Philosophy of the Catholic University. One family of five pays 28 pesos ($1.00 U.S.) for one room with dirt floor, with no lights and no water. The father earns 13 pesos a day, the mother 3. With this income of 2.58 pesos (about 8¢ U.S.) per day per person, the family has for breakfast: coffee; for lunch, broth and meat; for dinner—what is left over from lunch! All five sleep in the same bed. It is, of course, natural that such conditions as this put education for the younger members of the family far off in a gloomy future.

Another family of six has an income per person per day of 1.25 pesos (about 4¢ U.S.) and with this, get along on tea for breakfast, a single dish of meat or starchy food for lunch, and tea for dinner. Even worse cases than this are cited, one in which a family of five lives on 29 centavos (or one penny, U.S.) per day per person. The journalist asks, "How is it possible for one to eat on such a sum?" The answer is that the family doesn't eat, nor are its members able to think about bettering their condition or looking after their health and education.

Shelter, clothing, and food are the most vital necessities of these people, and they cannot have them without a living wage which will provide the family with twentieth-century living standards, and make possible the destruction of the conventillos and their replacement with modern sanitary houses.

Opposition to slum clearance in Santiago, I was told, comes from the Rightists, who are, usually though not always, the land-owners and also from the Church. These groups assist in maintaining the low level through slum ownership and ideological objections. Owners of slums profit well from the average charge of 70 pesos ($2.10 U.S.) per room with the barest of facilities. This should be compared with the 25 pesos (less than $1.00 U.S.) with bath, water and modern standards charged by the Chilean government housing projects. The Church itself owns about one-fifth of Santiago, according to authorities, who add that although the property is controlled by the Archbishop, it actually belongs to individual members of the clergy. Church ownership of land is said to be increasing through inheritance of property from its more pious and philanthropic members.

The housing problems in Chile were greatly affected by the extent of the damage by the earthquake of 1939. Even today, after a considerable amount of new housing construction, I was told of the need for at least 1,000 houses in the low-cost group in the small coastal city of Concepción alone. But from what I observed there, I would judge that the housing program hasn't begun to scratch the surface. One of the chief reasons for the lack of housing in the earthquake-destroyed area and throughout Chile is the shortage of building materials and the absence of an organized building industry. There was talk of promoting the lumber industry and developing a forestry program to provide building materials for low cost houses. Such steps are not only important but essential to the future economic and social well-being of the Chilean people.

In studying the problem of the conventillos of Santiago, Valparaiso, and other Chilean cities, we North Americans may well bear in mind a fact I mentioned before: In spite of huge investments of foreign capital in the mines and nitrates of Chile ($35,000,000 in the plant at Pedro de Valdivia) little of the wealth extracted has helped to raise the standard of living of the mass of the Chilean people.

In order to understand the housing situation in Buenos Aires, one must know that the middle class of Argentina is larger than that of any other Latin American country, and that wages are proportionately higher in relation to living costs. The average general income leaves but few with unsatisfactory incomes. For that reason the slum problem is not nearly so extensive as in Chile, yet there is much mediocre housing, though it is not so deplorably sub-standard that it requires immediate action as in the case of the conventillos of Santiago. This is true of much of the housing for some half-million people in the industrial Avellaneda section, which consists of one-story, single-family dwellings on small lots, spread over an extensive area. It is a suburban slum. Here the problem has been one of poor land use, jerry-building, and inadequate drainage, rather than a fundamental economic weakness.

Much of the ramshackle sub-standard dwelling construction on the outskirts of Buenos Aires is of wood or corrugated iron. There is not such a great amount of adobe construction as in Chile. However, there still remain areas of definitely sub-standard conventillos. Within the city itself, 65,000 adults and more than 50,000 children live in buildings of this type.

According to the figures of the National Department of Labor, the average industrial worker pays 25 percent of his salary for housing, and generally for inferior housing, which would suggest the economic possibilities for house building on a huge scale. The National Department of Labor's statistics show that 106,598 workers in Buenos Aires alone, whose salaries are no higher than 120 pesos (about $30.00 U.S.) per month, pay as high as 31 pesos (about $8.00 U.S.) or *one-fourth of the income* for a *single sub-standard room* in slum sections. *High standard public housing facilities* are provided in the United States at *one-fifth of the client's income.*

Dr. Alejandro Bunge, in the First Pan-American Congress on Low-Cost Housing, held in Buenos Aires in 1939, said Argentina needed a total of 2,500,000 houses to replace sub-standard dwelling. By 1939, they had built 24,000. Allowing an average of four persons per family or dwelling unit, Dr. Bunge's estimate indicates that in rural and urban areas, better than *two-thirds* of the 13,000,000 people of Argentina are in need of rehousing, according to twentieth-century standards.

During this same housing conference in 1939, Mario Saenz, Argentine Deputy, said that "housing in general in Argentina is inferior to the economic capacity of the country, and that the housing accessible to the working class is shameful for its high price, and for its deficiencies in sanitation, space, and comfort." He points out that "only ten percent of the working and white-collar employee classes own their own homes," and that there are "150,000 cases of families with children who must live in a single room in demoralizing over-crowdedness. . . . Such conditions are morally intolerable." Of the 1,000,000 families of workers in the country whose incomes are considered insufficient to live on, Saenz said that 150,000 families have more than four children and live entirely in one room. Figures of Dr. Alejandro Bunge show that out of a typical one hundred families of the 150,000, thirty families

74

had five or six children; twelve had seven or eight; while three families had nine to eleven children, all of them sleeping, eating and living in the same small room. Saenz continues with Dr. Bunge's comment: "It takes only a little force of the imagination to take into account the calamity that this represents from the moral, spiritual and physical point of view." Further data by Saenz shows that out of a group of 3,490 cases of children between the years of six and fourteen selected at random from families of low income, 19 percent lived with families of five in one room; 240 cases or 6.9 percent lived with families of six in a single room; and 82 cases or 2.3 percent lived with nine in a room. In 702 cases, the child slept with two other persons; in 196 with three; in 70 with four; and in 27 cases, with five or more persons. Can we tolerate a postwar world in which large portions of the population sleep six to a bed?

Mario Saenz quoted from André Gide, whose remarks on housing conditions in Paris apply as well to Buenos Aires, New York, San Francisco, or any other city where inhuman standards of shelter exist. Gide wrote: "Bad housing is more than an attack on man's comfort; first it is on health, and then on morality. Standards of cleanliness and decency are practically impossible to maintain in the sordid living quarters and promiscuity of the pigsty." He pictured typical conditions under which renters and sub-renters live together in one room, sleeping, resting, sometimes working there. "In it collect the drunken men, the sick, and the crying children; in it remains the corpse until it is taken away. It is difficult to imagine the degree of loathesomeness which these conditions must arouse in one who has not lost his sensitivity, but it is worse to imagine the degradation of even greater numbers who, having become so accustomed to this existence, are no longer affected by it."

Argentines with whom I spoke summed up the obstacles in the way of slum removal as being two-fold: financial and technical. They said there has been no real allocation of funds for studying the problem, nor has there been sufficient use of the funds in the Argentine Central Bank and those of private capital. What is needed, they said, is to circulate existing money and solve the housing problem at the same time. From a technical point of view, absolutely essential is a fully developed building industry, especially for low-cost materials. These Argentine technicians said the country needs research for making use of local materials, experiments with wood which can be obtained from Argentina and Brazil; a study of pre-fabrication; training of builders and technicians. There is not yet enough local building to make possible a large scale, low-cost housing movement, either public or private. Industry has been directed toward money-making opportunities rather than toward satisfying the needs of the Argentine people.

Uruguay's low population density (2,100,000 people in the entire country), and the generally high standard of living, make this advanced republic the least slum-ridden of all the South American countries. In direct contrast, the slum problem in Brazil's cities is one of the most extensive in South America.

One rough check-up estimated that 75 percent of the people of Rio de Janeiro live in houses which would be considered substandard according to minimum housing standards in the United States. For Rio, it was estimated that the "better" residential sections like Copacabana, Ipanema, Tijuca, and others, house not more than 600,000 persons in up-to-date dwellings, while the remainder of the 2,000,000 inhabitants of Rio live in housing that either has been reduced from a higher standard by more intensified use, or was sub-standard from the start. Most North American visitors in Rio de Janeiro know the delightful apartments and hotels of Flamengo, Botafogo, Copacabana, with their balconies and magnificent views. But they seldom know of the sub-standard housing in which the larger portion of the populace lives.

A prevalent type in the old, blighted sections of the city is the *Cabeça de Porco* (Pork's Head), so-called because of the endless possibilities of dividing into smaller portions. Large old homes of the Victorian era were taken over and rooms rented to families, using curtains for partitions and setting up simple cooking and sanitary facilities. Six, eight, or ten persons may share a single room.

The *vila* is used by people of slightly higher incomes (about $20.00 U.S. per month). Store clerks, typists, and workmen live in these long pedestrian alleys, dead-ended, with little one-room and two-room apartments along one side. In plan, they are much like the conventillos of Chile. Although as a rule they are more substantially constructed, they are yet below minimum standards of light, air, and space requirements. These have been built until recently with permission of the city, although with somewhat improved standards. Since land in Rio was originally sold by frontage, which accounts for the long, slender shape of the lots, these vilas are very well suited to present ownerships. Some vilas, built according to good standards, are quite desirable for privacy, quiet, and off-street play space, but this cannot be said for the majority of them.

One finds many dwelling places upstairs above commercial property on the side streets of the central business district in buildings that are usually forty or fifty years old. These downtown flats are now inhabited by many more families than were ever intended.

The *favella* has the lowest standard of all. There are two kinds —those of the squatters who are allowed to stay on unused public land by paying off the police and inspectors, and are otherwise ignored; and the renters, who live on land which was once pur-

Portion of Colonia Buenos Aires, whose name when translated means "good air."

"Shopping center" in Colonia Buenos Aires.

Another squatters' village in México City.

COLOMBIA: *A community of "ranchos" or adobe huts, on slopes of Monserrate above Bogotá.*

PERU: *Barrio Leticia, a sub-standard district on the slopes of Cerro San Cristobal in Lima.*

CHILE

A "conventillo" of the better type in Santiago, Chile, above; at left, children in another Santiago conventillo; below, a third conventillo.

BUENOS AIRES

Above, typical Argentine conventillos around courts (Buenos Aires); right, interior court surrounded by corrugated-iron dwellings, La Boca, Buenos Aires; below, slums in the suburbs: Buenos Aires, near the Avellaneda district. On facing page, general views of corrugated-iron dwellings in La Boca, one from inside court (below) and one from outside (above).

BRAZIL

... of slums in Brazilian cities
Above, a "cortiço" in São Paulo
left, a "favella" near one of Rio d
Janeiro's lagoons; below, typica
"vila" in Rio de Janeiro. On facin
page, top, Favella Hill, Rio d
Janeiro, at right of photograph
facing some imposing contemporar
buildings (including the Ministr
of War) at the left; left cente
baby sunbathing in favella nea
lagoon (see frontispiece, this chap
ter) and right center, general view
of this same favella; bottom,
single faucet supplies water for
favella hard by Rio de Janeiro'
luxurious Jockey Club.

Two more views of slums in Rio de Janeiro: above, favella on Lagõa Rodrigo de Freitas, near Le Blon; below, close-up of Favella Hill.

chased by a single individual and on which shacks were built for some twenty-five dollars each and rented for around $2.00 a month. With such a rapid return on investment and with practically no problem of maintenance, a very neat profit is to be made. Much of this latter type of favella, expressly built with minimum standards for maximum profit, is to be found in Recife to the north.

I found favellas in Rio which made our Okies' camps in California look like garden cities. Many of these crown the more conspicuous of the hills in the built-up area. The best-known of all is that on Morro do Providencia, the hill just above the new railway station and overlooking the verdant Praça da Republica. Another favella, Praia do Pinto, is located in the midst of the Le Blon area, one of the wealthier residential districts, just beyond the Copacabana district. The favellas (as all Brazil) know no color line, and the blackest of persons live in them in harmony with the whitest.

In the Le Blon favella (removed since my visit in June, 1942) on the edge of the beautiful lagoon, Lagôa Rodrigo de Freitas, I was greeted by a typical sight—a young girl of not more than sixteen years smoking a pipe and looking after three small children who were playing alongside a drainage ditch full of yellowish, stagnant water. There were *4,000* people crowded into this favella in an area of about two square blocks. I estimated that about 200 people lived in a similar area of two square blocks of the adjoining middle class residential district. The city is beginning to crack down on landowners who are thus exploiting a social problem, and has torn down one similar favella and built a temporary, planned community for the inhabitants. This action is due to the initiative of a group of socially-minded individuals, but as yet hardly represents a governmental policy. The city was forced to do something in the interests of public health protection when the high disease rate in these favellas began to menace nearby areas which were rapidly filling up with high-priced homes of upper and middle class types. I was told that because of such bad housing conditions, ten percent of the population of Rio is tubercular.

For these poor housing facilities, from the Cabeça de Porco down to the favella, the *Carioca* (native of Rio) pays a general average of one-half his income in rent. This fact in itself indicates the scarcity of and the demand for housing facilities of *any* kind—even a glance at the favellas tells you that there are no vacancies. It is not that these people *want* to live under such conditions, but that they simply have no choice: there is nothing better to live in that fits their wages and other living costs.

The housing situation in São Paulo, the industrial center to the south, is not as critical because the superior site of the city has allowed plenty of space for growth. In addition, most of the city was developed at a later period than Rio, when higher standards existed. However, one authority estimated that sixty percent of São Paulo lives in sub-standard dwellings, while another claimed forty percent. Even an average of these figures seemed conservative to me after an inspection of working class districts of the city. That the higher estimate is more likely is borne out to some extent by figures of the Municipal Office of Social Documentation of São Paulo which found areas of one-story buildings where the population density was as high as 2,000 persons per hectare or about 800 to the acre.

The inhabitants of these congested areas live in *cortiços* and *vilas*, the two typical slum types of São Paulo. The lowest of these, the cortiço, which means "bee hive" in Portuguese, is similar to the conventillo of Chile. With a friend from one of the municipal offices, I visited several cortiços. In one we found sixteen families living in a space about thirty feet wide by eighty feet deep, in a one-story building which enclosed a tiny courtyard. I spoke with a little Spanish lady of eighty-one years who told me she had come there twenty-six years ago and gave *graça de Deus* (thanks to God) daily for the good *patrão* (landlord) who let her live there free all those years in exchange for cleaning up a little. The average rent is seventy milréis ($3.50 U.S.), which gives the *patrão* an income of 1 conto and 120 milréis, or about $56.00. These families generally earn about 250 to 500 milréis a month ($15.50 to $25.00 U.S.) and could afford to pay more and live in better places if they were available.

Another cortiço I visited took up an area of about one hundred and fifty by ninety feet in which lived forty-two families. This was a one-and-a-half story group with basement dwellings, about four or five feet below the street level, and four or five feet above. Those on the basement level cost sixty to seventy milréis per month; those on the upper floor were ninety. All were one room only—some with four to six or more persons—and *all* family and domestic activities took place in that single room—sleeping, eating, working. (Chalk drawings of pornographic subjects sketched unashamedly by the tiniest of youngsters on the sidewalk outside, rather bluntly verified familiarity with the facts of life at a tender age.) Community facilities, such as laundry tubs for washing clothes, dishes or food, are all toward the middle of the court. Cooking is done on a charcoal stove arrangement just outside the door of the dwelling.

The vila is the next better slum type in São Paulo and, like those of Rio, consists of a number of single-family units of two or three rooms each, all in a row, and under one roof. All sanitary facilities are indoors; there are no community facilities at all. Rent for two rooms is about 150 milréis ($7.50 U.S.) per month; for three rooms, about 200 milréis. Coverage is practically 100 percent, except for narrow access ways and small courtyards.

78

Donald Pierson of São Paulo has conducted several case studies of bad housing conditions in that city. Three sections were chosen— Bexiga, Moóca and Canindé, as representative of the lower level of housing to be found, in contrast to those splendid sections like Jardim América, Pacaembú, and Higienópolis. Statistics for housing standards in these sections offer such comparisons as the following: Average lot size per dwelling in Moóca, 1,539 square feet (these are approximate figures converted from the metric system), and in Jardim América, 16,229 square feet. Average monthly rent per dwelling unit in Moóca, 91 milréis ($4.55 U.S.), and in Jardim América just about twenty times that sum. An average of six families in Moóca uses a single courtyard, with not a single garden anywhere in the district, while each family in Jardim América has its entire plot of ground for its own use. Out of twenty-five cases chosen at random in the Moóca section, as many as eleven persons were found to sleep in the same room, while the lowest number to share a sleeping room was three persons. Of the same number of cases likewise chosen at random in Jardim América, the average number of persons per bedroom was about 1.2 persons. Typical cases were found in Moóca where grown sons and daughters slept in a single room with their parents. Here are some instances cited by Pierson: mother, father and three sons, 27, 22, and 16 years old; in another case, the parents and two grown daughters of 30 and 25 years; another, the parents and a son of twenty-four years; and in other cases, younger children. The average distance to toilets from the door of the dwelling unit in Moóca was found to be 33 feet, with as many as twenty persons of different families for the use of each facility. In Jardim América, 78 toilets, each within the dwelling and of first-class standards, were found to exist for the use of 78 persons.

The survey likewise took a poll of radios, phonographs, musical instruments, and automobiles, and found the same scarcity of these items in the Moóca section and their abundance in Jardim América as in the case of toilets, beds, living space, etc., mentioned above.

No figures are available on birth rates, but all through the cortiço sections of Sao Paulo my guide and I found children in such amazingly large numbers that child-bearing would seem to be a ceaseless process. Although seemingly sturdy and rugged, the children of the cortiços were actually older than they appeared. They were poorly dressed and lacking in bodily nourishment, to say nothing of mental food. Fascinated with my camera as by a Pied Piper's flute, dozens of them followed us down the street and in and out of the cortiços. The children sometimes had diseased eyes or sores on their hands, mouth or feet (none wore shoes), but in spite of this, they were always cheerful and helpful, intelligent and thoroughly disarming.

São Paulo has its own "foreign" sections: Spaniards keep to one area; Italians to another; Lithuanians to a third. One Spanish woman had been living for thirty years among her country folk of the cortiço area, and had never learned to speak Portuguese, so isolated had she been in her compact island of Spanish culture and tradition. The cortiços and vilas are all marked with the date of construction over the entrance; one finds the years 1903, 1906, 1912, predominating—making these buildings as much as thirty to forty years old. These were the years of migration from Europe, the same years which caused the building of tenements in New York. In the old country, before they came to the New World, these people had never lived in anything better. Even now in the year 1943, they do not live in dwellings worthy of the twentieth century or the New World. Only a broad program of education and rebuilding will lift them up to a decent living environment.

Those who have studied the housing problem in Brazil list many causes for the favella and cortiço of Rio de Janeiro, São Paulo, and other cities, and know only too well their effects on the people. They point to the lack of general education, and to the meager understanding of the need and benefits of improved housing, on the part of both the people and the government. Actually, the slum dwellers of São Paulo could pay for better homes if they were to be had. Some blamed the government for approaching the housing problem as a source of investment of public or semi-public funds, rather than as a social issue.

The other basic obstacle in the way of good housing in Brazil is the low income of the mass of the people. Look at this indication of widespread poverty: there are roughly 4,000,000 contos ($200,-000,000 U.S.) in circulation in Brazil. If this money were to be stopped from circulating and then distributed equally among the 40,000,000 people in the country, each Brazilian would possess just about $5.00 U.S. But compare this with a similar hypothetical experiment in the United States: divide the $10,000,000,000 in circulation in our country among the 130,000,000 people, and each of us would have around $77.00. It doesn't require a penetrating knowledge of finance to see how such a low economic level retards housing for the masses on either a public or a private basis. Nor can industry in general flourish. No complete building industry has as yet developed in Brazil. Wood houses, for example, would stimulate local industry and the production of lumber; yet the building code in Rio, I found, doesn't even permit wood construction, except, of course, in the favellas where building is done outside the law. Although the danger of termites is often used as an objection, it is claimed by some of Brazil's architects that these can be controlled and that certain native woods which could be used are not touched by termites. In any case, Brazil needs to experiment with such possibilities for more widespread use of her existing timber, and even with planting forests of imported trees which may adapt themselves.

Brazil *cannot develop industrially without first creating a local consuming market* by raising of wages and housing standards of the mass of her 40,000,000 people.

Throughout all the cities of Latin America, the splendid parks and boulevards which adorn the "better" residential areas and business sections can be interpreted as an indication of the unbalanced economy of the cities. "Better" residences and business can afford to pay for the parks and boulevards, but the mass of the people still live on an economic level that is too low to permit a satisfactory level of housing and community planning.

3. Rural Housing Problems

Before closing this chapter, I would like to acquaint the reader with what I learned of rural housing conditions. Latin America is generally an agricultural continent. The pattern of agricultural practice comes from centuries of various traditions, but for the most part, in most countries, the land is held in large ownerships and those who work the land are tenants, much as in parts of the West and South of the United States. For this reason, the need for agricultural housing has been subject to exploitation as is likely to be the case in a feudal agricultural economy. However, there has been a tendency in many countries to break up the old colonial pattern and replace it with one based on the use of farm machinery or hand labor planned in such a way as to make production more efficient and more closely related to human needs. I shall discuss the agricultural backgrounds of Ecuador briefly, and of Chile in more detail, in order to suggest the extent of the housing problem outside urban areas.

The Ecuadorian hacienda, the unit of that country's agricultural pattern, is an enormous land holding running into hundreds of square miles in area. The Indian worker lives on a small plot of land called the *huasipango*, for which he pays rent by working so many days a week in proportion to the size of the plot. Houses are primitive and traditional, much like those of pre-Columbian times; those of the mountains are of adobe with thatched roofs. In one remote section, I remember how the loose straw roofs hung down over the eaves like fur on shaggy sheep-dogs; one village of several hundred houses resembled a pack of them resting on the hillside. Life on the huasipango is colorful, but as hard as life might be in the most backward sections of Asia. This particular village stood near a lake and the red ponchos of the Indians dotted the landscape against the blue of the water. Little boys carried huge packets of reeds on their backs, trailing them along the ground; the women carried even larger ones. To pass through rural villages in Ecuador is like going back several hundred years.

One-half of Chile's 4,000,000 inhabitants live on farms. The lives of many of these people have been deeply influenced by colonial agricultural patterns which are today out-dated and inefficient, and have caused many related social and economic problems. The backbone of the traditional pattern of agriculture in Chile is the *fundo*, which in many ways resembled the "rancho" or ranch of early California (not to be confused with the *rancho* or hut of Colombian slums). Actually, the fundo is feudalism carried up to the 20th century, at times operating in the best sense of the word and at other times in the worst. The owner or *patrón* is often the great-grandson of the original Spanish settler. The tenant worker or *inquilino* may also be the descendant of one of the original workers on the fundo. The inquilino receives from the patrón a small plot of land, a house, all the bread he needs from the community oven, and sometimes a few domestic animals, in exchange for working the land. In addition, he is paid a small sum of money depending on the size of his plot of land and the number of family members who work on the fundo.

Through the kindness and hospitality of friends in Chile, I had an opportunity to make several visits to El Principal, one of the oldest and most beautiful of the fundos. It lies back toward the foothills some twenty miles from Santiago, in a countryside that is green and fertile, where blue mountains, framed by towering poplars, form a majestic backdrop. This fundo, owned by the Izquierdo family, houses about 700 people, or 200 families, and operates effectively as a complete agricultural community. Twenty-three newly constructed, well built houses with large windows and concrete floors indicate that El Principal carries on the best of the paternalistic colonial tradition.

Driving out to the Izquierdo fundo you are projected back into an earlier period by the sight of old-fashioned horse-drawn stage coaches which pass you trailing clouds of dust in the warm summer air. The *huasos* or Chilean cowboys ride by, gaily dressed, wearing the characteristic small poncho that covers no more than the shoulders. As the road enters the gate into the large open plaza of El Principal, you are aware that this is no accidental collection of farm buildings which might have been added to little by little as by a New England farmer who has bettered his economic position. Here is a well-planned farm community consciously laid out for the use of a closely knit social group. Surrounding the plaza stand a church, school, clinic, small store, and other buildings: housing offices, stables, storage space, etc. Opposite the main gate stands the low, rambling house of the patrón enclosing a courtyard garden some 120 feet square. The house itself, built about 130 years ago, in excellent Chilean colonial tradition, is in the form of an *H* with a long colonnaded gallery or *corredor* the length of the courtyard, and a low tower marking the center of the building. Passing under the tower to the opposite side of the house you find a similar corredor and a smaller courtyard shaded by a huge eucalyptus tree. A gate leads you through the enclosing hedge to the orchard, which is crossed by a luxurious grape arbor several hundred feet long, covered with ripening grapes and banked on each side with huge mounds of hydrangeas in bloom. Half way down the length of this vine-covered walk, a similar arbor crosses at right angles and in the four quadrants stands the orchard of peach, plum, and apple trees. At the end of this main axis, an informal swimming pool of river water is set in a grove of green sycamores and beyond, an avenue of poplars goes off to the fields.

Life on a Chilean fundo reflects the delightful existence of colonial times. The family takes tea late every afternoon in the dining room, where the table is always bountifully set for twelve. Looking down on us are life-size portraits of family ancestors whose bodies, painted in Chile 130 years ago, have faces painted earlier in Spain. Afternoon tea, called *onces* in Chile, may include sandwiches, toast, pie, cake, tea, and fruit. Chileans are known for their hospitality; an afternoon visit to El Principal extends to include swimming, onces, horseback riding, dinner at nine-thirty, and after dinner an hour of singing huaso songs with guitar accompaniment.

Life on a well managed Chilean fundo may be advantageous to both patrón and inquilino, but viewed in relation to the 20th century, such a charming agricultural pattern becomes a survival of a once-needed paternalism which is today out of joint with social, economic, and political changes throughout the world.

This becomes particularly true in looking at more typical Chilean fundos where conditions unfortunately do not come up to the levels of El Principal. In the average fundo the houses of the inquilinos are of windowless adobe walls, contain no more than two or three rooms, and have dirt floors. Cooking is done over a fire in a hole in the floor of a separate building so that smoke may be kept away from the dwelling. Consequently, living quarters are without heat in the winter. All inhabitants must sleep with their clothes on in order to survive the blasts that come down from the Andes. The minimum sleeping quarters are further congested by the fact that families frequently take in single men as boarders to augment their income, and crowd them with parents and small children into one or two rooms. Sanitation is quite unknown. Piped water is never available and there is seldom a reliable drinking supply. Polluted water from sewage-fed streams, or from irrigation ditches, is often used for drinking, so that typhoid constantly recurs. Pneumonia, rheumatism, and arthritis are prevalent.

Diets are generally unbalanced, seldom include meat or milk. Although green vegetables are plentiful in Chile, my friends, who had worked with inquilino families and knew their habits well, told me that these people need to be educated to the use of them.

Wages of the inquilino have remained at the same level in recent years in spite of the fact that the Chilean peso has dropped in value and living costs have risen. The inquilino's wage of from 1.80 to 7 pesos a day (about 7¢ to 25¢ U.S.) keeps him in economic and social servitude.

But the general picture of agricultural life in Chile is changing. In the larger fundos of the Santiago region, where conditions have been most difficult in the past, many of the owners who once lived abroad have come back to Chile and are taking a more active interest in efficient operation of their land. Many who once lived abroad as Parisians, Londoners, or New Yorkers rather than Chileans now live on their land and are forced by public opinion to improve the standard of living of the inquilinos who also live on their land. In the area north of Santiago, where there are fewer large fundos, the land is gradually being subdivided more and more, and a new class of independent farmers is developing which will eventually challenge the continuation of the traditional fundo system.

In addition to the inquilino, there is the *obrero agricola,* an independent farm worker who either owns his own house or pays rent and works by the day for wages. Although he gets more money and is more independent than the inquilino, he must provide his own rent, food and clothing out of his wage of around 15 pesos per day, or about 55¢ U.S. money. About one-third of these workers are migratory, following the seasonal crops, coming to the cities in the winter, where often they find neither housing nor work.

Labor organization among agricultural workers in Chile has not been at all effective because the initiative comes from the industrial unions rather than from the farm workers themselves. Since the agricultural laborer is more conservative, and by experience suspicious of exploitation by others, he has no trust in the offers of trade unions. What is needed is a labor organization on the fundo that comes from the inquilino or the obrero agricola himself. But even this must be preceded by education so that rural workers may see the advantages of collective bargaining and group independence. They will learn that in comparison with rural conditions, industrial wages and housing standards are high. Organized labor and labor legislation have secured for workers at Pedro de Valdivia, the northern nitrate plant, wages of 22 to 30 pesos (75¢ to $1.00 U.S.) per day, and two weeks vacation each year.

Space does not permit a discussion of the agricultural background of all Latin American countries, but in many conditions are similar to those described above. The *estancias* are to Argentina what the fundos are to Chile. There is a similar need to subdivide the land, to resettle and rehouse the gauchos and peons, to educate them to a new standard of living, and create a more democratic agricultural pattern geared to modern times.

Brazil's problem of agricultural housing is an enormous one, particularly related to the need for general social advancement and education. Some agricultural workers on the *fazendas* or large plantations are paid as little as ten cents (U.S. money) per day. Others never see money at all, but are paid in beans, rice and other necessities from the fazenda store in return for certain labor units.

4. Obstacles and Their Meaning

In summing up the chief social and economic obstacles that stand in the way of providing good housing for the average Latin American, we find among them the following: Low wages virtually force the worker to live under slum conditions. It was unanimously agreed at the First Pan-American Housing Congress in Buenos Aires in 1939 that the first requisite to good housing is the provision for a decent living wage. Wages realistically adjusted to living costs can make possible the purchasing of good housing by the mass of the Latin American people.

Yet an increase in wages and an improvement in housing conditions must come along only with general education in standards of living. Long periods of sub-standard living have rendered the slum-dweller insensitive to his surroundings. Increased income too often goes to purchase temporary escape from his environment—some wasteful extravagance—rather than toward bettering his economic status for the long pull. A program of social education pointed toward higher standards of living will assist Latin American slum-dwellers to find their own way out of the slums.

The lack of a sufficiently developed building industry has made impossible the production of locally manufactured building materials at a price the common man can pay. In addition to building materials there is also a need for skilled building technicians and workmen—carpenters, plumbers, and others—in larger numbers. There are other reasons, too. The sudden increase of urban population in recent years has caused housing shortages in many cities; among the new comers are many European refugees; but the majority have come from rural areas. Since Latin American cities are far older than those of the United States, it is natural that there should be more old and worn-out buildings and so far there have been no large-scale programs for rehabilitation of such districts. Building ordinances in many cities are inadequately written and poorly enforced and there is too little knowledge of the extent of bad housing conditions.

Under such conditions as these, no real social advance can possibly be made in the direction of true democracy throughout the Western Hemisphere. As long as unhealthful, unsanitary living conditions remain in the conventillos of Santiago and the favellas of Rio—in slums, wherever they exist in the Americas—there are outposts of Nazi infiltration and threats against hemisphere solidarity.

Strangely enough, this fact was brought home to me over and over again as I had my shoes shined or bought a paper. Invariably the bootblacks, the newsboys and all the other little men of the street, well on their way toward adulthood as *rotos chilenos,* proved to be victims of a housing policy based on exploitation. Invariably these youngsters turned out to be four or five years older than I would have supposed, and just as consistently, they were thin, with narrow, canary-bird shoulders. Their legs were spindly from lack of proper nourishment; they were sleepy and dull from lack of a decent bed, and morally cynical from the lack of the stimulus that comes from a decent environment.

I leave with you the case of one young fellow whose attitude sums up the significance of the situation. As this lad shined away at my shoes, I judged him to be about nine years old and asked him his age. He said he was fourteen. It was noon time and I asked if he went to school. Yes, at night for two hours, he told me, between coughs which I thought would bring up his lungs. I asked him who he thought ought to win the war, and he answered without hesitation that he thought it would be better for Chile if Germany won. The lad was in rags and quite dirty, but he was intelligent. I asked him where he lived and he said he lived in a conventillo not far from the center of town.

Frontispiece for Chapter 5 (overleaf) shows a drawing of a portion of the Civic Center for the new city of Goiania, State of Goyaz, Brazil. Though an extension of an existing small village, most of Goiania has been built from scratch, and in this portion follows almost exactly the original conception. Goiania is the newly developed state capital in country which was almost inaccessible except by airplane, so the airfield was one of the first elements to be planned and constructed. Attilio Corrêa Lima, architect, laid out the city.

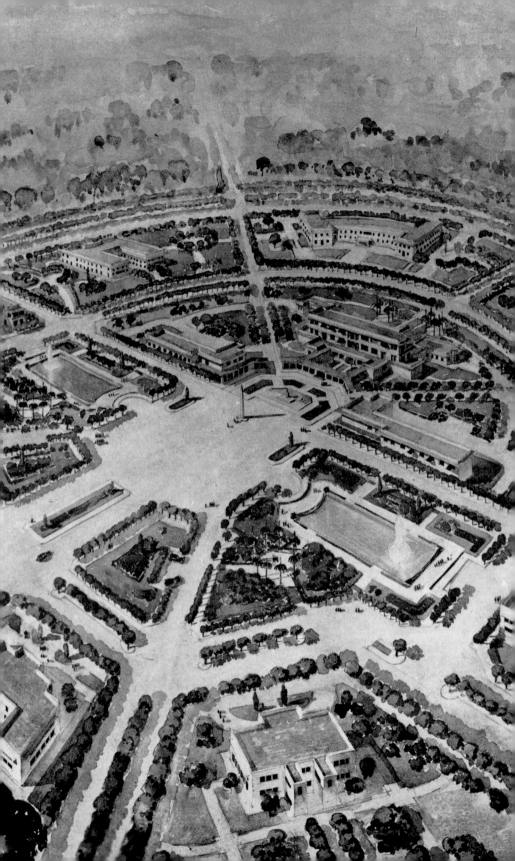

chapter 5

New plans for old cities

1. Background for Planning: U.S.A. and Latin America

Now the picture is not really as black as the foregoing might suggest, for in opposition to the forces responsible for these problems in Latin America there exist aggressive groups of technicians, actively interested in planning better cities. I met many men and women of these groups who know their urban problems thoroughly, who are facing them realistically and working effectively to combat them within the limitations of national difficulties. As a matter of fact, in spite of her urban problems, her particularly tough housing situation, the complexities of her economy, and her hazardous past, Latin America has in some ways won a moral victory over us. Taking all factors on each side into consideration and weighing our natural advantages with their handicaps, Latin America's city builders have been bolder, more imaginative, and more effective than have those of the United States.

I shall tell you something of the kind of cities Latin American technicians are planning to meet the needs of the people, of the methods they are using and the ways in which they surpass us in the matter of city building. But first, one thing should be made clear. It is my belief that the complexities of modern cities cannot be effectively handled without coordination through some sort of planning process. The chaotic heaps of construction which we live in today and call our cities are proof that more is needed in the future than trusting to mere chance and struggling, self-centered individual initiative. Therefore, in discussing the accomplishments of the Latins, I shall place greatest emphasis on those works that have been achieved through application of the *planning* principle. When I went down to Latin America, I didn't go merely to find out what was "happening," but to learn what was being *consciously* done to improve the urban environment.

In comparing the planning of the cities of Latin America with that of the cities of the United States, it is at once apparent that her technicians have profited by closer contact with Europe. The result has been the development of two divergent types of cities in the Western Hemisphere: those of the United States, impressive but ungracious; and those of the Latin American countries, historic and Old World-like, but thoroughly delightful and human. Different standards have been employed. Latin American cities, particularly those of the West Coast, give one the definite impression that planning techniques have been imported wholesale from Europe from the earliest laws of Charles the Fifth for the founding of colonial cities, to modern city planning practices developed in Central Europe after World War I. The cultural and technical influence has been from Europe, where there has always been a greater recognition of the need for planning. Consequently, Latin American cities have had a much longer tradition of public control of the city's growth than have ours.

Because of their cultural ties with the Old World, urban technicians and professional men have been trained in Europe, and know and put to use the techniques of outstanding European planners. It is significant that when the planning department of the city of Santiago was re-organized in 1934, none of the city fathers considered looking to the United States for technical advice in city planning. Instead, a European contact was used and Carl Brunner of Vienna was called in. The studies made under his direction are being carried out today and show not only an extensive European influence, but realistic understanding of urban needs.

The process of city planning in the United States, on the other hand, has taken a course away from European influence along with many of our other traditions and institutions. We have few of the urban parks, spaciously arranged public buildings (with the exception of Washington, D.C.), public plazas of well-considered architectural design, and broad, tree-lined boulevards, all of which are just the urban features which we admire in European cities and the loss of which we mourn when we read of a new blitz over a Rotterdam, London, or Paris. We in the United States have placed greater emphasis on the desirability of a democratic technique for providing those qualities, rather than on the desirability of the qualities themselves. In doing so we have built up a remarkably complex legislative organization of planning techniques at various governmental levels based upon full participation of an informed citizenry. A glance at the physical unpleasantness and economic instability of many of our cities invites a comparison of the actual effectiveness of that process with its true possibilities and opportunities.

But for the moment we are concerned with the cities of Latin America. The planning process in the Latin American republics differs from that of the United States in that, generally, it is not practiced with a comparable degree of democracy and is not based on the principle of citizen action to counterbalance official action. The public-at-large in the U.S.A. has at hand a unique opportunity to improve cities and better urban environment through a systematic and practical application of urban and regional planning law, based on common sense action by an informed citizenry. This opportunity the Latin American public does not have.

In a few cases, however, their planners have come into contact with our techniques, and where the general degree of democracy in practice is fairly high there has been some introduction of that feature into urban legislation. Generally, the United States is looked upon in Latin America as having developed the most complete system of legal methods for the control of urban growth. But on the other hand, and for this same reason, it is sometimes difficult for a North American to explain to Latin Americans why it is that in spite of our advanced legal control our urban centers are frequently congested, inefficient, disorderly, and economically unstable.

While talking about these matters with Latin American planners I had the feeling that many of them were thinking: "What we could do in the way of city building had we the wealth, the legal background, and the enlightened public of your county!" But I found that, even without these advantages, planners of the cities of Latin America have demonstrated imagination and a flair for molding the city into a desirable place in which to live.

2. City and Regional Framework

Before discussing in more detail the framework for city and regional planning used by the Latin Americans, I should like to review for the reader the legal methods in the United States by which the physical content and form of our cities and countryside may be controlled. Unlike the planning process in Latin America, ours is based on a thoroughly decentralized principle, placing chief control in the hands of local governments. Most of our large cities have City Planning Commissions, composed of representative citizens and certain key officials. These men and women meet and discuss current problems which are placed before them, acting in accordance with recommendations of a technical staff. Enactment of state enabling laws makes legally possible the formation of such commissions and, in some cases, actually requires their formation. Groups of these commissions may come together to form Regional Planning Commissions, and many of our larger metropolitan centers—New York, Chicago, Los Angeles—have taken this step to help solve common problems in complex areas made up of many towns or cities. Many of our states provide for County Planning Commissions which study the problems and prepare legislation to control the growth outside the incorporated cities. In all cases in the United States, the planning setup is decentralized as far as the Federal government is concerned, and provision is made for active cooperation of an informed citizenry.

In Latin America, this is not the case. There are very few citizen commissions and most city or regional planning offices operate as technical planning staffs under direct control of the municipal or even the federal government. In each country the legal organization for planning differs and control is centralized in varying degrees. A review of the various types of organization for planning of cities and regions may serve as a basis for an understanding of planning accomplishments in the field of urban development.

Mexico is the only Latin American republic which has made an attempt at a decentralized planning organization similar to that of the United States. This is due simply to the fact that one architect-planner, Carlos Contreras, has had long and close contact with the United States and believes in the democratic processes as an aid to planning. The result is a system of planning laws and citizen planning commissions more or less like ours in the United States.

Mexico City's program is under the direction of a Planning Commission of thirteen members made up of both citizens and officials. Subject to its approval is a separate commission which directs the technical office of the master plan, whose official name is *Oficina Controladora de Crecimiento de la Ciudad* or "Office for the Control of the Growth of the City." This title explains the function of the office more effectively than our word "Master Plan." In addition, there is a third commission, "Mixta" (composed of members of other city departments) which looks after financial planning and the budgeting of funds for carrying out the Master Plan.

These three commissions may be supplemented by independent executive committees, appointed to do special studies or projects. For example, a committee of three members is appointed from the property owners in a certain defined district in which a new street is to be opened. These citizens are held responsible for the entire financing and construction of the project according to the general plan of the Commission. They may hire their own technicians, planners, architects, and engineers. This system has operated effectively in opening important new streets and plazas, because it has the full cooperation of the area's property owners whose representatives are in direct charge of the work. Financing of these and other types of projects is based on the principle of *plus valia,* a tax on the increased value of the property due to the public improvements. Much formerly wasted land has been rendered useful and many blocks of needed streets have been opened by this method.

City planning activities center chiefly in Mexico City because it is not only the Federal District, like Washington, D.C., but the chief cultural center as well. However, Monterrey, capital of the State of Nuevo León, likewise has a planning commission and planning legislation under way. Nuevo Laredo, at the Texas border, has set up a planning commission with necessary planning laws for a Master Plan which, when carried out, will make Laredo, Texas, look like a poor relation. Acapulco, the resort town on the Pacific, has organized planning in order to preserve the natural scenic features of its beautiful setting. Tasco, the old silver town, is protected with a plan and legislation setting the town aside as a National monument. Vera Cruz, on the Gulf of Mexico, is laying out a new planning program under the guidance of Carlos Contreras.

Under Mexico's policy initiative to formulate plans is left to local governments as in the United States, but in two countries, namely Peru and Chile, the reverse of this procedure is practiced. In these republics, central planning offices have been set up by the governments to do *all* the town planning throughout the country with the aid of local offices in the larger cities.

Civic discipline in Peru has had a head start over that of many other countries. As early as 1549 the citizens of the newly built town of Lima submitted to the principle of private loss for public gain, when Diego de Torres Alarife, architect, was put in charge of removing all buildings which extended over the new street lines designated by law. In 1902, the first general planning law passed in Peru obliged each city in the country to make a Master Plan for its development. No aid was given to the cities, however, and the law was very loosely enforced. The following rough translation indicates that the law did contain the essentials of good town planning:

"Town Planning Decree for the Towns of the Republic—Sept. 26, 1902:
 'Because of the narrowness of streets, the lack of plazas and poor alignment of streets, causing unhealthy conditions in the towns, because of lack of adequate circulation and movement of air, because of poor drainage of water, and . . . in the interests of removing these conditions . . . IT IS DECREED . . . that the Municipalities of the Republic will each survey existing streets, plazas, etc., of the towns and show lines for future extension of streets, plazas, etc. . . ."

The remainder of the decree set forth specifications for the work to be done, methods of financing and administration, and permission for the use of expropriation laws in the interest of the community.

Today, planning in Peru is placed under the direction of a special office called the Section of Urban Studies. This is one of the best directed planning offices in South America, and is entrusted with city planning for all the towns and cities of Peru. The director, Emilio Harth-Terré, is an able and energetic architect who has been the mainspring in advancing the planning idea in Peru for the last twenty-two years. In this office, a competent staff studies land use control through zoning, regulation of subdivisions, and in general, acts as an effective planning force for the entire urban region of which Lima is the core.

The particular task of the Section of Urban Studies is that of coordinating into a regional plan the growth and development of the forty separate municipalities that make up the Lima region. Some of these (in addition to Lima, which has its own planning office) are Miraflores, Callao, San Isidro, Chorrilos, Magdalena, San Miguel, Bella Vista, each of which is autonomous, with officials appointed by the President of the republic. In addition to making plans for modern Lima, Harth-Terré and his staff have the difficult task of planning for the development of old towns like Cuzco, Trujillo, Arequipa, Chiclayo, and Huancayo, and others throughout the republic.

Chile's planning process resembles that of Peru. In 1929, Chilean planners were successful in having enacted the first comprehensive planning law, one which required all cities of over 20,000 inhabitants to make city plans. New impetus was given to planning in 1936 by the formation of a central Department of Urbanism in the Ministry of Development, with authority to make plans for all cities of over 8,000 population. This office, under the direction of Luis Muñoz Maluschka, carries on planning studies for some fifty-five Chilean towns and cities. Legislation for each city becomes law when the plan is approved jointly by the city authorities and the federal government, but such legislation operates without a citizen planning commission. Several of the larger cities, including Santiago, Valparaiso, Concepción, Osorno, and Valdivia have their own planning staffs which cooperate with the government's Department of Urbanism. Such centralized control is an advantage in Chile, in that smaller cities which could not afford to maintain planning staffs have the services of experienced and well-trained planning technicians. Comprehensive studies are made in two steps: first, the collection of basic data and preparation of a general plan in the Department of Urbanism; later, the development of detailed plans in the cities themselves. A typical set of studies for the city of Valparaiso included such subjects as land use, land values, and zoning; building values, building heights, and popula-

92

tion density; parks, major traffic arteries, and street widening lines. Presentation of the studies was simple, clear, and graphic; office personnel seemed well-trained and capable.

Although no regional planning is practiced in Chile as it is in Peru in the Lima region, technicians in charge of the growth of Santiago recognize the need for a regional planning organization to coordinate the separate municipalities that cluster about the city boundary. In this matter of regional planning, Chilean planners are particularly anxious to know more about United States' practice in the New York, Chicago, and Los Angeles regions.

Unlike Mexico, Peru, and Chile, a number of the countries, I found, had no consistent governmental policy in regard to planning, but were doing some effective work in isolated instances. Among these are Colombia, Bolivia, Argentina, Uruguay, Brazil.

In Colombia, planned city development is found in centers like Bogotá, Medellín, and Barranquilla, and reflects the energy, initiative, and vision of the aggressive Colombians. Through a well established planning program, Bogotá has developed an interesting and attractive city. This planning work was first initiated by Carl Brunner, who was called from Santiago, Chile, in 1934, to organize a permanent planning department and to do special civic improvement work for the city's fourth centenary. Using data and plans prepared by John Marr, who had been sent from the St. Louis office of Harland Bartholomew a few years earlier, Brunner laid the framework for a master plan, planning legislation, and administrative facilities. Today the permanent office is established and the master plan is being put into effect.

Medellín, Colombia, down at the lower elevations of Tierra Media, is likewise approaching planning with vision and thereby developing what promises to be one of South America's most lively and beautiful cities. Medellín's is an unusual program, the result of citizen action through the efforts of an especially effective group known as the *Sociedad de Mejoras Públicas,* or the Society for Public Betterment, led by Ricardo Olano, a retired industrialist. Nutibara Hill, rising high in the center of the valley of Medellín and overlooking the city, has been purchased by the municipality and is being planted with trees. The low area west of the city is being drained, streets are already laid out, and new facilities for the city's two universities are being planned. These projects are the result of the efforts of the Sociedad de Mejoras Públicas.

Bolivia, like Colombia, finds it to her advantage to study the urban needs of her capital, La Paz, but unlike Colombia is carrying on little planning work outside the capital.

La Paz' first planning legislation was passed as early as 1914, but was comparatively ineffective, as were most planning efforts of that time in all cities in both North and South America, because of inadequately trained personnel and an unrealistic approach. The science of urbanism has progressed considerably since those times. A new planning office was established in La Paz in 1934, and when the building boom began in 1936, the need to re-vitalize the planning program became urgent. In order to control the recently increased growth and to profit by new economic activity La Paz reorganized her Department of Urbanism about four years ago. In a special section of the Department, devoted to urban studies, a technical staff, which includes Mario del Carpio and Federico Castillo, both trained in Chile, is assembling a good background of basic data and laying out a program of urban legislation. Members of the staff are typical of many younger technicians in Latin America who have initiative and ideas and are anxious to overcome the economic and political obstacles that stand in the way of more effective action. These men in La Paz have an avid interest to learn from our experience in the United States.

It is incongruous that South America's most mature republic, Argentina, has no standardized or official national policy on the promotion and encouragement of city and regional planning. Those cities which do have planning under way acted entirely on local initiative. In Buenos Aires, the master plan office or *Plan de Urbanización*, now directed by Carlos della Paolera, was established about twelve years ago, and is one of the largest and best equipped in South America. La Plata, the nearby capital of the province of Buenos Aires, was so well planned when it was laid out that only a small planning staff is needed. Rosario, with its phenomenal growth in the last fifty years, to almost a million inhabitants, recognizes the need of developing a master plan, and has taken steps in that direction, but as yet has established no official city planning office like that of Buenos Aires.

Mendoza, far to the west in the shadow of the Andes, has an excellent beginning in planning. There, the whole problem of future growth was laid before a staff of four consultants, two from Buenos Aires and two from Montevideo, Uruguay. These men have completed a preliminary comprehensive study of the city's needs from economic expansion all the way through to public building locations. This first stage was in the course of approval during my visit, and is being followed by detailed work, part of which will be the establishment of a permanent planning office to administer and carry out a flexible master plan.

Regional planning is not practiced in Argentina as yet. But its necessity for the huge metropolitan area of Buenos Aires with its four million people has been talked about for years and in 1942 the task of organizing regional planning studies was given to Carlos della Paolera of the Master Plan Office of Buenos Aires.

The best equipped and most thoroughly staffed planning office which I came upon was that of the *Dirección del Plan Regulador* or Master Plan Office of Montevideo. Their budget for 1942 was 146,-280 pesos or about $73,000 U.S., which is large for a South American city. Their staff consists of *95* persons from the Architect-Director and his assistants down to draftsmen and file clerks. This budget, and especially the size of the staff, is generous compared with that of a city of similar size in the United States such as San Francisco or Seattle. Members of the staff are well trained; the engineers and architects are all graduates of either the *Facultad de Arquitectura* or the *Facultad de Ingeniería,* both among the finest of the architectural and engineering schools in Latin America. Under the direction of Américo Ricaldoni, the office is wisely authorized to study the entire Department of Montevideo (roughly corresponding to a large county) and actually constitutes a regional planning office. The population of this area is over 700,000—about one third of the population of the country.

Of all the countries of Latin America, that which could profit most from an official government policy on planning—not city and regional planning alone, but state and national as well—is fast-growing Brazil. Unfortunately, however, no such policy exists. Much good planning work has been done in certain cities of Brazil —Rio de Janeiro, Belo Horizonte, São Paulo, Goiania, and others, but most of this is the result of the efforts of either local civic-minded individuals or private planning offices. The city planning which is practiced in Brazil hardly represents a general policy of the government.

Since Rio de Janeiro is the capital, it is there where most attention is given to city planning. The so-called "planning commission," the *Comissão do Plano da Cidade,* is actually composed of city officials and a technical staff, appointed by the Mayor (who in turn is appointed by the President) with no citizen representation as in the United States. Such a staff has the advantage of operating on a purely technical basis, free of interference from small interests, and the disadvantage of being open to political control without participation of representatives of the public-at-large. As far as I know, the United States is the only country which makes widespread use of the citizen commission arrangement. The present city planning program in Rio was begun through the efforts of Dr. Edison Passos, when he overcame the original objection to establishing a permanent official planning agency by convincing the Mayor that he should visit Buenos Aires' Master Plan Office. This the Mayor did, in 1937, and immediately upon his return to Rio established the Comissão do Plano da Cidade. That office now has under way elaborate plans for molding Rio de Janeiro into the Number One show capital of South America, as well as solving some of the circulation problems resulting from the unusual site on which the city is built. The technical staff is studying many problems of congestion, over-building, and uncoordinated land use caused by the great granite mountains which impede natural expansion.

Several realistic planning studies have been made by capable planning consultants for the coastal city of Recife (Pernambuco) to the north, but political obstacles have kept these plans from being used. São Paulo to the south has under way what is perhaps the most elaborate planning program in South America, entirely under the direction of the Mayor Prestes Maia whose work will be discussed in detail later on. Smaller cities like Curityba and Porto Alegre in the south, and Belo Horizonte to the west in the rich mineral state of Minas Geraes, are undertaking studies for planning their future growth, but none of these have established well-rooted planning programs as yet. In a country as large as Brazil, they lack the impetus that might come from a coordinated national policy on city and regional planning recognized by the government and guided by an official or semi-official federal agency. Brazil's planning technicians are certainly not lacking in the talent and drive needed to organize such a program.

Two smaller countries I visited had practically no city planning under way at all. These are Ecuador and Guatemala. I found in Ecuador that although there is no organized planning for Quito, the capital, city officials are interested in beginning a planning program and are anxious to secure technical data and consultation. In fact, early in 1942, a young Uruguayan planner, Guillermo ("Bill") Jones-Odriozola, was about to be hired to do an *ante proyecto* or study for a Master Plan.

Guatemala's strongly centralized government wields what is probably the strictest national discipline in Latin America. The results are order and prosperity to a superficial degree, at a sacrifice of democratic evolution. After a six-hour flight from Mexico, Guatemala City, the capital, seems as clean as a pin, neat and orderly. Streets are paved and swept, buildings are in good condition, parks are green and luxuriant, and there is a general air of industry. This is the result of President Jorge Ubico's super-efficient administration of the last ten years. Throughout this period Ubico's chief planner has been Arturo Bickford, Mayor of Guatemala City, Chief Engineer and Planning Commission all in one. Bickford's planning has produced paved streets, low-cost housing projects, new parks, boulevards, bridges, highways, and water and power lines. Plans are being considered now for the changes that will take place with the opening of the Pan-American Highway. Guatemala is actually more interested in the highway as an aid to agricultural development and for defense purposes than as a potential money-maker from tourist travel. There is little need in a country as small as Guatemala for city planning on an extensive scale, but rather there is needed over-all planning methods on a regional and national scale.

3. State and National Framework

Before discussing methods of carrying on planning at the broader national levels in Latin America, I shall review for the reader what is the practice in our own country. In addition to city and regional planning in the United States, we have developed an understanding of the need for broader planning at the state and national levels. Most of our more heavily populated states, like New York, Illinois, and California, have established state planning boards responsible for the coordination of the work of county and city planning commissions, state agencies involved in flood control, agricultural conservation, highway, state park, and resources development. War conditions have hampered activities of these boards, but the recognition of their need remains a step ahead in the direction of more rational use of resources. The United States government has undertaken planning studies on a national level through the work of the various regional offices of the National Resources Planning Board.* The problems studied by this Board were of inter-state nature, affecting the entire national economy. In all, there are five possible levels of government in the United States where planning might operate to fulfil different functions: city, regional, county, state, and national.

In Latin American countries, there is no such well-patterned organization at a variety of levels. In only one case, Mexico, is there any appreciable attempt at the application of state and national planning as a logical outgrowth of local planning in cities and regions. But I found that Latin technicians in general were anxious to know more about state and national planning in the United States in order to apply a similar principle of rational development to the needs of their countries. They know well that planning on the city or regional level is futile if it is not tied to a broad program for the entire country. However, most countries have made some attempt at resources planning on a national level.

I have said before that the general planning pattern in Mexico resembles that of the United States. Mexican planning law actually provides for all levels, but for political and other reasons practice is somewhat spotty. National planning, organized by Carlos Contreras in 1932, even before that of the United States, operated in the form of a National Planning Commission, but, unfortunately, this body has since become inactive. State planning legislation exists for about five of the more important states of Mexico and is spreading gradually as architects and engineers with a knowledge

---

* Killed by Congressional action in 1943.

97

of planning practices and needs are beginning to come from the University in Mexico where courses in planning are given, and from North American universities. One must realize that the Mexican government has much more centralized power than has the United States, and that the States of Mexico have much less of the freedom of action of those of the United States. The government occasionally does some city planning as in the case of Nuevo Laredo, where a town plan was made and a planning commission set up under direct Federal initiative, and Ciudad Juarez, where similar action has been taken. Mexico's government is not without its planning bodies: federal agencies like the National Foreign Trade Commission, the Agrarian Bureau, the National Bank of Ejido Credit, the Federal Electric Commission and others are necessarily concerned with broad planning, but these function without the advantage of a central coordinating body.

Both Colombia and Ecuador have established National Economic Councils for the purpose of studying economic development. That of Colombia has been operating since 1931 and in 1940 its powers were broadened. That of Ecuador came into existence in 1935, in the wake of the depression, when the Council of National Economy was established by presidential decree.

In Peru, Emilio Harth-Terré, in charge of the Section of Urban Studies of the Ministry of Development, has urged a national planning organization like the United States' National Resources Planning Board. But so far, no such steps have been taken. However, several government agencies such as the Council of Subsistence and the government monopolies on tobacco, salt, alcohol, and other materials, operate in a sense as economic control groups.

Bolivia comes close to having a national planning agency in the National Economic Council provided for by decree in 1937, but most of the responsibilities of the Council have to do with national credit, with social and labor laws, rather than with rational planning of resources, so important to a country like Bolivia.

Chile's *Corporación de Fomento de Producción* (Corporation for the Development of Production) is one of the agencies most closely approximating a real national planning body. The Corporación was organized in 1939 partly as a means of helping to guide Chile out of the earthquake damage of that year. Its purpose is statedly "to develop national production in order to raise the standard of living of the people through taking advantage of the natural conditions of the country and diminution of cost of production . . . maintaining due proportion in the development of activities in the fields of mining, agriculture, industry, and commerce, and satisfying the needs of the different regions of the country." A board representing the government, Congress, private groups, etc., directs the activities of the Corporación. A branch office has been established in New York and works closely with various government agencies and with private groups in the United States in the interests of adapting our experience to the development of industry in Chile. A study of fish hatcheries and the fishing industry on the Pacific Coast is typical of studies being carried on by the Corporación which have a direct bearing upon planning new industries in Chile.

Argentina has no central agency for the purpose of planning on the federal level. However, national planning along the lines of that practiced in the United States has been promoted by the progressive *Centro de Ingenieros,* of which Luis Migone is President. For that reason, a national planning agency for Argentina lies within the realm of possibility. But State planning, which would have to be passed voluntarily by each province, is consequently far off in the more distant future.

Uruguay has no centralized governmental planning board, but does have a large number of public corporations for carrying out the progressive policy of federal intervention and state control of the larger industries. In this respect, Uruguay has gone farther than any other Latin American country.

At Brazil's stage of development, planning possibilities on a national scale could be enormous, but such planning work is practiced only in many uncoordinated agencies. A National Economic Council, to be composed of representatives of various branches of production, was provided for in the Constitution of 1937 for the purpose of advising the National Parliament and the President. But the government has not availed itself of widespread use of this agency nor has it made moves to promote state planning. The state of Minas Geraes opened a well-staffed planning department several years ago to do work for all cities in the state and to study state problems. It is significant that this took place under the coercion of Washington Azevedo, who received his training in planning at Harvard University. With the death of the Governor of Minas Geraes who had made the idea a reality, the office was discontinued.

4. Master Plans: Urban, Regional and National

I have discussed the various methods of organization and types of implements for planning at various governmental levels. In order to understand how effective this machinery has been we must look within the framework of these various organizations. Following the order given below, I shall tell something of the accomplishments of the Latins and suggest how their planning developments compare with ours:

Collection of Basic Data and Background Information
Land Use Planning and Zoning
Circulation, Streets, and Traffic

Subdivision Design and Neighborhoods
Parks and Recreation Facilities
Public Buildings
Earthquake Replanning
Plans for New Cities
Development of Modern Architecture
National Resources Planning

COLLECTION OF BASIC DATA AND BACKGROUND INFORMATION

One of the chief difficulties involved in carrying on a program of urban planning in Latin America is that there simply is not enough information available about the cities, the people who live in them, the urban land, and buildings. The result is that plans must often be made without thorough investigation of existing conditions. Since this requires time, money, and trained personnel, most of which do not always exist in large amounts in Latin America, it was my observation that planning was insufficiently related to a true picture of existing conditions.

However, in two instances I did find some very unusual examples of completed investigations supplying thorough background information. Buenos Aires' *Plan Catastral* or "Census Plan" is actually a census in map form giving an accurate representation of the location of streets, sidewalks, buildings, trees, property lines, and railroads. In addition, detailed data on the buildings themselves includes land coverage, type, condition, use, number of rooms, water, light, etc. Air maps were used for checking accuracy of the field work. Although three years—from 1938 to 1941—were used to complete the work, the results may well compete with similar material in a large city in the United States.

An even more complete piece of work, although on a much smaller scale, is the census and inventory which was being prepared for Montevideo in the spring of 1942. Data included a wide variety of subjects from fifth columnist hideouts to housing conditions and cultural facilities. One department, headed by Raul Lerena Acevedo, was devoted to urban problems and had been formed through the initiative of the Montevideo planners. Personnel, made up of architectural and planning students from the *Facultad de Arquitectura,* recorded data on transportation, streets, property uses, land values, housing conditions. When finished it will be the most complete census of any city in South America.

In the collection of information basically essential to city and regional planning, the United States, in general, surpasses the Latin American cities. But, at the same time, our excellence in this respect reflects one of our weaknesses: we frequently place more emphasis upon the means to the end and completely by-pass our objective, a livable city.

Land Use Planning and Zoning

The cities of Latin America differ from those of the United States in the degree to which land uses are controlled. Where our cities have developed a somewhat consistent segregation of uses through the practice of zoning and other municipal regulations (though we still have a long way to go) one finds in Latin American cities a much greater mixture of all kinds of uses—urban and rural, residential, shopping, and industrial—intermingling and overlapping.

A rather humorous instance repeated itself for me in a small way in a number of cities in Latin America. Most urban communities of the United States forbade the keeping of fowl in residential areas many years ago, while I found such practice common in many cities south of the border. In Santiago I remember all too vividly the garden outside my dwelling place in Los Leones, one of the modern residential sections. In back of the house stood a large shed for chickens and ducks which awakened us at dawn every morning without fail. This inconvenience was coupled with the annoying thought that the rodents and flies that bred would gather to infest our kitchen when activities among the poultry became dull for them. I had a similar experience in Rio de Janeiro. Next door to my quarters a few blocks from the luxurious Copacabana Palace Hotel, a large hen mothered a family of baby chickens and during my stay there the chicks grew into adolescence. Fortunately, I left before they reached adulthood and the ability to add to the early morning din of the mother hen and those others kept by the owner of my pension.

Widespread as this and other practices may be, most of the Latin American cities do have zoning laws which function with varying degrees of effectiveness, depending upon their drawing up and administration. In general, planning technicians and officials in the larger cities I visited are apparently realizing more and more the need for increased civic discipline and many new controlling ordinances have recently been passed or are being prepared at present.

Mexico City's zoning law, passed as recently as 1941, was urgently needed to assist in the guiding of new expansion. The law is related to a comprehensive Land Use Plan and is primarily designed to protect residential areas from encroaching industry. However, it has not yet been detailed or related to actual property lines, as have the zoning ordinances of the United States.

Harland Bartholomew of St. Louis, Missouri, as I have said, made a master plan for the city of Bogotá, Colombia, about 1930, but no sustained procedure was set up to carry out the plan. Recently, under the program organized by Carl Brunner, the city passed a new zoning law for purposes of general land use control, locating

101

areas for industrial, commercial, and residential uses. Height limits were established in relation to the width of the street. One excellent feature of the law limits the area for urban growth of the city of Bogotá; accordingly, no new subdivision of land is permitted beyond a certain established urban limit incorporated in the land use plan. Such a limiting of urban growth economizes upon the expensive utilities, permits more efficient land uses, and stabilizes land values.

Land use has been well developed in the Lima area, thanks partly to Pizarro's wise site selection 400 years ago and partly to careful land use control on the part of the city during recent years. The industrial section is located close to shipping facilities; the residential districts are well separated from manufacturing areas; the business and shopping center is located conveniently to both the other chief uses.

As part of her new planning program, La Paz, Bolivia, has made a careful study of land uses. It is interesting to note that these studies show that the greater percentage of land in the city has been put to urban uses for over one hundred years.

The zoning law of Santiago, Chile, is quite comprehensive in certain respects—area requirements, land coverage, height, land use. Special building height regulations in the vicinity of parks and historic monuments protect the effect of these public features and prevent them from becoming dwarfed and crowded. Two examples are building height limits protecting Cerro Santa Lucia and the San Francisco church. Because of the danger of earthquakes Santiago limits building heights throughout the city. However, my own observations and experiences suggest the need for the general application of detailed zoning restrictions of a more practical nature relating to important health and economic factors.

Argentina is more advanced in land use planning and zoning control. In 1939, Luis Migone, President of the Engineer's Center of Argentina, came to the United States, studied our building and zoning laws over an extended period and returned to write a book about them. The result of his work, *Las Ciudades de los Estados Unidos* (The Cities of the United States), is a new zoning law for Buenos Aires, approved in January, 1942, and based on the principles of zoning laws in the United States. One of the co-authors of the new zoning law told me that the zoning theory of the United States could be applied more easily than that of Germany because of the strong sense of property rights of the people of Buenos Aires. With an almost colonial sense of land ownership on one hand, and an urgent need for land use regulations on the other, the new zoning law for South America's greatest metropolis has yet to be proven in use.

In a general sense, Montevideo, capital of Uruguay, leads in progressive policy with regard to planning. The studies made in the *Dirección del Plan Regulador* are the most complete that I saw in any Latin American city. The land use plan was particularly good. It realistically defines land use types, confining them to clearly marked regions, provides for agricultural green belts and satellite units for future expansion. A detailed zoning law, which promises to be excellent, is being prepared, based upon the more generalized land use plan.

The difficult site on which Rio de Janeiro, capital of Brazil, is located has almost forced a natural segregation of types of land uses. Industry has developed toward the inner part of the great bay adjacent to rail and shipping facilities, while the apartment and residential section has naturally grown up along the park areas of the waterfront district within easy access of the downtown business and shopping section. In this way Rio had a good start from the beginning in distributing land uses. In addition, the city provides for general control by law, limiting changes from the basic pattern, but as yet Rio de Janeiro is without a zoning law.

São Paulo seemed to me to possess more jumbled land uses in a small area than any other city I visited in Latin America. This confusion is the result of rapid, planless growth in the last twenty years. However, São Paulo has adapted a fairly adequate zoning law, the only one in Brazil at all similar to those of the United States. The law was drafted with the help of Washington Azevedo who made a special study of zoning while at the Harvard City Planning School.

The state of Rio de Janeiro has asked Attilio Corrêa Lima to prepare a regional land use plan for the area of some 25 kilometers which parallels the Parahyba River where the first large steel mill in South America is now under construction for the *Companhia Siderurgica Nacional*. At the two ends of the ribbon-like area stand the towns of Pinheiro and Barra Mansa, while in the center lies Volta Redonda, site of the steel mill. A complete survey has been made of the existing conditions in the area, and plans for its development will include segregation of industrial, agricultural, residential, and recreational uses according to their most appropriate locations.

In the matter of land use control and zoning, it is apparent that our techniques and their effectiveness in the United States have been developed further than those of Latin American cities. Neither is there enough understanding in Latin America on the part of the people and the officials of the advantages of careful land use control, nor does zoning have the established legal standing that it has in the United States. Zoning may often be used effectively to put over an esthetic point, such as the control of building height near an historic monument or park, while ignoring an important health or economic factor such as light industrial uses or the keeping of fowl in a residential section.

CIRCULATION, STREETS, TRAFFIC

If Latin American cities are lacking in the orderly arranging of land uses with which North American planners have made some progress, they do excel in the matter of streets, boulevards, and avenues within urban areas. Latin American engineers and architects have done great things in the past by way of broad, tree-lined boulevards and spacious avenues, and judging by the amount of new work which I saw in progress everywhere down there, they are still keeping up the old standards. I can say truthfully that every city of importance which I visited had more new street work actually in progress than any one city that I know of in the United States has had in the last five years. The things I saw in Mexico City, in Bogotá, in Lima, in La Paz, in Buenos Aires, and particularly in São Paulo, amazed me for their daring and bold approach to the problem of freeing urban traffic—vehicular and pedestrian—and to the need for giving cities the graciousness that comes from generous standards of space for movement. In their boldness and completeness of approach to this problem Latin American planners surpass us.

Mexico City has taken advantage of her recent building boom, and through the use of a master plan is redeveloping blighted areas by widening streets and making new openings. This work has been done through the unique, effective system of Executive Committees, of which I spoke earlier (committees composed of three members, appointed by the City Council and chosen from the property owners of the area involved, equipped by law with full powers to buy and sell land, buildings, etc.) Since the Executive Committee, when properly appointed, generally represents the property owners to be affected, opposition to direct municipal action is automatically avoided. The actual plan for the area to be rebuilt is made by the city's Planning Commission, but changes may be proposed by the technical consultant for the Executive Committee. *Plus valia*, the name for the method of financing such projects, resembles our too-seldom-used process of excess condemnation. Under the *plus valia* procedure, the improvement sometimes increases the value of the property to such an extent that more funds are collected than are actually needed. This is often applied to the cost of another phase of the improvement which might have been done for esthetic reasons alone and which could not otherwise pay for itself. In this way a public works project may accomplish both practical and esthetic results and pay for itself in the bargain. Re-valuation of the property is adjusted in proportion to the benefits derived from the improvement and a standard scale of compensation is worked out according to depths and widths, and resulting usability, of the properties. An endeavor is made to judge fairly and scientifically. At least one committee with whom I spoke had an excellent record of cooperation from property owners and immediate agreement from them in almost every case.

Through this use of Executive Committees and the *plus valia* principle, a number of important streets have been completely re-modeled. Calle San Juan de Letrán (and its prolongation—Niño Perdido) was widened from a narrow street of colonial dimensions to a major metropolitan artery. Calle López was widened and extended, and is now a street of secondary importance. Carlos Contreras acted as planning consultant for both these projects. Today his finished work shows admirably the result of consistently applied effort—and patience—in the attainment of city planning objectives. His accomplishments in the difficult task of street widening in the built-up heart of the city indicate that in order to make planning effective more is required than engineering and design ability alone. Contreras *believes* in the principles by which he works. In the case of these two streets, costs to be shared by property owners were sometimes contributed in the form of the property itself, which would then be sold for cash by the committee to help defray costs. In theory, the city was supposed to pay one-half the cost of the Letrán project, but actually, paid about two million pesos in gifts of property, or liens against property, rather than the necessary cash. This left a rather complicated financing problem up to the committee, a problem which was nevertheless overcome. I tell of this instance to indicate the extent of responsibility often assumed by the Executive Committees.

One integral part of Mexico City's Master Plan is the new Avenida 20 de Noviembre leading south from Zocalo, the historic center of the city. Nine blocks of new street have been opened by an Executive Committee, where before there was a blighted, congested maze of narrow streets and old buildings. The further extension of the new avenue is now under way, with plans for a plaza and two diagonal boulevards which will provide easier access to outlying sections. In this particular case the city agreed to pay one-third of the cost to the Executive Committee. Vicente Urquiaga was the architect and planning consultant in charge.

Where this opening affected the Zocalo itself, Urquiaga made architectural studies for the treatment of new public buildings which would tie into the old colonial architecture of that plaza. These were part of a plan for redesigning the layout of the Zocalo itself by means of a competition for architects and planners. The plan called for an air-conditioned underground garage, redesign of surface facilities, and re-routing of traffic in the entire area surrounding the plaza.

Another replanning project on an even larger scale, done by this system of Executive Committees, was undertaken in preparation for building the Monument to the Revolution just off the Paseo de la Reforma. This project seemed to me an unfortunate expenditure of public funds, when one considers the relative need for other facilities such as low-cost housing in Mexico City. Nevertheless the comprehensive approach—replanning of streets and rehabilitation of the surrounding twenty square blocks—makes up in some degree for the relatively questionable significance of the monument.

One of the most damaging leftovers from colonial periods in Latin American cities is the typical narrow street, which does not meet today's needs. I found a number of examples of a usual method of street widening in many other cities of Latin America. The new street width is laid down by law, and any new building must conform to the altered building line, which is called *ante-jardin*, or set-back. The remaining space between the old and new property lines along the sidewalk may be three feet or thirty, and is often left unused for many years, until the remainder of the block is rebuilt. The sides of projecting buildings become places for advertisements; often this indented space becomes a convenient collector for rubbish or homeless noon-day sleepers. Bogotá, Colombia, has widened many narrow streets through this process. In Bogotá, if the piece of land is only a narrow strip the city takes it free; but if it is a reasonably large piece the owner is compensated. However, the owner must pay his share of any public improvements which increase property value.

A project of this type which is nearing completion in conformity with Bogotá's master plan is the widening of Avenida Jimenez de Quesada, which passes through the center of the downtown area, to from seventy to one hundred feet in width, and the opening of several new plazas—a feat achieved by covering the old river channel. Much of the new construction in Bogotá is taking place along Avenida Jimenez de Quesada. This boulevard will become the main east-west thoroughfare and will connect the central business section with the new Avenida Caracas, one hundred and twenty feet wide, which comes from the north residential section. More work of this nature was being pushed for the Pan-American Conference originally scheduled to be held in Bogotá in 1943.

Contribution of private land for public uses seems to be much less painful in Latin America than in the United States. Citizens of Medellín, Colombia, through an organization called the *Sociedad de Mejoras Públicas*, aroused interest in the idea of building a parkway along each side of the River Medellín, which was in the process of being channelized. The owners of the land adjoining the river were so attracted to the plan, which included other features as well—parks, university, etc.,—that they have given to the city a right-of-way, some two hundred feet on each side of the river, over a length of thirty-five miles—absolutely free. With Ricardo Olano, one of SMP's leaders, I drove over a portion of the boulevard (only a small section is complete) and, seeing the site for the development, I could understand why the beauty of the riverside inspired the owners to cooperate with the plan. In this case, it would have been difficult for even the most hard-boiled North American property-owner to refuse to contribute his share of land. This is just one example of the lesser degree to which mercenary standards have taken hold in Latin America than in the United States.

For years the heart of old Lima, Peru's capital, has been full of streets in process of being widened by this time-consuming *ante-jardin* method, but today there is an especial reason for impatience to grip the city. New, broad openings are worming their way like hungry termites through the thick mud walls of the old buildings. This special reason is the mayor himself—Luis Gallo Porras—who, for years, has taken an active part in the planning of Lima. Under his guidance, one and one-half miles of widening are under way on Avenida Tacna, increasing it from alley width to about a hundred and ten feet. A new bridge across the Rimac will extend the boulevard to the opposite bank at a total cost of 2,500,000 soles ($400,000 U.S.), of which the government pays 500,000, the city pays 500,000 and the remainder is paid for through *plus valia*. Another widening to be carried out is Avenida Abancay, east of the center of old Lima. The two boulevards will be joined by a new *Malecón* (a road following the water's edge) along the Rimac. These drastic changes will form an inner circulation ring around the central business section, and will be augmented by a new shopping street from Avenida Tacna to the Plaza de las Armas. This street is to be arcaded—that is, lined with covered sidewalks—with provision for new shops. The city is making an effort to free shopping congestion in the older section, and at the same time rehabilitate run-down areas.

One basic cause for the need of such a replanning program in the heart of old Lima is that the city suddenly exploded some years ago, spreading its population over the great triangular delta that makes up the Lima region. Widespread use of automobiles and extensive construction of concrete highways have made it possible for a person to live in Miraflores, ten miles from downtown Lima, yet work and shop in the city. This network of highways, which has caused Lima to spread out to such an extent, has been well planned partly through the efforts of Emilio Harth-Terré of the Section of Urban Studies of the Ministry of Development, mentioned early in this chapter. Avenida Salaverry, one hundred and twenty feet wide and parked in the center, one of these magnificent boulevards leading out of the city, was planned to deviate from a straight course in order that it might pass through a grove of eucalyptus trees.

Harth-Terré has other plans under study. The Pan-American Highway, almost completed in Peru, is to by-pass the center of Lima and connect with the central interior highway just above the heart of the old city. This portion will be one hundred twenty to one hundred fifty feet wide, with freeway control over abutting property. In connection with the highway, Harth-Terré is planning a much needed park-forest reserve of 500 hectares. Lima needs forested areas and parks—there is no natural tree growth. The city has had a long tradition of civic discipline; and as a result, it is probably better adapted to 20th-century living needs than any other city on the West Coast.

High in La Paz, Bolivia, I found only one street widening project under way, but that one was great enough to dwarf any other single undertaking I had seen up to that time. It involves construction of a thirty-foot underground concrete culvert to control the rampant river which raced through the center of the city. When the river has been literally buried alive, the Prado (main boulevard) will be extended seven blocks over the path formerly occupied by the river. Financing is also being done by the successfully used *plus valia* method. Many-storied modern buildings are being erected on the newly improved property.

I have said that because of the difficult site, La Paz has grown awkwardly. But today the city is spending large sums of money to remedy past errors and make the most of the difficult terrain. Plans are in progress for developing an inner-loop boulevard to link the two sides of the canyon in which the city is located. The planners of La Paz are thinking in broad terms of facilitating the entrance of produce into the city from the rich Yungas Valley by means of a by-pass which would go directly to the markets and industrial sections of the city, avoiding the congested center.

In Buenos Aires, typically "American" problems of congestion, traffic, and overcrowding, exist in the central area. These need bold-stroke planning, nothing less, and some mighty bold, if expensive, strokes have been made. Here are some of them: The Avenida 9 de Julio, cut five blocks long and four hundred and twenty feet wide through a solidly built-up but blighted area near the center of the city; the splendid, spacious public garage constructed under this wide, short boulevard; the new Diagonal Norte, with its excellent building height and design control; the waterfront parkway development of the old and the new Costanera along the shores of the brown Rio de la Plata. That which tops all others is Avenida General Paz, the eighteen-mile-long parkway, three hundred feet wide, that belts the city at its boundaries. Many of these and other works have been under study by the office of the Plan de Urbanización, under the direction of Carlos della Paolera. This office has published much of the excellent research done during the last few years, particularly on the problems of congestion, sudden urban expansion, and the need for open space in this startling maze of built-up urban area.

The opening of Avenida 9 de Julio is the result of long argument on the need for providing adequate open space in the very center of the city, and of a demand for cutting through wide arteries. A portion of the blighted ring around the central core of the city was chosen for destruction and five square blocks were removed. Underground was built a magnificent garage for over a thousand cars, one of the finest examples in the world; and overhead, on the surface, the urban parkway was built, one entire block wide. Since my visit in Buenos Aires demolition of several more blocks has begun in preparation for extending the parkway. Eventually Avenida 9 de Julio will extend through the city and form an inner belt parkway (like the *Ringstrassen* of Vienna and Frankfort) linking with the outer circumferential parkway, Avenida General Paz.

This latter project—Avenida General Paz—is the work of a section of the National Highway Department which is doing important planning in various cities in Argentina and bears the dramatic title of *Departmento de Acceso de Grandes Ciudades* (Department of Access to Large Cities). This section is entrusted with the designing of all highways entering and leaving the major cities of Argentina. Pascual Palazzo, whose unusual imagination is responsible for the planning of Avenida General Paz, is the engineer in charge of the office. He began the parkway in 1937, and finished eighteen miles of it by 1941, at a cost of twenty-five million pesos or about $6,250,000. Palazzo's first problem was to convince officials that the principle of the freeway was sound, but once it had been demonstrated, all opponents were won over. According to this principle, access to the parkway is permitted only at planned intersections where grade-separations are designed with ingenuity. One, the "Double Lassoo," is an original method of eliminating left-hand turns and an excellent substitute for the expensive, space-consuming cloverleaf. Plans for the continuation of the present section of the parkway, now well along, call for its extension to the Riachuelo, the river, on the eastern, industrial side of the city, and through —to the Costanera at the Rio de la Plata—completely encircling the city. Four kilometers of this new section will have a six-hundred-foot-wide longitudinal park, the result of clever planning: fill needed to raise the level of the parkway will be taken from a shallow pit alongside the right-of-way on land purchased at less expense than the cost of hauling in fill. This strip will then be drained and planted with trees to form a useful, well-located park on the edge of a residential section housing industrial workers.

Palazzo speaks of eventually bringing this type of parkway right down into the heart of Buenos Aires. He envisions a series of radials entering the city from various points along the circumferential boulevard and linked together by an inner ring parkway. For these radial arteries he plans to acquire a strip a full block wide, use only the interior one hundred fifty feet for the freeway, and resell at a higher price the remaining property on each side, thereby paying for the new trafficway. He demonstrates the potential saving to motorists by pointing out that starting and stopping cars on ten blocks of Calle Maipú in downtown Buenos Aires uses one hundred twenty percent more gas than would be used in driving the same distance on the proposed freeways, to say nothing of the time lost.

For the cities of Rosario and Córdoba, Palazzo's office is planning similar ring parkways. When built, Rosario's will be twenty miles in length, three hundred feet wide throughout, and will link a series of existing parks to which will be added other park areas providing a total of six large recreation grounds with public picnic areas, planting, and playgrounds. Palazzo looks at highway planning only as a means to an end—a means of raising the standard of living both by getting people in and out of the city quickly and by making available new recreational and living areas.

Brazil, though not nearly as advanced in highway planning outside the cities as Argentina, is making great strides within Rio de Janeiro and São Paulo. Work done in past years in Rio de Janeiro, in parkway and boulevard development along the waterfront, is in itself almost fantastic; but what is now being planned and actually started *in the interior* of the city, reads like a page from Baron Haussman's plans of the last century for Paris. This work when carried out will influence the plan of Rio to almost the same extent as Haussman's did. New circulation lines will establish an integrated city pattern, bringing order out of the chaos of urban congestion in those areas lying behind the beautifully built waterfront. The major project is the new two-mile Avenida Presidente Vargas, two hundred and fifty feet wide, which will free traffic movement in the forgotten interior of the city, and rehabilitate a very extensive blighted area. Several blocks in the vicinity of the new railroad station at Pedro II have already been removed and demolition has begun down in the center of the city. The building wreckers will continue through a congested, blighted section as far as the railroad station, and there meet that portion of the avenue already opened. An entire city block on each side of the boulevard itself has been expropriated; here the buildings are being removed. This property will be re-subdivided according to up-to-date principles and sold by the city for rebuilding, but only under carefully planned restrictions. One of the most popular songs of the famous Rio Carnival concerned this Avenida Presidente Vargas, how it is surging through the city and how the Praça Once *já acabou*—is being swallowed up in the onslaught. The raucous *já acabou* at the end of the song suggests that the Brazilians are shedding no tears over the loss of the old Praça and are all for the new Avenida named after their President. This and other projects equally as bold will go far toward giving new life to the extensively run-down areas of the city away from the bay and seafronts.

Costs of expropriating land from Avenida Presidente Vargas are to amount to ten million dollars. The development is expected to bring to the city a surplus of about $1,750,000, through increased valuation of land, the result of improved, more efficient site planning. Where the former lots were as narrow as twenty feet, with buildings averaging two stories, new lots will be sixty feet wide, and well spaced buildings will rise to ten and fifteen stories. The plan is to define clearly the portions of the lot which may be built upon, completely controlling the height and general form of the apartments, even though they will be built by private builders on privately owned land. The plan will allow a height of ten stories throughout, except at plazas and main intersections where the permissible height will be fifteen stories. The apartments will serpentine in strips forming great inner patios, open on one side of the avenida and generously planted with luxurious Brazilian vegetation. Planted areas will remain under the control and maintenance of the city. Buildings will be uniformly free of the ground, standing on *pilotes,* or columns, in the Corbusier tradition, allowing for free circulation beneath them, and protection from rain and sun. This particular project is imaginative—one of the most complete in conception of any I saw in Latin America.

Another project, part of the general plan for improved circulation in Rio, is the new Tunnel do Leme, paralleling that already in use and providing for improved access from Botafogo Bay to Copacabana Beach on the ocean. The completed project will thus provide a double-tube, tunnelled boulevard. Other tunnels are planned under the granite mountains which isolate one section of Rio from another. Although such boulevard planning is approached from a less scientific point of view (in that less reliance is placed on factual data concerning traffic volumes and movements) than is true in the United States, the work shows more imagination in the matter of actual design than we use here.

Because the booming city of São Paulo to the south of Rio de Janeiro has done so little planning in the past, the work being done today by the *Paulistas* (natives of São Paulo) seems even more amazing than that of Rio. Having developed rapidly, through hard work, the city is now turning some of its wealth and energy toward making itself a more attractive, efficient place in which to live and work, to untangling some of the urban snarls of traffic and congestion.

The planning program is largely in the hands of a brilliant, ag-

gressive engineer who is none other than the mayor himself—
Mayor Francisco Prestes Maia of São Paulo. Prestes Maia's plan is
detailed and far-reaching. Most attention is being concentrated on
the circulation system, which will be based on an inner and outer
circumferential boulevard and a number of radial links. The inner
"ringstrasse" will be a parked boulevard, varying from a hundred
and twenty to a hundred and eighty feet in width, and encircling
the Triangulo, the heart of the central business and financial district, where high land costs prevented cutting straight through.
This ring-parkway is well under way, in some portions complete,
in others with land already expropriated or purchased. The second
circumferential boulevard will follow the outer edge of the residential fringe of the city, where land is already being acquired as
subdivision goes on. In addition to these two parkways, radial
arteries are being built to link the center of the city with the open
country. These follow the beds of old drainage channels formerly
built up but now blighted due to inaccessibility; great viaducts
above the boulevards act as natural overpasses and grade sepa-
rators for traffic. This system of interlacing parkways and viaducts, rapidly becoming a characteristic feature of São Paulo, will
also serve to link a number of existing parks close to the downtown
area—Parque Dom Pedro II and the Praça da Republica.

Another important part of Prestes Maia's plan for São Paulo is
the channelization of the Rio Tieté, which in its meandering course
frequently overflows its banks. It will be shortened from twenty-
eight to sixteen miles. Rail lines which now cut through the city, im-
peding traffic, will be placed along the banks of the new channel;
three railroad stations will be combined and a central rail terminal
will be built on new land formed by reclamation along the banks of
the river. Nearby will be built a new airport. The old rail lines will
be taken over for use as highways leading in and out of the city.

Without doubt, in planning urban streets, boulevards, and traffic-
ways, Latin American cities score well over ours for boldness
and imaginative approach. Has New York City a block-wide, tree-
planted boulevard uniting Times Square with Central Park? Mexico City has its splendid Paseo de la Reforma linking the downtown
section with Chapultepec Park where on Sundays *charros* and
china poblanas ride their blooded horses.

Is there in San Francisco a chain of waterfront boulevards,
recreation areas, and parks linking the Ferry Building at the foot
of Market Street with Yacht Harbor and the Presidio? Yet, Rio de
Janeiro has built its magnificent developments of Praça da Paris,
Gloria, Flamengo, and Botafogo which together with Avenida
Atlantica, link the city's airport with Copacabana Beach and other
residential sections and provide the most glorious waterside recreational areas in the world.

Boston has its waterfront cluttered with gloomy wharves and warehouses shutting out access and view to the Bay; Montevideo has planned an orderly, out-of-the-way industrial waterfront with the remaining ocean frontage developed for public uses of a recreational and residential nature. The magnificent Rambla sweeps around the Boston-like peninsula on which the city is built and carries you along the water's edge out to the beaches to the north, where you may travel for miles with an uninterrupted view of the Atlantic.

Look back of the wealth and splendor of the Michigan Boulevard in Chicago to the internal congestion and lack of open space of the famous Loop district. Can you find there, as you do in Buenos Aires, an Avenida 9 de Julio, boldly cut through the city a whole block wide and five blocks long, only the beginning of a system of cross-city freeways and interior greenbelts?

We could well use many such applications of European civic traditions, which we have too often spurned in building the cities of the United States. This work of the Latins bids us look to what laurels we have.

SUBDIVISION CONTROL AND NEIGHBORHOODS

In our cities of the United States, we too often take for granted the spacious areas of residential subdivisions which extend out into our suburbs and forget that these exist only because we have developed a large middle class. When one considers how small is the middle class of most Latin American countries, it is not surprising to find that few Latin cities have large areas of such subdivision; however, where the process of industrialization is developing a broader distribution of wealth, as in São Paulo, Brazil, and Buenos Aires, Argentina, enormous areas are being subdivided at a rate of speed not seen in the United States since the boom days of the twenties. But we have had much more experience in residential subdivision work; in quality ours exceeds Latin America's.

Most cities of Latin America have subdivision laws similar to those of the United States, under which plans for opening new streets and selling residential lots must be approved by city authorities and planning technicians. Such approval is generally in accordance with a master plan for the city.

However, the Latins do have the edge over us in one phase of urbanizing new land: there is a greater willingness on the part of property owners to cooperate in the public interest and to contribute ample land for wide streets and for park space in newly subdivided areas. I was always astounded to see the extent of parks deeded to the city as part of the process of subdividing new sections of Mexico City, Bogotá, Lima, and other cities.

In Mexico City, fifteen percent of subdivided property must be

113

given for parks. In Bogotá, Colombia, as much as thirty-five percent of the land is given to the city for public use (including streets and avenues), which results in a conspicuous, widespread distribution of open green areas in the new residential districts.

Peru, as I have said, has a long-established sense of civic discipline. Her land subdivision law, first passed in 1926, controls the spread of urban development by permitting urban lots only to a certain limit outside a city. Beyond that, lots must be of rural size, restricted to rural use. This device for controlling uneconomic over-expansion may well be noted for use in the United States. The law requires thirty-five percent of the land to be set aside for streets and avenues, and ten percent for parks or school sites, making a total of forty-five percent of the subdivided land actually put to public use. In the United States, a city does well to obtain twenty-five percent of such land for public purposes. Some of the most beautiful residential suburbs in Latin America are the result of such laws. It is no wonder that North American visitors in Lima favor living in sections like San Isidro, planned around a century-old olive grove in the center of what used to be the Monastery of San Isidro, or in a section like Miraflores generously planted with parks and built along bluffs overlooking the blue Pacific.

The point I wish to make is that while subdivision planning in Latin cities receives more generous cooperation from property owners, in general the design standard is not up to that of the United States. Street planning and lot layout have not reached the standards set by federal housing agencies and applied by some large-scale private developers in our country. But generous parks and planting in Latin American cities make up for this weakness.

Subdivision control probably goes further in Montevideo than in any other city I visited. Here, plans for subdivisions are made in the city planning office; the owner then puts in the streets according to the plan supplied by the city. One-third of the area is usually given for parks. Such close cooperation between the city and the developers makes possible a coordinated relationship in the newly opened areas. Thus, a man who wishes to subdivide his property into small city plots may do so only if his land lies within the zone provided for minimum sized lots. Radiating out from the center of Montevideo are other zones providing for lots of greater area. In this way, similar types of residences are kept in the same general areas, reducing the cost of extending public utilities,—streets, waterlines, electricity, etc. Again we may learn from Latin American practice.

In a few cases some good work based on United States design standards has been done. In the industrial suburbs of Rio de Janeiro I visited Cidade Jardim Hygienopolis, a complete garden-city subdivision, well-planned, with contour streets, cul-de-sac dead-ends, playgrounds, school-sites, and shopping centers laid out along the lines of Radburn, New Jersey. The reason for the use of North American standards is that Washington Azevedo, designer of the community, was trained in planning at Harvard University and is familiar with the best of the English and American land-subdivision practice.

Likewise, up in São Paulo, other excellent work has been done by the City Company in suburbs like Jardim América, Pacaembu and others. These neighborhoods have been built according to the best English and North American standards of design, and the best Latin tradition of spaciousness. The suburbs of São Paulo are gradually extending into the nearby, open, rolling countryside. One subdivision company has built a splendid divided highway through the open country to the edge of Lake Guarapiranga, and has under construction beside the lake a satellite garden city known as Inter-lagos. The first unit for some six thousand people is now complete with streets, parks, beach, and boating facilities. Interlagos is a remarkably well done job of modern subdivision planning.

To sum up, the U.S.A. excels in the design of residential communities and subdivisions simply because we have had more experience in this field of housing our larger middle class groups. But where an advanced economy has made it possible, the Latins have developed some excellent examples of residential community planning and have set a particularly high standard with respect to provision of parks, wide streets, and other public space.

PARKS AND RECREATION

Latin American people seem to be more conscious of the need for urban parks than are we North Americans, but generally use them for more passive recreation than we do. The downtown sections of most South American cities are almost always provided with at least one fairly large park where one sees reflected much of the Latin way of life. Here the chief activity is nothing more ambitious than the delightful *paseo,* which, as the reader may know, is the all-important institution of relaxation among our southern neighbors; it may amount to a five-minute walk in the plaza or may be a two-weeks' vacation in the Chilean lake district. Here is Appleton's translation and definition of *paseo*: "Walk; promenade; stroll; drive; ride; ramble, mall; turnout, parade." And for the verb form, *pasear*: "to take a walk; to ride or sail for pleasure; to promenade; to make a pleasure trip; to walk up and down." What a wide variety of recreational activities the word covers! If there were only one thing which we were to absorb into our cities from Latin America in exchange for those we have to offer her, my first recommendation would be the "paseo." If we could learn how to "pasear," and then could provide places in our cities—small parks, plazas, boulevards

—in which to "pasear," our cities and our lives would be enriched immeasurably.

In addition to many downtown parks, most Latin American cities have a much larger one farther out from the center. In Mexico City, all North Americans know the beautiful Chapultepec Park crowded on Sunday with the colorful *charros* (horsemen) dressed in colonial trousers, jacket, and sombrero, riding with girls who wear *china poblana* costumes, brilliant with colored spangles. In Santiago, there is the Parque Cousiño and the even more popular Cerro San Cristóbal which you ascend on a toy-like funicular to one of the loveliest urban views outside of Rio de Janeiro.

Besides these parks, many more plazas, boulevards, and streets are planted with trees and flowers. Yes, this *is* an Old World idea, and a very good one—a very necessary part of the equipment of any city in which people wish to live as human beings—Old World or New World, North or South.

Although Latin cities surpass ours in provision for downtown parks, we excel in the matter of providing facilities for more active recreation, whether on a large scale or in small neighborhood centers. The reason for this is obvious: few other peoples in the world are so completely taken with the idea of practicing active outdoor recreation as are we in the United States. Social customs in Latin America prevent the widespread distribution of neighborhood playgrounds, tennis courts, etc.

Many of the cities which I visited were extravagantly planted with trees, shrubs, and flowers—more like the New York World's Fair than downtown New York. Lima resembled a permanent Treasure Island in contrast to the drabness of downtown San Francisco. All of the Lima area, excluding only the small core of Old Lima, was practically one huge flower garden. In all the United States and Europe that I have seen, I have never run across such an array of color. Every home (Lima, unlike other Latin American capitals, has many single-family homes of moderate cost) has a garden of some kind. It may be small, with only a patch of front lawn and a bright flower border over the low wall; or there may be a great rambling garden surrounding a huge house. Lima is unique for having broken with the Latin tradition of the high wall surrounding all homes. Each garden, small or large, was remarkably well kept. Geraniums were growing as I've never seen them before; they had more blooms than leaves. Red bougainvillia, snapdragons, coreopsis, canna, roses, every flower we know in California and then some, grew there.

In addition to private gardens, the municipalities that make up the Lima region, including Lima itself, maintain a luxurious planting of lawns, flower beds, and trees in all public areas. I saw jacaranda trees, a solid mass of blue blossoms, planted in four rows all the way from Lima to San Isidro on Avenida Arequipa, the four-mile boulevard from Lima to Miraflores overlooking the Pacific. The Plaza Bolognesi was the most colorful—the great center circle, three hundred feet in diameter, was planted solidly with cannas in three concentric circles, each circle in a different color: first row, yellow; second, salmon-pink; third, deep red. The planners of Lima have been generous and imaginative in providing space for planting; the gardeners and nurserymen have shown skill in the use and maintenance of those spaces.

In Santiago, Chile, recent park work has aided in rehabilitating physically and economically run-down areas near the center of the city. Such new parks pay for themselves through *plus valia;* the increased value of adjoining property is used to finance the improvement. Several of these projects have shaken old, blighted areas out of a static economic condition: for example, the excellently laid out Parque Japonais, designed by Oscar Prager (who did Lake Merritt Park in Oakland, California); the Plaza Italia development; and the great new Barrio Cívico, the new federal building center. A new park is being planned on the site of the old railroad station and electric rail line which formerly entered the Plaza Italia. A new parked boulevard will provide access to suburban areas.

Before leaving Chile, the reader may be interested to hear something of a broader field of recreation planning. Because of Chile's natural scenic advantages, possibilities for recreational planning on a national scale, outside the cities, are enormous. The government has already done a great deal in this field, though in a somewhat unplanned, uncoordinated way. In the private field, a young architect, Santiago Roi, has done an outstanding job that is worthy of attention because it suggests a policy that might well be adapted to future recreational development in Chile. This job is Farallones, the ski center, six thousand feet in the Andes overlooking the city of Santiago. Although my visit there took place in the Chilean summer, I shall not rest until I return for a visit in the winter.

Ten years ago Santiago Roi and his friends used to drive half way up the mountain, then go on mules through the snow to these magnificent slopes, part of a large *fundo* above the valley where the city lies. After five years of such primitive access, Roi bought the property for a small sum, planned a complete ski-town, and started building a road. Farallones has been a success and today is the most accessible and popular ski spot in Chile. It is only about thirty miles from Santiago, but the trip takes an hour and a half in a car because of the steepness of the climb. You follow the Rio Mapocho back into a deep canyon of the Cordillera. The road continues through rugged country; high, treeless mountain peaks, still spotted with patches of snow, soar above canyons running with clear, green water. You drive back closer and closer to the snow

117

peaks, and high above, on a shoulder of the mountain called El Colorado, you see the cliffs of Farallones where the chalets seem to teeter on the edge. A zig-zag road takes you to the top of the cliffs.

The planning and architectural design were done by Roi himself, and the result is a unique example of winter resort planning which shows more imagination, though on a much smaller scale, than examples in the United States, including Sun Valley, Idaho. Roi has used native rock for the walls of his buildings, flat pieces of shale for the roofs, and boulders laid about to hold the roofing stones in place. Huge windows of steel frame open out on wide terraces overhanging the cliffs and slopes. Completed to date are: a hundred-bed *refugio* for the Ski Club, about thirty private houses, a store and restaurant building. Although there is no real need for a church—the whole mountain-top is a natural cathedral —a picturesque chapel, named the "Virgin of the Snows," has been built as an integral part of the scheme. Roi has complete plans drawn for paving the road, constructing a large hotel with swimming pool and tennis courts for summer use and a ski lift to the crest of El Colorado for winter. Farallones is destined to become one of the outstanding ski spots in the hemisphere when postwar conditions permit.

At the end of my visit in Farallones, when the sun had gone down, a sprinkle of misplaced stars down on the valley floor was pointed out to me as the lights of Santiago. As we made our way down toward them, Roi outlined to me other plans based on his experience in planning Farallones. He knows that among Chile's greatest assets are her scenic and climatic resources, but he believes that these must be properly developed. He would like to promote *turismo*, or tourist travel, not only for foreign visitors but for all Chileans as well. Roi wants to see provided facilities inexpensive enough for the average man, and planned to meet the recreational needs of all classes. Resulting increased travel would not only make possible the needed recreational outlet, but would also provide the average Chilean an opportunity for bettering his knowledge of the country. Roi proposes a ten-year program, based on a careful survey of possibilities. He recommends three steps: First, establishment of a planning unit to survey the field, make recommendations, and lay out plans; second, setting up a unit for administration and maintenance; and, third, providing means to make the facilities known to the people for whom they have been planned.

Santiago Roi is interested in the national park systems of the United States and in our State and County Park developments, and believes that they could well be used as examples for Chile. Such young men as Roi, part of the large younger generation of good neighbors, should be brought to the United States to see what we have done, for with them lies the success or failure of our future relations with Latin America.

Although I admired the facilities for *turismo* recently developed by the Chilean Government, I could not help but feel that much of the program was unplanned. Fifteen million pesos, I found, had been spent on the luxury hotel at Puerto Varas and a large sum on that at Puyehue. Both of these are open only during the summer months, while nearby are some of the finest ski slopes in all Chile. The eighty-bed hotel at Lago San Rafael far to the south in the Canal region of the fiords, has in use, it is said, only six to eight beds each summer because of a lack of coordination in providing activities nearby.

In crossing from Chile into Argentina by the southern route through the Chilean Lake district one sees the most beautiful part of Chile—forested mountains, snow-capped volcanoes, and magnificent lakes—but all of it is without needed protection which could be offered by a system of national parks and national forests. Over the Argentine border, however, the similarly beautiful mountain country is a part of a system of Parques Nacionales which are as well developed and maintained as those of the United States. Argentina's national park movement goes back to President Theodore Roosevelt's visit many years ago to the southern mountain region surrounding Lake Nahuel Huapí. Roosevelt encouraged Argentine nature enthusiasts who wished to preserve and protect this scenic area, and some six or eight years ago the movement crystallized. A National Park Department was formed and a number of scenic areas were set aside. The largest and most popular of these is the Parque Nacional Nahuel Huapí adjoining the Chilean lake regions. Here, the National Park Department controls all private architecture and uses excellent standards of design on park structures. At first small towns within the park areas opposed the federal government's action, but some of them, like San Carlos de Bariloche, where a delightful civic center has been built overlooking Lake Nahuel Huapí, have profited so much in recent times by the popularity of the park that today all are in favor of the national park idea.

Buenos Aires is, curiously, the most congested city in Latin America, and at the same time one of the most spacious. At first the visitor is impressed by the great number of green areas near the center of the city and by the large number of private recreation clubs further out in the vicinity of Palermo and along the rivershore toward the beautiful Tigre waterland. Buenos Aires' clubs are unique in the Western Hemisphere and provide recreational facilities of all kinds for all classes of people. But actually, these have come about as a result of the congestion, lack of open space, and scarcity of public recreational facilities in the city. The Master

Plan Office under Carlos della Paolera has done some illuminating studies of this problem. Maps contrasting built-up areas and open spaces in Buenos Aires, super-imposed over those of Berlin, Madrid, London, and Paris, show a lack of open space in Buenos Aires that is startling, but no less so than would be a similar comparison of those European cities with Chicago, New York, or San Francisco.

I have said that most Latin American cities do not provide public facilities for active recreation to the extent that we have in the United States. Montevideo, Uruguay, is one exception to this rule. This Uruguayan capital has done some significant work in urban park development in relation to social needs. Montevideo's park system is the most complete and up-to-date in Latin America. Parks are simple, functional, practical, and designed to fit the people's needs. In addition to existing playgrounds, there has been started a new system of community houses, each of which will act as a nucleus for the neighborhood unit it serves. Tajamar, a community house and restaurant building recently completed, is the first of these, and will act as a center for tennis courts and sports facilities recently provided in Carrasco for the use of the citizens as well as for summer visitors.

Juan Scasso, in addition to acting the rôle of a Bob Moses as director of the City Park Department, is also a leader in the Institute of Urbanism and Professor of City Planning and Landscape Architecture in the Facultad de Arquitectura, of which he is a graduate. In contrast to Buenos Aires, which is so densely built up in residential areas, Montevideo is more spacious. I was impressed with the large number of flower gardens. To my surprise I found that the Park Department gives free seeds and plants both to private homeowners and to renters of houses in the government's low-cost housing projects in order to encourage garden planting. The department also holds competitions each year for best garden designs and finest home-grown blooms.

In the development of Montevideo's recreational attractions, the city's Master Plan Office works closely with the Park Department, and together they have developed and protected the beautiful beach resources by intelligent planning and careful control of private uses of land. The Rambla, the waterfront boulevard which follows the ocean front from the industrial embarcadero north to the suburb, Carrasco, ranks with the Rio de Janeiro bay front as one of the finest pieces of waterfront planning in the western hemisphere. In decided contrast to similar waterfront areas in the United States—Miami Beach, for one—no private property other than public sport centers or small pavilion restaurants is allowed between the Rambla and the sea. The beaches are open to all, for both view and use.

Montevideo's city planning office is preparing a new coordinated program to take care of the 200,000 tourists who come to the city each summer. Using the United States National Park system as the example, they are looking toward the development of many other sections for sports facilities, scenic attractions, and historic resources. They plan to build *paradores* or small, economically managed stopping places for picnicking, camping, or over-night lodging for all classes. In this way, tourist trade will be increased, and the most scenic areas will be made available yet protected from private exploitation. Montevideo has already done much to attract tourists through a subsidized program of construction of beach hotels for summer use. Many of these hotels are built and owned by the city.

Another park feature in Montevideo is the Parque Nacional at Carrasco, a most unusual scheme of naturalized large-scale tree planting. Developed in a drained swamp twenty years ago according to a plan by a French landscape architect, the park has only been open to the public for about two years—that is, since the trees have matured. A long narrow strip of land is planted symmetrically on each side of a central axis, but the imaginative placing of trees in patterns—long curves going off to infinity, crosses, squares, open ovals, diamonds, and combinations of different tree heights—make this a fairyland of trees, a kind of ballet wherein the ballerinas are leafy trees.

The only comprehensive plan I saw in Latin America for development of recreation on a national scale was that of the *Comisión Nacional de Educación Física* in Uruguay, though it was not carried out in full. With architect Julio Vilamajó as consultant, this physical education commission outlined a program of recreation to include three types—social; recreational; physical education and competitive sports. The program included detailed plans for developing recreational centers for Montevideo and all towns of the republic.

This review of Latin American urban recreation facilities indicates that the Latins have a more widespread use of public parks in downtown urban areas, as well as a truer understanding of their need and location in relation to use. But in the matter of providing playground space for active recreational needs, we have progressed further.

PUBLIC BUILDINGS

Latin American cities far excel us in another way. They have had a long established tradition of well located public buildings arranged in an orderly manner. Their developers have placed more emphasis on the need for a suitable, dignified setting for the grouping of governmental and municipal structures than have we. With the exception of a few errors in certain cities, from a functional, as well as an esthetic, point of view the general policy is of high standard.

Just over our Mexican border, in Nuevo Laredo, stands a striking contrast between the Latin approach to location of public buildings and ours. The Mexican government began a plan for the location of public buildings in this border town and finished with making of a master plan for the entire town. I know of no analogous policy or plan for Laredo, Texas, U.S.A. A similar plan is under way for Juarez, also on the border.

The planners of Lima, Peru, do not consider adequate the well designed, spacious grouping of public buildings about the Paseo de la Republica, built on the site cleared for the celebration of the city's fourth centenary in 1935. Luis Gallo Porras, Alcalde (Mayor) of Lima, showed me a plan for redeveloping the entire area facing the Palacio de Justicia (Palace of Justice). The plan included removal of the massive penitentiary and acquiring additional private property for public use, while a small portion of unnecessary park area was being sold to help defray cost of the project.

A consistent policy of city planning in the early days has caused many of the public buildings in Latin American cities to be grouped around the original plaza at which the city was founded; this was likewise the practice, though less consistently, in the towns of Spanish California, with their plazas, and those of New England, with their Commons. Mexico City, Bogotá, La Paz, and many others still maintain this tradition. Some of these cities have improved and made larger the plaza; others have moved some of the buildings to a more spacious site. La Paz, for example, has a plan for enlarging the size of the Plaza Murillo by setting back the government buildings on one side and replacing private buildings on the opposite side with a new public building set back from the present building line.

Several years ago, the Chilean government selected a new site on which to group federal buildings away from the old center of Santiago. This new center is known as the Barrio Cívico and includes the *Moneda* (the White House of Chile), the Ministry of War, and other federal government agencies. The Barrio Cívico is the finest grouping of public buildings to be found in Latin America, in that it achieves dignity without monumentality.

In Argentina I found an overlapping procedure of public building design and a variety of staffs, resulting in a lack of coordination. This accounts for the unwise location of the new Ministry of War, in direct contrast to many good examples. Buenos Aires can boast of her Plaza de Mayo with its *Casa Rosada* (literally Pink House, the White House of Argentina), the old Cabildo, and other public buildings well related to the Palace of Congress at the far end of the Avenida de Mayo.

Montevideo, Uruguay, has recently constructed a new city hall based on a plan which was conceived through a public competition open to all architects. Mauricio Cravotto was awarded first place, and his design, which is now being carried out, includes not only the details of the building itself, but treatment of streets, plazas, and park area in the whole district surrounding the new building.

The Brazilian government showed commendable foresight when plans were laid for the development of the area in which formerly stood the hill, Morro Castelo, removed in the early twenties. Plans included a large area reserved for governmental structures arranged in functional relationship. Many are now under construction; the most outstanding is the Ministry of Education and Health.

Few of our cities in the United States have the character and integrity which comes from the proper placing and grouping of public buildings, not only in relation to each other, but in relation to the city plan as a whole. This the Latin planners of cities have achieved in general, and in this respect their efforts surpass ours.

NEW CITIES

About ten years ago the Government of the State of Goyaz in the interior of Brazil decided that a new, more centrally located state capital was needed. A site was carefully selected in a new, undeveloped region within a stone's throw of an insignificant village of several hundred persons. Construction began in 1934. In that year the rolling site was as clean and free of civilization's development as the native Indians living a few miles away were completely devoid of clothing. Photographs shown to me, of both the vacant site and the naked Indians, present a startling contrast with the city of Goiania, with its avenues, parks, and buildings, and its 48,000 well-clothed, well-fed Brazilians.

The first work started on the airport, making Goiania the first city, perhaps, to be built on a direct airline rather than a main rail line. Although the distance inland from Rio is only about six hundred miles in a straight line, the train trip from the capital takes four days, while the plane trip is only six hours. By 1937, most of the streets were laid out, the major buildings were constructed, and residential building had begun.

The plan of the new State Capital (not to be confused with the national capital once proposed for the State of Goyaz) represents the work of several Brazilian planners and three different schools of planning thought: first, the tiny village follows the gridiron plan of Portuguese colonial tradition; second, the new section now completed, representing the French school of diagonals and radials, the work of city planner Attilio Corrêa Lima; third, the Radburn-

123

like section designed by Dr. Armando Godoy, distinctly North American.

Construction was undertaken by Coimbra Bueno brothers, engineers of Rio de Janeiro. The city plan provides no fixed population limit but the present layout allows for about 100,000 inhabitants. As new units are needed, they will be planned and added on sites separated by the natural greenbelts of the wooded canyons, which are being preserved and developed for recreational use.

There is no other example of a new city to rival Goiania, but in connection with the preparation of the Regional Plan for the Volta Redonda area, Corrêa Lima has prepared plans for the new town to be built for 20,000 workers adjacent to the new steel mill. The town is to be built in a small, picturesque valley leading into the main river canyon about 2 kilometers from the steel mill itself. Corrêa Lima's skillful, efficient planning includes a minimum number of main avenues, and a maximum amount of pedestrian walks and central green areas. The plan in general follows the Radburn principle of providing walkways and play space and eliminating drives and traffic ways.

Chile's central planning office has made plans for two completely new towns, Chacabuco and Cisnes, both near Aysen in the south. These are part of the Government's plan to coordinate economic development with physical planning, which is part of the reason for the existence of the centralized planning office. These plans were made at the request of another government office, the *Caja de Tierra y Colonizacion,* in the belief that possibilities exist for populating this interesting region.

EARTHQUAKE REPLANNING

A very special kind of planning must be mentioned here because it is particularly significant to planning in general. I speak of the replanning that was done after the great earthquake of January, 1939, in Chile. The reconstruction work of the 300-mile-long region south of Santiago devastated by the *terremoto,* made possible some very unusual planning work.

The extent of the damage is difficult to imagine. In one town alone—Chillan—10,000 houses were shaken to the ground in five minutes, leaving the city fifty houses with walls, twenty with roofs. The damage done there in five minutes of earthquake was more than the German Luftwaffe could do in five days. One can imagine the destructive effect on the morale of the people, to say nothing of the problems of health, food, and water that developed immediately after the catastrophe. One man I spoke with had flown down a few days after the quake, and when he stepped out of the plane on the edge of town, found it necessary to return to Santiago immediately because of the smell of putrifying bodies. Many towns were wiped out and will never be rebuilt. Others lost only the oldest, most poorly constructed buildings.

Shortly afterward, twin government corporations were set up to rebuild the region: the *Corporación de Reconstrucción y Auxilio* and the *Corporación de Fomento de Producción* (Corporation for Reconstruction and Assistance, and Corporation for Development of Production). In the first lies authority for making all necessary plans, laws, etc., relative to the physical replanning of the area. Emphasis is on sanitation and health improvement, circulation, zoning and land use. Several towns are actually being abandoned and rebuilt on better sites. The twin agency is concerned with the industrial and economic redevelopment of this region, and also with planning a wider, better use of Chile's industrial resources in general. This will be discussed more fully.

Actual reconstruction has been slow for a number of reasons: the psychological shock of the earthquake froze people into a refusal to act; lack of any fully-developed building industry has caused a real scarcity of building materials. Although Chilean architects can proudly point to buildings constructed entirely of national materials, there is not yet enough material to go around, particularly now that the war has cut off foreign supply.

I visited Concepción, the third city of Chile (population over 75,000), south of Santiago on the coast at the mouth of the Bio Bio River, which winds through green hills framed with lines of Lombardy poplars. The damage from the earthquake of 1939 is still very conspicuous. You see facades of what were once four-story buildings, now cut down to one story, with temporary roofs of tin. You see a great many ruins of adobe and brick buildings, and once in a while false Corinthian columns broken in half. About forty-five percent of Concepción was destroyed, but in 1942 only about five percent of that had been rebuilt in permanent construction.

However, Concepción, a growing industrial center, is looking forward to considerable rebuilding, including a new railroad station and widening of the approach street leading to the central plaza. A *pasaje* or pedestrian passage with shops will lead from the plaza for two blocks to a new Barrio Cívico or Civic Center, from which a diagonal boulevard will extend to the Plaza Universitaria in front of the University of Concepción. These elaborate plans are being carried out, but nevertheless stand in striking contrast to the rebuilding to be done in the remainder of the city and particularly to the need for improved housing.

The government corporation to reconstruct and replan includes a planning section called the Sección de Urbanismo under the direction of Federico Oerhens, who is making the most of this opportunity to introduce modern planning into these ruined cities, originally planned during colonial times. The area defined for reconstruction work is larger than the actual area destroyed and within it, the law gives complete powers to the Corporation just as though it were the owner of the land. All plans are obligatory for the cities once they have been approved by the Federal Government. Master plans are being made for all of the capitals of the provinces in the area—plans for Chillán, Los Angeles, Cuquenes, Talcahuano, and Concepción are finished. Inadequate basic data has been an obstacle; one and a half years were required just to map streets, record conditions of buildings, and collect other facts needed for making plans. In their preparation the two prime considerations have been circulation and sanitation. The colonial gridiron plan of streets is generally being maintained with occasional widening of more important thoroughfares, and all cities are being comprehensively zoned into use-districts for the first time. The program includes excellent plans for acquisition of greenbelt and recreation areas. Rings of agricultural land are being reserved through rural zoning around urban areas, to make for compact, economic growth in the future. Lots in rural zones are not permitted at less than two hectares (about 5 acres). Increase in population will be provided for by more efficient land use and a general building height of two stories instead of one. Recreational areas are being reserved by refusing permission to rebuild on certain lands needed for that purpose pending their acquisition by the city. Areas which are not fully studied are allowed buildings of a temporary nature only.

Planning such as this will stop the tradition of cities which have actually migrated from one site to another over a period of generations through frequent earthquakes. Such migrating cities will now be held in place by sound construction. One small town, Yumbel, will actually be rebuilt on a new site, completely abandoning the old town.

Although this work of replanning is accomplishing a great deal to assist in rebuilding more soundly, it is not all that it could be. The law could have permitted a much broader social objective but it was passed during the first months of President Aguirre Cerda's liberal administration, before Popular Front principles were fully established and reactionary practices of the previous government eliminated. The law was actually written to protect the large property owners, and profiteering in land transactions has retarded reconstruction. Quibbling over the ideological significance of collective apartments for workers has also held up a really effective low-cost housing program.

This program of planning illustrates the general lack of preparedness everywhere for the job of replanning. A gradual education of both the public and the government is necessary if planning is to be an effective means of providing a really twentieth-century

126

environment for all peoples. Earthquakes or no earthquakes, a broader ground work must be laid by those who believe in planning.

The extent of destruction in Chile and the need for rebuilding has no real counterpart in the United States, except for the earthquake and fire of 1906 in San Francisco, the Chicago fire, and other more recent disasters. But a comparison of Chile's standards of replanning and rebuilding with those demonstrated during our limited experience, particularly in the great opportunity offered San Francisco, places Latin America unquestionably ahead of us in foresight and vision.

MODERN ARCHITECTURE

What the Latin Americans are doing in the field of architecture in relation to city development cannot be overlooked. Trends in building design are important because the form and character of each individual building help to determine the form and character of the entire city. We gain our impression of a city more by the three-dimensional appearance given to office buildings, apartments, and residences by their designers, than by the two-dimensional pattern of streets and property lines. Thus, when we think of New York, we think of skyscrapers; New Orleans is identified by its grilled balconies; and the New England towns bring to mind a prim, neat quality: white walls, green shutters, brass knockers. Seldom do we visualize the basic plans of cities and towns.

The city today depends upon architectural design more than at any other time in history, for ours are the most complex, the most consciously created cities of any century. Early urban architecture depended primarily on natural, rather than on man-made, forms and decisions—thus the architecture of Athens was built of the most available medium: stone. Early California villages were of a simple, harmonious architectural character because of the general use of adobe construction. A limited choice of building material permits only a limited variety of structural forms, and the result is bound to be one of harmony throughout each entire street and the whole community. But today in California this character— which once gave to Spanish colonial towns and early mining villages alike a kind of integrity, or agreeable personality—has been replaced with the harsh force of competitive, *consciously* conceived building forms. Yet, in thousands of simple villages in Mexico, Guatemala, and all through the Andean regions where modern techniques have not yet been introduced one still finds this same harmony of form and materials. Modern building techniques are so widely varied and permit such a range of esthetic possibilities that for the first time in the history of city building, man has found it

127

necessary to think consciously in terms of the *design of one building in relation to that of another*. Now those who believe in this, rather than in following blindly the scraps of a decadent architectural tradition unrelated to twentieth-century needs—those men have arrived at the conclusion that it is only through the frank use of today's building materials in ways planned to meet the needs of today, that this harmony of older times may again be given its rightful place in the city. Those men are the designers of a contemporary architecture, a thing distinct from mere up-to-date, modern stylism.

In Latin America, the architects who so believe have acted with characteristic boldness and imagination. In centers where they have had the necessary technical and economic opportunities they have gone farther than we toward developing an architecture related to modern conditions.

Mexico began a modern movement in architecture during the early days of her liberal government and produced some interesting results in schools, hospitals, and residences. But this movement has become somewhat static in recent years and only a few of the new apartments and residences have the simple vitality of good "modern" architecture. These occasional examples stand out among extensive blocks of contractor-built "colonial" revivals in the newly subdivided areas.

Guatemala's stern but efficient dictatorship weeds out imaginative young ideas in favor of an official colonial style, which is generally well done, but certainly out of step with the times. More functional design is to be found in Bogotá, Colombia, where a group of younger men, several of whom have been trained in North American architectural schools, have had an opportunity to build office buildings, apartments, and residences. Ecuador and Peru have practically nothing contemporary, but have a wealth of fine colonial and Inca architecture. In fact, the buildings of the Incas bear out many of the tenets of modern architecture—simplicity of form; expression of structure, materials, and function. In Peru, Emilio Harth-Terré has done some residential and hotel building, in which are combined the modern point of view and colonial materials and forms. He effectively combines massive adobe walls and bold colonial moldings with large glass areas and functional planning.

Bolivia's younger architects have designed apartments and office buildings in La Paz—many of them showing a Swedish or German influence—but no one there has yet used the strange mountain setting to produce an architecture which is really part of that Andean metropolis. Chile has gone further in that direction in the ski resort at Farallones near Santiago. Architect Santiago Roi uses native stone combined with great glass walls which bring the Andean peaks into the room itself, huge timbers and the contrast of thin, cantilevered concrete balcony ledges—many details which are creative, bold and imaginative, and always indigenous both as to materials used and in feeling.

Apartment house design in Argentina, particularly in Buenos Aires, is a challenge to the designers of the apartments in our own cities, for the free use of balconies, simple fenestration, and imaginative treatment of reinforced concrete structural forms. Outstanding work has been done by Eduardo Sacriste, Alberto Prebisch, and others. The work of the Automobile Club of Argentina by Antonio Vilar is fresh in design and particularly bold in the use of reinforced concrete construction.

Uruguay could be called a hot-bed of architecture and architects. One finds in officialdom representatives of the profession from the ex-President of the country down to the Mayor of Montevideo and the entire staff of the city planning department. Many different, interesting types of work have been done: suburban residences, beach houses, semi-public recreation centers, and several successfully designed hotels in the new beach resorts. One use of indigenous building materials is the reed roof used for small residences, pavilions, and beach shelters—an idea taken from the homes of the Uruguayan farming people. Another characteristic native material is the brilliant white sand of Uruguay's beaches that shines through the stucco of modern apartments. Perhaps the most outstanding building in Montevideo, and there are many, is the unfinished *Facultad de Ingeniería,* the Engineering School, by Julio Vilamajó.

But of all the South American countries, Brazil's modern architecture is the freshest and most vigorous. The full story of the accomplishments of the Brazilian architects is told in Philip Goodwin's *Brazil Builds* (Museum of Modern Art, New York, 1943). A break with tradition on the part of a younger group has resulted in the most progressive examples of modern architecture in the New World, the forerunners of a new school of highly significant architecture. Oscar Niemayer, Lucio Costa, Attilio Corrêa Lima, Marcelo Roberto, and many others in Rio de Janeiro have gone far beyond anything we have done in the United States and have shown us what will be possible in a world of new architecture befitting the twentieth century. In São Paulo, Henrique Mindlin, Gregory Warchavcik, Rino Levi, and Bernard Rudofsky (who is now in the United States) have done outstanding work. The finest public building on the continent has been built in Rio de Janeiro—the Ministry of Education and Health—an eighteen-story office building which takes the lead in setting a new standard of functional architectural design and free site-planning. Likewise in Rio there is the Brazilian Press Association Building (popularly known by

129

the initials ABI) famous for its fixed concrete "sunshade" fins, and also the well-known Seaplane Station (also used for land planes) at Santos Dumont Airfield, where Rio's busy air traffic terminates.

Brazil's examples alone, to say nothing of the work of the Montevideo group and that of Buenos Aires' apartment house designers, give Latin America the edge over us in the designing of modern urban architecture. If we are to implement our New World philosophy with cities built of a New World architecture, we must be willing to do more of the kind of pioneering begun by Latin American architects.

NATIONAL RESOURCES PLANNING

Planners in Latin America realize that physical planning alone is futile, if it is not geared to some kind of planning for the development of economic resources. I believe this to be more widely recognized in Latin America, where there is such a need for it, than in this country where development of economic resources is something taken for granted, whether planned or not.

Earlier in this chapter I spoke of various agencies provided in some of the republics for studying resources development. What these agencies have accomplished, I found, did not reach a degree of effectiveness which most Latin American technicians in the planning field would like to see. The chief obstacle lies in the realm of politics, in the lack of a clearly defined policy on the part of the governments, as to the role they should play in promoting economic and social well-being on a national scale.

In the United States, the National Resources Planning Board (killed by Congress in 1943), the various State Planning Boards, Chambers of Commerce, Universities, and many similar groups have collected and interpreted material on the extent and condition of our national resources. In this respect we have gone considerably further than the republics of Latin America, but neither we nor they have begun the logical practice of taking inventory of resources on one hand, national needs on the other hand, and budgeting an efficient economy.

However, Lewis L. Lorwin * says correctly that, "The idea of national planning—physical, economic and social—has played an increasing part in the making of national policy in Latin America during the past decade." A look at some of the accomplishments of established agencies will suggest how small that part has been.

In Mexico, economic planning might have been effective in the National Planning Commission had political stability allowed it to continue to function. Mexican planners realize this misfortune, but

---

* "National Planning in Selected Countries"—By Lewis L. Lorwin. National Resources Planning Board, 1941.

today there is little coordinated effort toward planning the development of Mexico's resources. The most highly integrated national plans (today almost non-existent) laid out in Latin America were the First and Second Six-Year Plans of Mexico for the years 1934-1940 and 1941-1947.

Colombia's agency, the National Economic Council, is studying the economic problems of the country, but as yet has not reached the stage of actual planning, or laying down a policy or program. This agency has considerable promise, but I was told that one of the obstacles in the way of effective action is the lack of sufficiently trained technicians to do the necessary study of resources.

Ecuador's National Economic Council, badly needed in that problematical country, seems to have gone by the boards and operates with little effectiveness. Peru has not established similar economic councils, but does control certain commodities such as tobacco, salt, alcohol, etc., through government monopolies. The National Economic Council of Bolivia has shown little activity in recent years.

In Chile, as we have seen, the earthquake of 1939 pointed out the need for putting the country on a more self-sufficient industrial basis and the *Corporación de Fomento de Producción* was set up. Along with the central Planning Office of the government, there is an opportunity for really combining planned industrial development with physical planning, but this, as far as I could see, was not being done. It is true that the Corporación de Fomento is developing industry, but it is not *planning* the development of industry. Economic and industrial planning is not being coordinated with physical planning, although a promising law proposed during my visit would set up a special department for industrial planning in the Corporación de Fomento to work in the earthquake area and to complement the program of physical replanning.

As I have said, Argentina has no central agency, although a number of controlling offices have been set up for the regulation of major industries. The Pinedo Plan, a "New Deal" for Argentina, proposed by a former Minister of Finance, was a plan for strengthening Argentina's economy. His proposal of public works was met with acclaim by planning technicians and engineers, but the program also met with too-powerful economic and political opposition. Argentine planners would like to see (at the very least) a planning and housing policy similar to that of the United States applied to Argentina in order to give her new economic life.

Although Uruguay has no central planning agency, her methods of government control are further developed than those of any other South American country. They are described by Lewis L. Lorwin: "Government intervention and control in Uruguay have been developing on an increasing scale for a number of years. One of the characteristic features of this development is the establishment of public corporations, state-owned plants, and government monopolies for various industries." I found that these cover marketing of fuel, manufacture of cement, electric distribution, telephone system, refrigeration and distribution of meat, distribution of tires, rubber goods, and milk. These semi-public agencies are well-implemented with technical staffs of high standard.

5. Final Score

A more complete review of all work in Latin America directed toward the planning of a better environment should, of course, cover many more than the items herein discussed. I have chosen only those most closely related to the problems of cities. A very important phase of development indirectly affecting cities would require a special investigation; this is the field of conservation planning—soil, timber, and water resources protection and development. Latin America, as a group of agricultural nations, will one day have to face the matter of industrialization of farming methods. On a broad scale, this will have to include the harnessing of the great water power of the Andes, the distribution of electricity for fuel, the practice of modern methods of soil conservation and agriculture. Few Latin countries have looked deeply into the possibilities of forestation in sections where trees are rare and the waters run off the land from the melting snows only to carry down to the lowland rivers the most productive soil.

Before going on to a look at housing achievements by our neighbors, a summary of the score between the United States and Latin America will reveal that in spite of our technical achievements in city building, we do not excel by very many points the work of Latin American city builders. Taken point by point, throughout the ten items we have discussed, it looks as though the score is just about a tie—that we have as much to learn from them as they have to learn from us. In fact, on my return to the United States I could not honestly escape an impression that Latin American planners had actually done more for their cities than we have, when one takes into consideration the relative breaks we have had in the past, and Latin America's turbulent social and economic history.

MASTER PLANS: Mexico City

One architect-planner, Carlos Contreras, is responsible for much of Mexico's advanced planning principles and legislation—Mexico's program takes advantage of citizen participation in the planning process. Mexico City has a Planning Commission made up of both citizens and officials; a second technical body whose name, translated, is "Office for the Control of the Growth of the City"; and a third commission, the "Mixta," composed of members of other city departments, which directs financial affairs of the master plan.

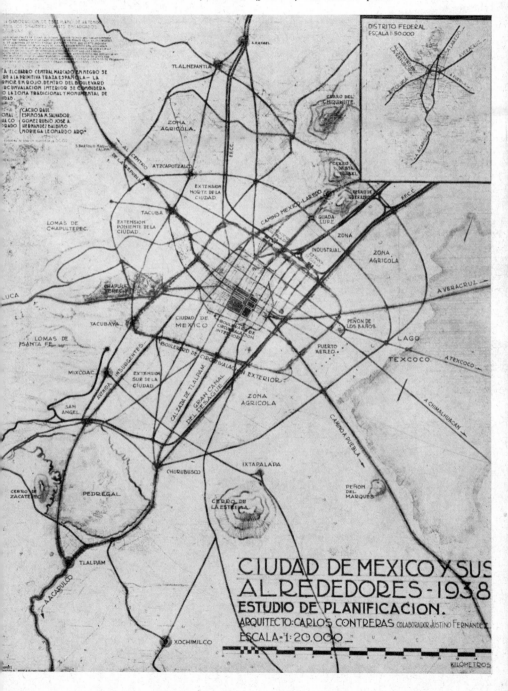

CIUDAD DE MEXICO Y SUS ALREDEDORES · 1938
ESTUDIO DE PLANIFICACION.
ARQUITECTO: CARLOS CONTRERAS COLABORADOR JUSTINO FERNANDEZ
ESCALA · 1: 20.000

KILÓMETROS

GRAN SANTIAGO
ESTUDIO REGULADOR

MASTER PLANS: Chile

In 1929 Chile enacted legislation requiring all cities with populations exceeding 20,000 to make city plans. In 1936, a central Department of Urbanism was established in the Ministry of Development. This office, directed by Luis Muñoz Maluschka, has authority to make planning studies for all municipalities with populations exceeding 8,000. Above, master plan for Santiago; below, for Valparaiso.

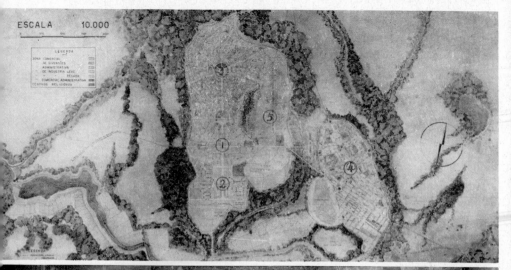

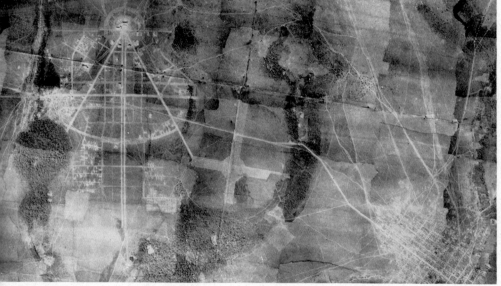

NEW CITIES: Goiania, Brazil

Top, master plan of Goiania, new industrial center and capital, State of Goyaz, Brazil. Old village is at right, separated from new development by the airfield. Center, air maps of Goiania showing progress in 1937; airfield, civic center, southern portion well established.

Avenida Goyaz, Goiania, is built and planted; government building in background.

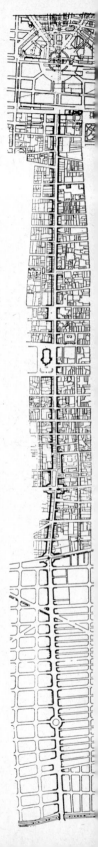

Street widening and other developments: Above, Monument to the Revolution, Mexico City, has necessitated widening Avenida Revolución. Right, ambitious plan for widening and connecting several streets, Mexico City. Center, below, Avenida Salavery, double laned, runs from the center of Lima, Peru, to the sea. Bottom, Avenida Tacna, Lima, being widened; old width visible as black strip at right.

Avenida 9 de Julio, Buenos Aires, is for some distance the widest street in the world. Air view, above, shows relation to surrounding city; the Avenida is being extended. Below, center, closer view showing Obelisk and side islands, some of which contain entrances to the underground parking garage (bottom) which underlies the entire Avenida.

Avenida General Paz, encircling Buenos Aires: above, grade separation and access roads with parkway depressed; below, "double lassoo" intersection for important cross highway, with parkway elevated. This scheme was devised by Pascual Palazzo.

On facing page is a plan of São Paulo, Brazil (above), showing proposed ring road widening at city's center, to provide starting point for radiating highways. Below, on facing page, construction progress on a radial highway, with viaducts for cross traffic; building in center being removed for highway extension.

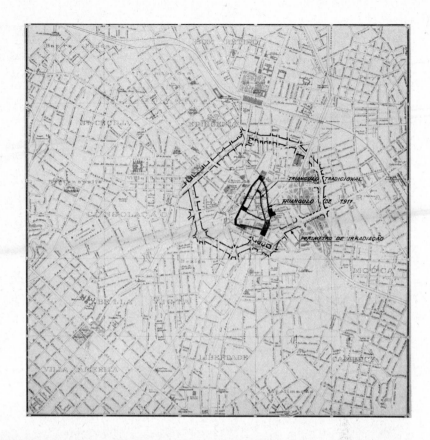

TRIANGULO TRADICIONAL
TRIANGULO DE 1911
PERIMETRO DE IRRADIAÇÃO

an highway reconstruction to improve circulation brings up collateral
...lems in São Paulo: facing page, above, viaduct over new boulevard; below,
...ble-tube traffic tunnel leading out to new residential areas. This page, above,
...el for new railroad station, bridge, and construction to control the Rio Tieté;
...w, the bridge materializes.

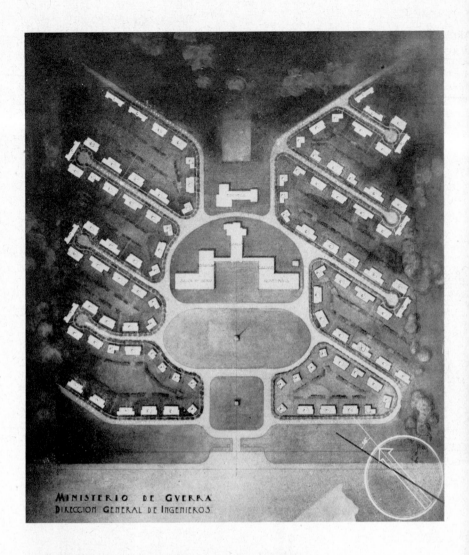

MINISTERIO DE GVERRA
DIRECCION GENERAL DE INGENIEROS

Neighborhood unit near Buenos Aires: Barrio Sargento Cabral, a planned community for military personnel, Campo de Mayo. Plan above, general view at left.

ARKS: Buenos Aires

t right, park near Plaza de Mayo, Buenos Aires.
elow, two views of the Old Costanera, Buenos
ires. Contrast these and photographs on following
iges with commercial waterfront development in
ost United States maritime cities.

PARKS: Rio de Janeiro and Montevideo

Above, day and night views, Praça Paris, waterfront park built on fill from Morro Castello, the hill that was leveled to make building sites and an airfield. Below, fishermen's boats drawn up on Copacabana Beach; full city development just across the marine drive behind the beach. These are portions of

some 8 miles of bay and seafront park developed for public recreation. At right, above, are two views of the Rambla, Montevideo's parked boulevard along the waterfront; below, another portion of the Praça Paris, Rio de' Janeiro. (Photos by D. I. P. Brazil)

PUBLIC BUILDINGS and DESIGN DETAILS

The new Ministry of Education and Health, in Rio de Janeiro, was designed by Niemeyer, Vasconcellos, Reidy, Leão, Lucio Costa, and Moreira (all architects); Le Corbusier, consultant. Its south wall is almost all solid glass; on the north side, where intense sunlight might have been a problem, the wall is an expanse of movable horizontal louvers which act as sunshades; behind these is a glass wall. On facing page, top, statue, small pools, mosaic sidewalks in Rio de Janeiro; center, characteristic mosaic pavement and bougainvilleas, Rio; below, Barrio Civico, Santiago, Chile.

chapter 6

New houses for old

1. Achievements of the Latins

We in the United States came face to face with the reality of the housing situation when we began our first public housing program in 1933, with limited funds allocated to the Housing Division of the Public Works Administration. A full program did not come until 1937 when we passed the United States Housing Act. I found in Argentina that the first public housing project in the *western hemisphere* was built in 1910 in Buenos Aires by the municipal government, just *thirty-two* years before my visit. This project, housing about one hundred families, was followed a year later by another. Both are planned according to the best standards in use today. They are of row-house type, with quiet inner plazas planted with trees, and I remember them as among the most pleasant housing groups that I have seen anywhere in North or South America. In Montevideo I saw two projects, one public and one private, which were built twenty years before.

The Latins are working hard to clear their slums. I was surprised to find, and was often reminded proudly by Latin Americans, that the other American republics have long been aware of the housing problem and had already made some progress before we in the United States hesitantly embarked on what seemed to some its primrose path to government-subsidized housing under the seducing influence of the New Deal. With all the materials, technicians, and wealth of our advanced nation, we went gingerly on our way, planning and building relatively few projects here and there, but not until Pearl Harbor brought war conditions did we really get into our stride and begin an "all-out" program of mass construction of low-cost housing.

Herbert Emmerich's figures in the following statement * indicate the extent of our war time housing program: "Low-rent housing (under the local authority program with loans and contributions from the United States Housing Authority) has provided for over *160,000* families. The public war housing program of the Federal Government contains about *676,000* units. Of these, 317,000 units, or nearly half the program, have been completed and are occupied. The remainder are rapidly approaching completion. The program will eventually house nearly *two million people.*" Technically we have proven our capacity in the field of publicly financed low-cost housing.

Latin Americans, with incompletely developed building industries in most countries, with a scarcity of technicians—of plumbers as well as hydraulic engineers—and with widespread national poverty in many countries (an average income at least one-tenth of that of the United States) have been doing public housing work without qualms. In spite of the scope and complexity of their problems, and in spite of the many social and economic limitations with which they are faced, the republics of Latin America are doing a valiant, earnest job of tackling the housing problem.

If you keep in mind the vastness of this problem in Latin America you will better be able to understand the various methods by which slums are being removed, how the programs differ from ours, and what types of dwellings are being built by the various republics. Because each country has different characteristics, housing occurs in varying amounts and with different types of programs. Several of the countries I visited have *centralized national housing agencies.* These are Argentina, Uruguay, Chile, and Peru. Many countries have developed *social security* to a higher degree than we, and often use the funds for financing housing. Those doing most of this type of thing are Chile, Brazil, Ecuador, and Bolivia. Still other countries have assumed no federal policy on housing, and in these cases initiative has been taken by some of the cities. Into this group falls Mexico, Colombia, Guatemala. In the general absence of a well-organized real estate and home-building industry like that of the United States, group housing has frequently been done by semi-public banks and by private companies.

2. Housing by the Government

The legal structure for government-sponsored housing in Latin America, like that providing for planning procedures, is not nearly as democratic or as decentralized as in the United States. In no

---

* In a talk entitled "Public Housing—Yesterday—Today—Tomorrow," given by Herbert Emmerich of the Federal Public Housing Authority on May 20, 1943 before the meeting of the National Association of Housing Officials in New York City.

country is provision made for local initiative to request funds through a locally formed city, or county, housing authority as we have provided for in our housing law. The Latins have learned much about public housing from Europe, but little, as yet, from the United States.

As I have said, Buenos Aires can boast of a long-established tradition of public housing, demonstrated by the fact that two of the oldest and best planned projects in *all* the Americas, built over thirty-two years ago by the city, are still put to good use. Argentina's *Comisión Nacional de Casas Baratas* was formed as early as October 5, 1915, under Law No. 9677, and has had minor revisions by law since that time. However, only within the last twelve years has much been accomplished. Several projects, such as the Guillermo Rawson group with its 135 dwelling units of both apartment and row type, date back to 1932, several years before the United States public housing program began. Most Argentine housing, however, is aimed at lower middle-class consumption and has not yet begun to reach large groups of the working class. Literally translated, the name of the agency is the "National Commission for Cheap Houses," but paradoxically the housing projects did not appear to be very "cheap," nor did the incomes of the tenants seem minimum. For example, I found that where a worker's salary begins at around 150 pesos a month, rents in the projects begin at 35 and go to 75 pesos, one-half of the worker's salary. Compare this with the one-fifth ratio in our public housing projects.

The Comisión is thoroughly centralized in Buenos Aires; no allowance is made for the development of state, county, or municipal authorities as in the United States. Construction is confined to Buenos Aires, and no program is being carried out in any other city in the country. Even in the capital, projects have not been built in large numbers, although they are perhaps the best constructed in South America. In fact, one project, Casa América, seemed almost luxurious. Casa América is of the *colectiva* or apartment house type, and is typical of the spacious standards of Argentine low-cost housing. Halls are of very ample width; rooms are large; windows wide. I commented on some attractive composition panelling on the doors of each of the apartments and was told that the material was imported from Italy. This was explained by the fact that materials which are to be used on the low-cost housing projects are permitted to enter the country free of duty, thus making possible purchase of imported building materials. This fact is significant because it indicates the shortage of building materials and the inadequacy of Argentina's own building industry.

Tenants are selected from a list of approved applicants by an unusual method—a *sorteo* or public drawing, but there is a tend-

135

ency to favor the middle class rather than really low-income groups. In spite of Argentina's wealth and its relatively high standard of general housing, the public housing program is not as large or as effective as it should be.

On the other side of the Rio de la Plata stands Uruguay, much smaller in size than Argentina and with a decidedly less complicated housing problem because of its low population density, high wages, and high standard of living. Uruguay's central housing office is included in the Ministry of Public Works as a special department and is called the *Instituto de Viviendas Económicas*. Since the housing law went into effect in 1937, nine projects have been built, including about one thousand dwelling units. Although Uruguay has no extensive slum problem, the progressive government has subsidized this housing program to relieve low-income groups, and to safeguard general welfare. Monthly rent is kept from 7 to 13 pesos ($3.50 to $6.50 U.S.) per dwelling depending on the number of rooms, and is in about the proportion to income required by the housing law of the United States, which allows a rental of about one-fifth of the client's income.

Projects are well-planned, and because development of Montevideo is spread out, consist of single- and two-family houses rather than the *colectiva* apartment type. Buildings in government projects—those of the Instituto—are generally of white stucco walls and red tile roofs. Montevideans use an especially clean white sand for stucco; in the bright sunshine, the walls of these buildings glisten like artificial snow. The two projects I visited on the fringe of the built-up section of the city had ample park and recreation space and well-planned streets following the natural contours. Gardens flourish in Montevideo's projects more than in any others I saw elsewhere in Latin America. A few *colectivas* are now under way near the more congested center of the city on land adjoining a newly built portion of the Rambla, the waterfront boulevard.

The city of Montevideo also does some low-rent housing through the municipal Department of Architecture. A number of projects consisting of single-family houses have been built. The city's architectural office also assists families of low income by supplying house plans and technical advice gratis where the total cost of the house does not exceed the approximate equivalent of one thousand dollars. Other group projects have also been built by the semi-public government monopolies, such as the petroleum distribution unit, known as ANCAP. (Uruguay's ANCAP is the government oil monopoly, the *Asociación Nacional de Combustibles, Alcoholes, y Petróleo*.) ANCAP's housing group adjoining the refining plant is patterned after government housing projects. It is a simple, well planned layout. I have said that Montevideo began low-cost housing over twenty years ago with the construction of two projects. These were built just after World War I, one by the government, another by one of the city's leading architects, who has for a long time advocated high principles of housing and planning: Carlos Perez Montero. Uruguay's progressive work in housing is the result of its progressive government, perhaps the most socially advanced in South America.

In Peru, the central government housing agency is the *Servicio de Arquitectura* in the *Ministerio de Fomento* (Architectural Service of the Ministry of Development). This office does other construction such as hospitals, schools, and the well known Popular Restaurants, in all parts of the Republic, but so far housing has been limited to the Lima-Callao area. Rents are kept as low as ten percent of the monthly salary in some cases (18 soles or about $2.90 U.S. per month for two rooms), and careful tenant selection is based on family health, income, general integrity of record, and size—there must be at least two children. This office had built about five hundred houses during the year prior to my visit in December 1941, many of them in the Callao district where a recent earthquake automatically demolished slum areas. Projects are one- and two-story row-house types, well planned, with play areas, private yards, and green open space.

We visited one of these *Barrios Fiscales*, as they are called, under construction on a site adjoining a boulevard near Callao. The buildings face the blue Pacific on one side and on the other, the ancient fort, Castillo Real Felipe, built in colonial times for defense against pirate marauders. Another project I visited, the *Población Obrera del Frigorífico Nacional*, built ten years ago by the National Refrigeration Plant, houses some six hundred people and includes a movie theater, store, central park with swimming pool, and planting of bamboo clumps and green lawns. The one-story houses, of row type, are of red brick with flat concrete slab roofs. Due to war conditions a shortage of building materials was holding up a program to continue building at least five hundred houses per year.

The Popular Restaurants, which bear an important relation to the social problem of housing, are financed by the government and assure every resident of Lima three square meals a day. One *Restaurante* which I visited serves 2,000 persons daily. A total of 10,000 are served in four such restaurants in the Lima-Callao area. School children wearing white smocks typical in all Latin America waited in line outside the building to be served their free lunch. The charge for adults is 20 centavos or about four cents U.S., and includes a roll, plate of soup, rice and lentils, a serving of meat and vegetables, and a choice of drink—coffee, tea, or milk. The building is large, modern, and light, and absolutely immaculate throughout. A special room is provided for feeding expectant mothers; food can be taken out to be served at home in case parents are ill or

137

working. The policy of cleanliness is emphasized in an attempt to set an example for care of homes. I was told that neighbors vie with one another to keep their quarters *"limpio como el Restaurante Popular"*—just as clean as the Popular Restaurants!

In Chile, the *Caja* (pronounced Ka-ha) *de Habitación Popular* (Popular Housing Fund) was set up by law in 1936,* although as long ago as 1906 the government had formed its first housing agency. The Caja, which has done more project construction than any other housing agency in Latin America, today acts as a central housing office and plans and constructs projects directly in various parts of the country. There is no decentralization of authority; all work is the result of federal initiative, but projects are not limited to the capital. During the last four years, the office has built, throughout the country, some 6,000 houses which are rented to workers with a maximum income of 1050 pesos per month ($35.00 U.S. but with a Chilean buying power of two or three times as much). The program seems to reach low-income group needs. The realistic administration of the Popular Front Government, and a fairly well developed building industry, are two factors which have made possible this large program. Through the Caja, Chile is beginning to clean up the *conventillos*. It is the most effective and the best administered program in Latin America.

Santiago has the most projects. In *Población Vivaceta* in Santiago (the word *Población* is used as we use "project") I saw three-room apartments which rented for 170 pesos per month (about $5.70 U.S.) and a four-room apartment which rented for 300 pesos (about $10.00 U.S.). This was the largest project built in the Chilean capital, and housed six hundred families in row-house dwellings with only a few apartments. I visited three other projects: *Población Pedro Montt*, adjacent to the huge Yurar Hermanos cotton mill; *Población Arauco*, with a new community house under construction; and *Población Huemul*, entirely of the *colectiva* or apartment house type, four stories high. This latter type had been objected to as being Comunistic, but practical aspects are winning out. Several projects have been built in Viña del Mar, the fashionable beach resort, which actually has a large industrial population (50 percent of the city). Here an interesting political

---

* A new Chilean low-cost housing law, passed in November, 1943, was promoted by Engineer Abraham Alcaino and greatly expands activities of the Caja. Its name is shortened to "Caja de Habitación"; it is allowed a total working capital of 250,000,000 pesos—about $8,000,000—a large sum for a country of only 4½ million people. The Caja may now: invest capital in any way that will further the purpose for which it was established; expropriate land for housing; borrow and lend money; use its own standard building code in place of that of the municipality where housing is to be built; inspect all housing, public or private, falling within a specified low-cost category.

split is to be found: votes along the seashore district of Viña came in Rightist in the last presidential election, while the inland industrial section voted Popular Front.

The names of Latin American housing projects are interesting in that they are almost always taken from outstanding figures in historical or political life. Here are some typical names of Poblaciones in Chile: Carlos Condell, Almirante Wilson, Sargento Aldea, Fermín Vivaceta, Pedro Montt, Bernardo O'Higgins. Contrast these with names of United States housing projects: Elm Haven, Lakeview Terrace, Hillsdale Homes, Harlem River Houses.

3. Housing by Social Security

I have said that some countries in South America have made use of social security funds to develop housing programs. The Latin American republics in general have had a longer experience with social security and have put the funds to a broader use from the beginning than has the United States. Our program was first put into effect in 1936, while Chile, to name one country, formed its social security organization as early as 1926. In the United States, the wage earner and the employer each contribute *one percent* of the amount of the wage-earner's salary, while in most Latin American countries from *two to five percent* is contributed not only by the wage earner and the employer alone, but by the government as well. While we include only industrial and trade employees (about 60,000,000 wage earners) many countries in Latin America cover public employees and professional people as well. Our program provides primarily for old-age retirement insurance, but in Latin America social security generally provides not only old age retirement, but also health insurance, free medical care, life insurance, loans for building purposes, and even housing itself. In the United States social security funds may be invested only in government securities; but in Latin America allowance is also made in most cases for the use of such funds for investment in land and buildings in order to encourage construction, stimulate industry, provide employment, and augment the income of the agency. The law in most cases was written broadly enough so that little revision had to be made to use the funds for low-cost housing. At first, individual home loans were made; the next logical step was to build group housing for rent or resale.

This social security housing program has its broadest application in Brazil, although Chile, whose social security laws are the oldest in the western hemisphere, has used it a great deal. Chile's *Caja de Seguro Obrero Obligatorio* (Worker's Social Security Agency) was first formed in 1926, and has since developed a splendid reputation for its health program and system of hospitals and clinics. It is limited to manual workers who contribute 2% of

139

their salary, while employers contribute 5% and the government 2%. To keep up with the needs of its 1,200,000 members, revisions have been made in the law. These now provide for four services: disability, health and life insurance, and housing. Some 1900 dwelling units have been built since 1935 by this agency. Projects are usually row-house types or *colectivas*, and, in general, are well planned. Four *colectiva* projects especially designed for the hot northern districts have been built in Antofagasta, Arica, Iquique, and Tocapilla. These were quite bold in design; in fact, the one which I saw in Antofagasta was by far the most modern building group in the town, the wonder of all who came to see. The Caja has also built projects in Lota, Puente Alto, and Valparaiso, in addition to those mentioned above.

This social security agency has provided free clinics for its members in all parts of the republic, from a one-room transportable *posta minima* for use in remote sections to the two large, modern clinics in Santiago. The Caja first rented buildings for use as clinics, then established an architectural staff to plan their own buildings, and in 1934 began to do housing. From now on this social security agency plans to discontinue the housing work in favor of the central housing agency, the *Caja de Habitación Popular*, turning over a certain amount of money to them each year for that purpose.

The *Caja de Seguro Obrero Obligatorio* is permitted to invest its money in building and land, and has constructed many of the large office buildings and apartments in Santiago. Such investments are not unlike those of the Metropolitan Life Insurance Company in this country. The Caja keeps a sharp eye for good buys, and six or seven years ago bought a piece of land near Santiago Sport Stadium (perhaps knowing the plans for its construction), for 2,000,000 pesos, which today is worth 60,000,000 pesos. This agency seems to be in a position to expend funds more freely than the *Caja de Habitación Popular*. The Caja's largest investments are in agricultural land. In 1942, 38,000,000 pesos had been put into *fundos* (farms), 90,000,000 pesos in housing projects, 32,000,000 pesos in clinics—altogether a total of close to 200,000,000 pesos or over $6,500,000 U.S. invested in land and buildings of all types.

One advantage which the Caja holds over private builders is that it has large funds with which to work. For example, during my visit this social security agency was planning to overcome the cement shortage by building a cement plant. This is to be the largest in the country, and will not only provide added income for the Caja but supply building material for the country.

The other social security agencies in Chile—those for private and for public employees—have also done housing on a smaller scale, but confine most of their programs to individual loans for private home building. Chile's broad use of social security funds is the most effective in South America.

On the Atlantic side of South America, in Brazil, housing has been slow to get under way, but it is coming now with the enlivened economic condition of the country under the Vargas administration. Since public housing in Brazil is a fairly recent development of government activity, it suffers from the usual opposition. But the use of social security funds has been a huge impetus and, in fact, is almost entirely responsible for all the low-cost housing being done in Brazil at the present time. There is no national housing office in Brazil to determine housing policy for the country, or to plan directly a program of housing construction, or to coordinate the work of existing agencies.

Brazil has begun to use social security funds for housing purposes only during the last three or four years, but has already built many dwelling units and is planning an extensive program for the coming years. However, an enlarged housing program is made difficult by the structure of the social security system itself. There are five major agencies or *Institutos*, each of which is autonomous and carries on its own program independently. The five are: Industrial Workers, Bank Employees, Commercial Employees, Maritime Workers, and Transportation Workers. Into the *Institutos* the worker pays three percent of his wage, the employer three percent and the government three percent. This enforced savings fund is paid back to the worker in the form of old-age retirement, free medical service, life insurance, loans for building, and an increasingly large amount of housing. Most of the *Institutos* have been making loans for private home building as a regular part of their activities but during the past several years have begun some group rental housing, in spite of the general government policy in Brazil, which has been to encourage private home ownership. The lack of coordination among the *Institutos* works to the disadvantage of housing. Together, they represent some 1,500,000 members, and hold about one-third of the money in circulation in Brazil, according to authorities. If these interests were pooled, there would be ample resources to develop a building industry large enough to supply the needs of the *Institutos*, and get under way a broader, more effective housing program. But that unification of action may come in time.

Meanwhile, several are experimenting in group housing. The Institute of Industrial Workers, or the IAPI as it is briefly identified in Brazil, has under way the largest program and is using the most progressive housing practices. It has built 2,200 units in three years, located in some three or four large projects in Rio de Janeiro, São Paulo, and Florianopolis. Rents are kept to one-third of the income, a percentage that is too high, but actually lower than the average in Brazil where fifty percent or more is common. Such a high percentage of rental allowance leaves an insufficient amount for food and education in the worker's budget.

The use of IAPI funds for housing and investment building helps the worker in two ways; by stimulating building activity, thereby providing employment; and by increasing the worker's housing facilities. Loans are made for private building of all types (to building contractors who are not members of the Institute), at a rate of nine percent rather than the banks' usual ten. In this way, IAPI has invested as much as $6,000,000 in building other than worker's housing. The new program of investment building is under way in other cities like Bahia, Belo Horizonte, São Paulo, Recife, and Goiania. Most of these structures are offices or apartments, well planned in sensible modern designs under the direction of an architect, Carlos Ferreira, and are a part of the program of construction of branch office buildings to serve IAPI in future housing construction in the capitals of the more important states. This will decentralize the housing program to some extent, but the new state offices will continue to act as branches of the central office rather than as separate state agencies. The purpose of this is in line with the Brazilian government's policy to develop the interior, to provide a more even distribution of the existing money in circulation throughout the country.

Elaborate plans are drawn by IAPI for the immediate construction of several very large housing projects; one for 3,500 families in twelve-story skyscraper units in industrialized São Paulo; another for several thousand families in four-story row-house units in the industrial section of Rio de Janeiro. The São Paulo project for IAPI is called the *Conjunto Residencial de Varzea do Carno* and will be a startling, significant contrast to the dismally blighted section of São Paulo in which it is to be built. The project is being planned by Attilio Corrêa Lima, who made the plan for the new city of Goiania, and who is also planning the workers' town for the new steel plant at Volta Redonda. The São Paulo project will consist of seven units of twelve stories each, with elevator stops only at every third floor for purposes of economy; in addition there will be a large number of four-story walk-up units. The plan for the project includes a school, clinic, and a small hotel and office building. The entire development is estimated to cost the equivalent of about ten million dollars, U.S.

The other large IAPI project in the planning stage is to be built at Penha, an industrial suburb of Rio de Janeiro. This is being done by Marcelo Roberto, and if built as now planned will be one of the most interesting in the western hemisphere. It is imaginatively, boldly planned for efficiency and practicality. By use of a row-house type in which two dwelling units of two stories each are

142

placed one above the other, making a four-story building, Roberto is able to reduce the cost to the equivalent of about $500 per unit—less than half of the cost of a traditional type of single family unit on the same site. This cost per unit includes a school, nursery, play areas, and all utilities, in addition to housing for 7,800 persons.

The largest IAPI housing project already built is that at Realengo, another industrial suburb of Rio de Janeiro. The project already houses about 12,000 persons in separate houses and two-family units. A new policy in building has begun with the construction of one four-story *colectiva* which now dominates the entire project with its massive scale. Workers pay about 100 milréis for rent out of a salary of about 240 milréis—close to half the salary. The project was built on the site of a former, poorly planned subdivision, which is the reason for Realengo's rather unimaginative layout. A new unit at Bangú, adjoining Realengo, will have a better general plan and an excellent social center including a cinema, cooperative store, school, nursery, and park, as well as a new railroad station. Other projects built by IAPI are *Saco dos Limões* at Florianopolis, and *Santo Andre* in São Paulo.

In contrast to this excellent beginning, another social security agency, the Institute of Commercial Workers (known as IAPC) operating since 1936, has only a few rental projects built, and for the most part makes a policy of directing its funds toward individual loans. Projects are conservative in design, and consist of single-family houses only. But IAPC's ambitious program for 1942-43 included group housing projects of 480 dwelling units for a site in Rio de Janeiro adjacent to the new bridge to Governor's Island; 480 units for Recife; 70 for Goiania; and several hundred for Porto Alegre, the growing coastal city in the south, capital of the State of Rio Grande Do Sûl. Branch offices of IAPC are being built in important cities throughout the country and will serve as nuclei for developing an enlarged housing program. This Institute of Commercial Workers has plans under way for a residential club for 1,920 single men, to be built in downtown Rio, somewhat like Y.M.C.A. facilities in United States cities, but on a larger scale.

A third *Instituto*, that of Banking Employees, with about 40,000 members, does no group housing at all, but limits its housing activities to approving plans for individual homes to be built on loans from the Institute. Funds may be borrowed by members up to 100 percent of the value of the dwelling when the plan is approved for resale possibility by the Institute. Six percent interest is charged rather than the banks' usual ten percent. The *Instituto* can afford to charge a lower rate because it derives income from investment building of other types. No control is exercised over the amount of monthly payments in relation to income, and sometimes these go as high as fifty percent of the client's monthly earnings. Group housing has been avoided due to a prejudice against so-called "socialized" living conditions in group projects. Home ownership through a twenty-year payment plan on an individual dwelling burdens the worker with a heavy responsibility. This constant state of debt might be presumed to occupy the worker with maintaining his small equity and discourage clear thinking about such important matters as changes needed to improve his living and working conditions.

Yet it would seem that group housing on a very large scale is the only logical answer in Brazil. A pooling of the resources of these five major *Institutos* could provide much more efficient and larger-scale production of houses, either in groups or individually. The success of IAPI in collective housing would indicate that this is the probable direction for public housing in Brazil if it is to become effective in raising housing standards. The fact that each of the *Institutos* has its own policy, reflecting the personal ideas of its officials and technicians, has caused a lack of coordinated action.

The following figures by the *Conselho Nacional do Trabalho* (National Labor Council), give an idea of the general increase in housing construction in 1941 by the various *Institutos*.

Instituto	No. of Dwellings Constructed Up to June 30, 1941	No. of Dwellings Under Construction on June 30, 1941
Industriarios	296	4,231
Commerciarios	311	905
Bancarios	188	622
Maritimos	101	233
Transportes-Cargas	195	130

In addition to the work of the *Institutos*, the *Caixas,* special savings funds of private utility companies—light, power, railroads, street car, water, etc.—have built as many as 3,232 houses. Most of these are individual houses, rather than group projects. With a proper coordination and direction, these agencies could be more effective in improving housing standards in Brazil, where bold-stroke, large-scale planning is the only effective kind. The Vargas administration is making rapid strides in many directions, but as yet has not taken the lead in establishing a clear policy on low-cost housing construction.

Little Ecuador, one of the most underdeveloped countries from an economic point of view, has been making good use of social security funds for housing purposes. There are two agencies: the *Caja de Seguro,* formed in 1938, requiring compulsory contribution for all private employees of all kinds, and the *Caja de Pensiones,* which operates similarly for public employees. Both Cajas provide health and life insurance and loans for individual home building, and have programs under way for construction of housing projects without government subsidy. The *Caja de Seguro* has built some five hundred homes in community units near the industrial areas in Quito, the capital. Rent is kept down to thirty percent of the monthly income of the client. Houses for sale include life insurance in the payments, giving the house as the endowment in case of the death of the head of the family. Incidentally, variations of this practice are also used in other countries. The *Caja de Seguro* is quite generally supported by all Ecuadorian employees and employers alike, each of whom is required to pay five percent of the amount of the employee's salary.

One of the projects I visited in Quito was *Barrio Alpahuasi* (Turtle House), whose name was taken from that originally used for the district in the days of Inca domination. This project included about 160 houses. Working with no help at all from the government, with a total capital of 1,500,000 sucres (about $98,-000 U.S.), the engineers who built the project were justly proud of their achievement. The prices marked on the outside of each of the new houses—figures such as $10,000 or $9,540 or $11,200—at first appeared ridiculous for a small three- or four-room dwelling until I became accustomed to reading "sucre" in place of "dollar" for the dollar sign. These prices in U.S. money would be between $500 and $700. Smaller homes sold for 6400 sucres ($416 U.S.) at payments of forty sucres per month, including life insurance. Barrio Alpahuasi is well located on high land near Quito's small manufacturing district. Considering the technical limitations in building materials, personnel, etc., these houses were well done, but it was apparent in their planning that the designers could profit by the experience of other countries, especially from agricultural and war housing work in the United States. While I was in Quito, the *Caja de Seguro* also had under construction a new clinic of some seventy rooms with a maximum bed capacity for one hundred and sixty patients.

Although many of the South American republics have social security legislation, not all of them use the funds for housing. Bolivia, for example, early in 1942 was just beginning the study of a large program of workers' housing through the use of these funds. Bolivia's social security agency has done some housing through individual loans to clients, but this is limited strictly to middle-class groups and does not provide housing for working classes.

Bolivia's most extensive low-cost housing work is in the mining areas, where standards are set by regulations of the Ministry of Labor and Social Welfare. This office, the *Ministerio de Trabajo y Previsión Social*, also has under way an elaborate program for the direct construction of worker's housing in the mining areas. The program of *Previsión Social* has a total working capital of about

$200,000 U.S., and during my visit had plans for some two hundred houses in La Paz, fifty in Oruro, fifty in Potosí, at a cost of about 40,000 bolivianos ($800 U.S.) each. They will be rented for about 100 bolivianos per month to workers who earn in the neighborhood of five hundred bolivianos—a reasonable proportion of rent to income. In addition to this working capital, funds from a special tax on beer, cigarettes, and local mail will be used. A special stamp, placed on all letters mailed within the country, shows the strong-jawed face of a worker before modern housing, and below, the words *Pro Vivienda Obrera*—For Worker's Housing. There was talk, of course, that this amounted to no more than a bluff, and that the money would never be used for housing. But political unrest may be enough to force the issue and see that the money *is* used for housing.

In fact, during my visit in La Paz there was held an *estado de sitio*, or state of siege which arose indirectly from the housing problem. Actually nothing unusual took place, except for censorship of the mails which led to frightful complications of the already complicated Bolivian post office. (There is nothing as irritating as some of the Latin American post offices. People who wait *on* you act as though they were doing you a special favor, and the people who wait *with* you believe strongly in first-come-first-served.) This *estado de sitio* was called because of a threat by the PIR (*Partido Izquierdo Revolucionario*), that they would "do something" if the money promised the city of Potosí for a water system and worker's housing did not come through by a certain date. The money was to come from an inheritance tax on the fortune of the eleventh richest man in the world—Patiño, the Bolivian Indian who once dug for tin himself, and who hasn't been in Bolivia in twenty years.

4. Housing by the City

In some countries, where there is no use of social security funds for housing and where no centralized national housing agency exists, local initiative has been taken by city governments. In this way a number of cities themselves have programs under way which do not necessarily depend on government aid or direction. This is true in Colombia, where there is no national housing agency. Bogotá developed a slum clearance project in 1937 to move several thousand families from the slopes of one of the hills overlooking the city. Five hundred houses were built in the *Barrio Centenario* (Barrio in Colombia is used as the word "project" in the United States) for the most worthy and dependable cases; these houses were sold for 800 to 900 pesos ($400 to $500 U.S.) with payments arranged in proportion to income. In general, the sale of homes, where economically feasible, has worked out successfully in South

146

America in that it stimulates interest in the care and maintenance of the home. These slopes, formerly covered with *ranchos*, are now planted with grass to stop erosion and the entire area is being maintained as public open space, bordering the scenic drive, Paseo Bolívar overlooking Bogotá. A few sections are still covered with *ranchos* but these are gradually being cleaned out.

I visited the Barrio Centenario, which re-houses many of the former slum dwellers, and I found very attractive dwelling units built in blocks of four in each square building, with one dwelling in each quadrant. Adjoining gardens were green with vegetables and colorful with flowers, and one tenant with whom we spoke said that she never realized what living meant until she moved into the *Barrio*. The city has also built housing for municipal employees in small groups away from the center of town. These run in cost from 6,000 to 8,000 pesos ($3,000 to $4,000 U.S.).

The city of Medellín, one of the most progressive in Colombia, has its own housing department, formed by municipal legislation in 1925. Small houses are built for about 800 pesos ($400 U.S.) and rent for as low as five pesos ($2.50 U.S.) per month. Where families can prove the existence of a steady income, houses are sold on a twenty-five year payment plan, but with the ruling that the house cannot be sold again *other than back to the city*. A total of 344 houses had been built up to November, 1941, under legislation which, though in effect since 1925, was unused up to several years ago. Municipal authorities wish to maintain a construction program of about one hundred houses a year in order to prevent the further building and continued use of substandard dwellings, as the city becomes more and more industrialized.

Guatemala City built about five hundred houses for slum eradication in 1940 and 1941, but these well built homes are probably too big an economic step for slum dwellers. This is often the case in South American housing, where exact data concerning the incomes and resources of clients for whom housing is being planned are not always available, and where the limitations of building materials permit little cutting of corners on cost.

The municipal government of Guatemala City, under the efficient administration of Arturo Bickford, Mayor and Chief Engineer, had 460 low-cost homes to show me. One group, *Colonia Ubico* (Colonia here is used as "project" in the U.S.), named for the president of the country, houses 136 families in simple, well built dwelling units of row-house type. These, I was told, were built for about one thousand dollars (U.S.) for each unit, which suggests rather strongly that the lowest income groups would scarcely be able to afford to rent them. However, standards of design and construction are good, and the housing program serves a purpose if only to pave the way for workers' housing after this first experience. Other home building in Guatemala City is done by a housing department in the Public Credit Bank.

I was surprised that Mexico, in spite of a liberal constitution, had no housing law passed by national legislative action; practically no money had been appropriated in the last ten years to carry out a program of low-cost housing. Yet as I have indicated, there is ample need for slum clearance; and judging from the amount of building of upper-class apartments and flats, there is no lack of money in circulation. During the administration of Mayor Aaron Saenz of Mexico City, 1932-1935, two excellent projects were built and more were planned, but no national housing agency was ever set up, and since that time those two remain the only projects to be seen in Mexico City. A special committee, called the Executive Committee for the National Housing Commission, had been appointed and late in 1941 was studying the organization of a permanent agency.

In Brazil outside the social security program there are few other public efforts in housing. Lacking a clearly defined national housing program for slum clearance, the city of Rio de Janeiro has had to take steps on its own initiative. A small temporary project called the *Parque Proletario*, for seven hundred families, was completed in the spring of 1942 for the inhabitants of one of the city's worst *favellas*, known as *Largo da Memoria*, that stood in the way of new middle-class residential development. This project has been the result of initiative of the Department of Health and Social Assistance. Depending on the success of this experimental community, others are being planned to replace the *favellas*, and at the same time improve the social and economic status of the class which lives in them. The directors of the program in this *Parque Proletario* are carrying out a carefully planned program of education, tenant selection, and project management for the purpose of initiating what was described to me as a "filtering-up" process of social betterment.

This filtering-up process takes the *favella* dwellers out of the worst of living conditions, where no sanitation facilities exist and no baths are provided (other than the lagoon); where there is no running water for washing clothes, no educational facilities, health or police protection; and in which all are under-nourished and without assistance for employment or training in any kind of trade. This program puts these people into houses of wood, built well above the damp ground; provides them with their first sanitary toilets, showers, tubs, and running water for washing clothes; it supplies health protection in a special clinic, a kindergarten and school for youngsters, night classes for adults, postal service, police control, and a restaurant and dairy service. *Parque Proletario*, the first project, now offers all those services. Each family is recorded as a separate case, listing habits of diet, health, schooling, and

148

occupation, and each case is being given the special kind of aid needed. Two thousand more of these simple accommodations were planned in July, 1942, to remove the *favella* Praia do Pinto, on the edge of the lagoon, Lagôa Rodrigo de Freitas, adjoining Rio's elaborate race track. Four thousand persons now live in this *favella*. The Department of Health and Social Assistance believes that the construction of at least forty thousand units similar to those of the *Parque Proletario* will be needed throughout the city to make a good start in the removal of Rio's social blight.

While I was being shown the *Parque Proletario*, my guide asked four of the new tenants how they liked the new quarters,—if they would prefer to go back to the *favella*. The reaction in every case was an enthusiastic "We like it here!" One woman looked up from her wash and said defiantly, "You can't send us back to the *favella* —you've burned it down for good!" The young social worker in charge of the small tots in the kindergarten lined them up for me, in the form of a train making the trip from Rio to São Paulo, to demonstrate methods of teaching them. Each child played the part of a car, and the leader became the locomotive. At each stop a special chore is done, and in this way the children learn how to brush their teeth, scrub their hands, and at the same time memorize the names of the stations between Rio and São Paulo. Prizes of wash tubs, buckets, or brooms are given each day to the mother who sends her child to school the cleanest. This kind of housing program—complete in its scope—is the only one that can reverse the degrading process of sub-standard living conditions from "filtering-down" to moral degradation to "filtering-up" to sound, independent citizenry.

Perhaps the combined efforts of the work of the social security *Institutos* and this beginning of *favella* clearance in Rio will converge in a coordinating agency to develope a potentially enormous industry: that of supplying twentieth-century homes for all Brazil's citizens.

5. Housing by Private Initiative

In the absence of federal housing legislation in many countries, and lacking a fully developed building industry, there has been a good deal of housing done through semi-private and private initiative. An outstanding example of semi-private work in the low-cost housing field is that of *Acción Social*, a cooperative group in Colombia which has operated with considerable success in Bogotá for the last ten years. *Acción Social* was first formed during the depression in 1932 under the administration of President Herrera to help the working people help themselves. The group is autonomous, self-supporting, and has its own plant for manufacturing building materials—brick, tile, woodwork, etc.—which it sells at cost to

149

clients who are approved and to worthy working-class families of low income. My visit to the building materials plant gave me a clear idea of the scope of the work of *Acción Social*. Efficient machine operation cuts cost and turns out ten thousand bricks per day. I was interested to note that a new piece of tile-cutting machinery, manufactured in Monterrey, Mexico, had just been received. Purchase of such machinery from the United States was prevented by the prohibitive cost. The low cost of brick production regulates the commercial price of brick in the city, and makes possible a lower cost in house building. *Acción Social* has two thousand client-members, who either rent or buy houses, not including others who purchase material for their own construction.

About nine years ago *Acción Social* built *Barrio Acevedo Tejada*, and on my visit I found it still functioning admirably. The community includes a central park, community house, small school and cooperative store. The group was enlarged recently with some twenty new row-houses built for a group of municipal workers, clients of *Acción Social*. Projects such as these carry out the policy of *Acción Social* in stimulating self-initiative and educating working classes in higher standards of living.

Large-scale group housing has been done extensively by private initiative throughout various parts of South America in connection with industrial plants and mining enterprises. These occur in many different sections, and the few with which I came in contact were of high standard. I found several communities built by progressive *Paulistas* in and around São Paulo, Brazil. One was a housing project consisting of some 200 houses, school, church, stores, parks, etc., built about 30 years ago by a progressive industrialist named Jorge Street. Another is the planned suburban town for workers in the paper mill at Cayeiras. This includes about 800 houses of two-family type, a church, recreation center, and swimming and boating facilities.

Large scale housing facilities have been essential to the operating of the mines of Bolivia and Peru, and for that reason, a number of planned communities can be seen. Chile has had a good deal of private housing. Some has been recent, perhaps the result of the example set by the government, while other housing has been built out of the necessity of providing decent accommodations in the nitrate and copper mining areas. Among the former is the new planned community for the carton box plant at Puente Alto, near Santiago, which has a central park and white cottages set in a beautiful site against the Andes.

Among the latter is Pedro de Valdivia, the most complete company town in northern Chile, in the nitrate area. It is interesting enough to merit a full description, for its establishment required the almost miraculous creation of a twentieth-century environment

150

for human beings in an ageless, lifeless desert. Pedro de Valvidia sits in the middle of the desert of Atacama, on high land called the *pampa*, north and east of Antofagasta, about three hours by car. The heat ripples the air and penetrates far into the scorched, dry, sandy gravel that makes up the landscape, and throughout the cool nights the earth remains warm. In the midst of this strangely beautiful setting is built a huge plant, a small village for the administrators, and a larger one for the workers.

The plant itself is ten years old, cost thirty-five million dollars, and was built by Guggenheim money to compete with artificial production of nitrates in the United States and Germany. At the beginning of our three-hour tour of the plant I saw huge boulders in loaded freight cars, each weighing 32 tons, dumped into a crusher and broken into eight-inch bits. Dust fills the air like a thick fog, but the six-story interior, where the powerful yet delicate machinery is housed, is as clean as a hospital, because constant air pressure keeps the dust from entering. Two more crushings reduce the rock to two-inch chunks which travel a half-mile in cars to huge vats of concrete, each 110 by 160 by 19 feet deep—ten of them in a row in the open air. These are filled with the rock and covered with water. Ducks occasionally take the vats for ponds and alight on them only to have their tail feathers burned by the nitrate in the water. When the water filters through, the left-over is scooped out by enormous derricks to be thrown away, miles off in the desert. Eight percent of the original material goes on in a liquid form through a system of pipes in which the liquid is cooled by a refrigeration plant—made cooler and cooler until crystals of nitrate are formed. These are pumped off into a spinner and separated from the liquid. The crystals are then sent on a traveling belt to furnaces and melted into a molten fluid that is sprayed into the air in a sixty-foot-high "snowstorm" chamber. The nitrate drops down little tapioca-like balls to a belt, and out to be sacked and shipped to the United States.

After our tour of the plant we washed the dust from our mouths with two huge glasses of ice-cold orange juice at the community recreation club, and went down to see the workers' town. The community center has a fine theatre, one of the best in northern Chile, a swimming pool, stores, a square planted with trees and lawn. The dwellings of the workers are single-story, and of row-house type. Over in the smaller "North American" village, so-called because it was originally built for North Americans, since replaced by Chileans who now run the plant, the houses are as good as those in any small town in the United States. Each house has two large bedrooms, a bath with tiled shower, a living room, equipped with radio, a dining room, and a kitchen with electric refrigeration. All furniture was brought from the United States.

In Latin America, unlike the United States, comparatively little speculative building is done by private contractors. Some of the larger cities such as Mexico City, Lima, Santiago, Buenos Aires, and others do have private companies which build homes and apartments on a speculation basis, but as yet the middle class in these countries has not developed enough to create a large market in this field.

In the absence of a highly developed home-building industry, middle class housing work in Latin America is often done by the banks, who find a sure return for investment in much-needed housing. Semi-private banks in Colombia have done an admirable job in middle-class housing. Several large, very well planned projects in Bogotá, Medellín, and Cali stand as a challenge and an example to investors in the United States, who might learn a good deal for use in planning for postwar rehabilitation and rebuilding of blighted areas in our cities. I was very much impressed by the progressive policy of Colombia, and the amount of local initiative taken by public and private groups to apply common sense to solution of the housing problem.

The Bank of Chile has also done a considerable amount of very excellent apartment-type housing for middle-income groups in Santiago.

6. Rural Housing

We have said that rural housing standards are generally low in Latin America. One reason for this state of affairs is that in the republics south of the border, in contrast to conditions in the United States, there is little individual farm ownership and much exploitation of farm labor, with its resultant problems of sanitation, health, and housing. Mexico's progressive agricultural program provided for in the Constitution of 1917 has taken steps to meet this situation, by breaking up large holdings or developing collective rural farms. Colombia, in a conservative way, is doing good rural housing through the *Instituto de Credito Territorial*, a semi-government bank. About seven hundred houses (or *casas campesinas*) have been built for farmers who own their own land. Loans are made by the bank at the rate of 4.22 pesos per month per 1000 pesos, borrowed over a thirty-year period. Part of this payment goes toward life insurance, with the house as the endowment. Houses are built by the housing office of the bank itself. There is no group housing as yet; the policy is to promote home ownership. This is an unusually good program.

Houses range in cost from 750 to 1000 or more pesos. Five hundred were planned for 1942, but the *Instituto* would like to plan one thousand a year as a consistent program in order to have a real effect on rural housing standards all over Colombia. Houses are of different types, according to location. Those for *Tierra Fria,* the high-land of the Andes, are of brick, while those of *Tierra Caliente* are of light frame and bamboo. I visited some of the *casas campesinas* near Bogotá and found them planned simply and sensibly. The country people who were about to move into several of them seemed so impressed with their new quarters that in one case, I'm sure they were tempted to use the house only to show off to the neighbors. In this particular case, a family of six had been living in a hovel of wood poles and thatched walls. In another, the family was living in a completely windowless adobe building whose interior was as dark as a gopher hole.

Agricultural housing in the Indian-populated countries of Ecuador, Peru, and Bolivia has changed little since the days of the Incas; any change has probably been for the worse. Chile has the best—in fact the only—government rural housing agency I found in South America. This is the *Caja de Colonización Agricola,* and performs very much the function of our Farm Security Administration in re-colonizing and improving the social and economic use of the land. The *Caja* has been in existence some twelve years, but received its greatest impetus during the popular front administration of President Aguirre Cerda between 1938 and 1941. A total of 300,000 hectares (750,000 acres) of large holdings of farm land have been subdivided, providing for eight hundred semi-cooperative colonies of eight to ten families each, with necessary housing and community facilities. The housing program consequently goes well beyond the physical needs and into the economic and social structure of Chilean agricultural life, because the *Caja de Colonización Agricola* is concerned with revising the land pattern and industrializing agriculture. In addition to the colonizing work, loans are made to private farmers who wish to work within the program of the *Caja.* Under Aguirre Cerda's administration these loans increased 400 percent in 1938-1939 over the previous year.

The colonization program has re-colonized about twenty-two hundred families (or roughly 10,000 persons) since its beginning. The scope of the problem is understood if you compare this figure with another: one-half of Chile's 4,000,000 people are agricultural. One typical colony I visited near Santiago is the Colonia El Noviciado, housing about one hundred families on 4,000 hectares (10,000 acres). Living quarters of a very simple *colectiva* or row-house type are located near the center of the project. There are an administrative center, school and sports field, and a number of single houses on half hectare plots. The planning was excellently done, but a great gap between building and management prevented the project from looking well. The *Caja* has built a total of about one thousand houses, and during my visit planned to build 2,800 more, plus fifty rural schools, by 1945.

The law requires that the *Caja* spend its funds proportionally in various provinces. Some of the funds budgeted for the northern desert section are being used for experimentation with the growing of crops in the saline soil through a continued process of leaching. If these experiments are successful, the economy of the northern desert section of Chile may be revolutionized.

7. Comparison with the U.S.A.

We have seen then that public housing in Latin America functions on quite a different basis than in the United States. Few countries have central housing agencies; those that do carry on programs with a great deal of centralization of authority since this is the practice for most other government activities. Actually, because of the relatively smaller size of the republics, each government functions more like a single State of the United States. Even some of the larger countries, too, have authority centralized in the capital. However, the opportunity for local initiative is not encouraged or provided for even where national legislation exists— although, where local or municipal agencies exist, they have been formed purely through local initiative. It would seem that this lack of provision for the use of local initiative is a reflection of a greater lack of democratic action; but this can not be expected to increase until the Latin American republics reach a more mature degree of economic development, provide more widespread mass education and achieve greater literacy. A public housing program similar to that of the United States is hardly possible or to be expected, as yet. Local governments do not object to the centralized control, since it already exists in so many other forms of government administration.

Decentralization of authority will come of necessity because of the size of some countries, such as Brazil, where it is beginning now. Decentralization will also come in others as communications are improved and new development of the interiors of the countries progresses. It will certainly come with the spread of public education and general improvement of the standards of living. As it stands now, the capitals of the countries are the focal points of the educated groups, the technically trained people, the advanced thinkers and doers.

However, although the general structure of housing organization in South America differs greatly from ours, the administration of housing programs compares quite well. Political influences are sometimes more prevalent than in our country, but by and large, standards of planning, financing, construction, and maintenance are fairly high, taking into consideration the many limitations with which the Latin Americans are confronted—limitations which frequently do not exist in the United States.

154

Another factor which makes the program differ from ours is that there is very little citizen-participation in government affairs in general, and in housing in particular. There are few groups organized to oppose housing, even fewer to come to its support. Popular support of housing in South America will come with the adjustment of the large masses of people to new levels of education and economic life. At the same time, housing itself can be an aid to this adjustment.

Before I begin to discuss the possibilities of working with the Latin Americans in the matter of housing and planning for the peoples of the western hemisphere, I would like to speak of people with whom we shall have to deal. I shall tell you something about the technicians, students, and citizens of the other American republics.

LOW-COST HOUSING: Mexico City

Above, one of two projects built in 1933; right, statue and plaque commemorating those responsible for the project; below, another view, Colonia Balbuena.

CHILE

Above, two types of government-established row housing built after the 1939 earthquake, Concepción, Chile. Below, housing built by private interests for workers at the nitrate plant at Pedro de Valdivia.

On facing page, top, two projects built by the Caja de Habitación Popular: housing at Los Andes (upper) and Vivaceta, Santiago (lower.) Bottom of facing page, housing by social security agency, Antofogasta.

BUENOS AIRES

Above, housing built by the city authorities in 1911; left, Casas Americas, multifamily apartments; bottom, housing as built today. The early example compares quite favorably with the late; an unexpected situation, since the prevailing public sympathies have seemed to favor commercial exploitation over social advance.

BRAZIL

Housing by social security agencies: above, Sacco dos Limões; below, row housing, apartments, and water tower at Realengo, industrial suburb of Rio de Janeiro. All of these were built by IAPI (Institute of Industrial Workers), one of five social security institutes for different classifications of workers. IAPI has the largest housing program; though well under way, all housing in Brazil is of more recent date than in most other Latin American countries.

COLOMBIA
Barrio Centenario, Bogotá, a series of buildings containing four dwelling units.

BOLIVIA
Postage stamps issued to promote housing for workers.

ECUADOR
Social security housing project. Quito. Condition of materials and attitude of workmen illustrate some difficulties encountered in obtaining satisfactory construction.

PERU

Top, housing project in Lima; center, highway planning and housing development proceed in conjunction. Each, though constructed by an agency independent of the other, is related to the other.

Municipalidad de la Ciudad de Buenos Aires
DIRECCION DEL PLAN DE URBANIZACION
EL SIMBOLO DEL URBANISMO

¡AIRE, SOL, VEGETACION! TAL ES LA TRILOGIA DE ELEMENTOS NATU-
RALES Y ESENCIALES PARA LA VIDA HUMANA QUE SE REPRESENTAN
CON EL AZUL PROFUNDO, EL ASTRO REY Y EL VERDE VERONES EN EL
SIMBOLO DEL URBANISMO

●

EN esas colmenas humanas que son las grandes ciudades modernas se ha roto el equilibrio razonable entre la obra artificial y los elementos de vida que generosamente nos brinda la madre naturaleza. Siguiendo los más variados rumbos en sus investigaciones, los urbanistas de todo el mundo han llegado a la conclusión de que es necesario reconquistar el aire, el sol y la vegetación para el ambiente de la ciudad moderna. Las teorías y realizaciones urbanísticas más opuestas concuerdan en el objetivo final consistente en asegurar la unión íntima de la ciudad con la tierra viviente, dando amplia entrada a la naturaleza entre las masas inertes de la edificación urbana.

La ciencia urbanística moderna ha puesto plenamente en evidencia que la utilización en la ciudad de los más maravillosos e inesperados recursos de la técnica no debe ni puede excluir el aprovechamiento intensivo de los elementos naturales. La ciudad como el árbol no puede desligarse de la tierra que la sustenta.

Durante mucho tiempo hemos creído, por una falsa asociación de ideas, que el progreso edilicio consistía en llenar con edificación todo terreno baldío. Pero de este error podemos por lo menos obtener una conclusión evidente y es que cuando la edificación compacta alcanza una extensión importante se produce en la ciudad un estado de desequilibrio que afecta profundamente la regularidad de sus funciones biológicas, vale decir, que hemos confundido progreso edilicio con desarrollo anormal o deformación patológica del organismo urbano.

El progreso urbano no consiste en invadir ciegamente los terrenos con la edificación sino en edificar conscientemente donde corresponde después de haber asegurado la formación y conservación del espacio en que debe dominar la naturaleza, facilitando la entrada del aire puro y del sol vivificante al interior de las viviendas y de los barrios que se crean. Permitir que las viviendas de los seres humanos se amontonen desorganizadamente, en medio de las impurezas de un aire cargado de humo y gases deletéreos y produzcan así ambientes antihigiénicos y nocivos a la conserva-

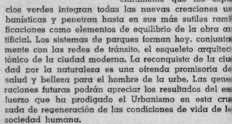

ción y mejoramiento de la especie, significa incurrir en un anacronismo que contrasta violentamente con el grado de adelanto a que ha llegado la civilización.

Felizmente la reacción salvadora provocada por el Urbanismo en estos últimos tiempos no ha tardado en propagarse por todo el mundo. Luchando al comenzar contra la rutina y el escepticismo, los urbanistas quieren que la vida entre con el aire y el sol en todas las viviendas y que el niño se desarrolle y vigorice en ambientes propicios en contacto íntimo con los dones y esplendores de la naturaleza. Todas las concepciones del Urbanismo moderno revelan esa preocupación fundamental. Desde la composición urbana de orden monumental hasta las más modestas organizaciones del tipo ciudad - jardín expresan hoy claramente que los espacios verdes integran todas las nuevas creaciones urbanísticas y penetran hasta en sus más sutiles ramificaciones como elementos de equilibrio de la obra artificial. Los sistemas de parques forman hoy, conjuntamente con las redes de tránsito, el esqueleto arquitectónico de la ciudad moderna. La reconquista de la ciudad por la naturaleza es una ofrenda promisoria de salud y belleza para el hombre de la urbe. Las generaciones futuras podrán apreciar los resultados del esfuerzo que ha prodigado el Urbanismo en esta cruzada de regeneración de las condiciones de vida de la sociedad humana.

La Dirección del Plan de Urbanización de Buenos Aires, creyendo interpretar fielmente el sentir de todos los que se preocupan por el perfeccionamiento de las aglomeraciones humanas, ha reunido en un sencillo símbolo de comprensión universal la expresión de los elementos naturales que integran el indiscutido ideal urbanístico. Realizado este paso inicial confía en la solidaridad internacional de nuestra causa para propiciar su uso y colaborar en su divulgación.

Noviembre de 1934.

CARLOS M. DELLA PAOLERA.
Director Técnico del Plan de Urbanización

The Symbol of Urbanism: sun against a background of blue sky and green earth; issued in 1934 by Carlos Della Paolera, Technical Director of the Plan de Urbanización, Buenos Aires, to promote popular support for city planning.

chapter 7

Technicians, students, and citizens

1. I Like the Latins

If you have followed me this far, you may have surmised that I liked Latin America. I did; and I liked best the Latin Americans themselves. They were always warm, friendly, and hospitable, and never could do enough to help me understand their problems. I like the Latins.

I became acquainted with all types and classes from the most privileged to the lowliest man on the street. But those whom I learned to know well are the practicing technicians, and the younger student generation, as well as a cross-section of the citizens for whom the planning is done.

In order to understand the future of the cities of Latin America, we must know something of the technicians who are building them, the younger generation who will one day take over, and the citizens for whom the cities are built. If future relations between ourselves and the Latins are to be sound, we must know and understand thoroughly the people with whom we are going to deal.

2. Technicians: U.S.A. and Latin America

It is obvious that the chief reason we, as a people, have known so little about Latin America is simply that we have had too little contact with Latin Americans. This is likewise true of the professional group among us, and the technicians who plan and build cities in both our land and theirs. Through these people, who actually build the cities we live in, contact must be made, if we are to achieve a better environment throughout the hemisphere.

On my return to the United States, a planning technician asked me, "What are the chief differences between Latin American

planning and housing technicians and those of the United States?"
I told him that I had found three basic differences: First, the city
planners of Latin America are much more influenced by Europe
than are ours; second, they are much more versatile and less
specialized; third, they work harder and more earnestly than we do.

Perhaps the most significant of these three is the first. For the
most part, Latin planners are either European-trained, or prepared
for the technical field in their own country by European-trained
professors. Technical education is thorough and technicians frequently have a broader understanding of their own and related
fields than would be provided in similar training in the United
States.

The builders of our cities have steered away from European
examples; Latin American planners have not been afraid to learn
from Old World practices. Perhaps it is for this reason that their
cities have a form and integrity which is lacking in many of ours.
Their European background leads Latin technicians to philosophize
about the significance of the city's pattern, about the broad, human
objectives of planning; and as a result, the application of their techniques tends to be more imaginative than ours.

I found that these technicians had too little knowledge of certain
practical planning methods in the United States and that few
planners had traveled or studied in our country, although there
were many who were thoroughly familiar with Europe. I spoke
with men who knew by heart cities like Madrid, Paris and Rome,
and who always thought in terms of their home town—Santiago,
Buenos Aires, or Montevideo—in comparison with the basic form
and function of those cities of Europe. But I found a minority who
were familiar with Chicago, New York, St. Louis, and San Francisco, through actual contact, and a large majority who had a
definite, sincere desire to know better the cities of the United
States.

The second characteristic difference, the greater versatility of
Latin technicians, may be the result of European training, which
provides a schooling period of broader, more general preparation,
followed later with specialization in actual practice. This type of
training differs from that in the United States where a technician
in engineering, architecture, or other related field specializes for a
particular job during his schooling period and graduates sup-
posedly full-fledged, ready to begin as an experienced man in that
field.

Because of the lesser degree of specialization in Latin America,
one technician frequently handles several different kinds of jobs.
Planning and architecture are thus very closely related professions
in Latin America, and are frequently practiced by the same individual. Architects and planners are a closely cooperative group, to

the mutual benefit of both professions. For example, I was impressed with the range of versatility of Mauricio Cravotto, one of the leading planners in Montevideo, Uruguay, who had just completed detailed plans for the new city hall, now under construction, for which he had taken first place in the competition held for its design. At the same time, Cravotto was working as one of four consultants on the planning of the Argentine city of Mendoza, a very broad study reaching into all phases—economic as well as physical—of that fast-growing "Western" city. In Uruguay, the smallest of the republics on the southern continent, there are by far the largest proportional number of such architect-planners. The Montevideo group has an enviable understanding of the relationship between architecture, planning, and landscape architecture. These men undertake major planning or architectural assignments with equal facility.

Another example of this broad ability of the Latins is to be found in the work of Attilio Corrêa Lima of Rio de Janeiro, Brazil, well known for his delightfully open, spacious planning of the Seaplane Station at Santos Dumont Airport. Just before completing plans for that building, he had designed the larger portion of the new city of Goiania, built in the wide open spaces of the interior as the new capital of the state of Goyaz. Over in Peru, Emilio Harth-Terré, Director of the Section of Urban Studies of the Ministry of Development, showed me the work he was doing on the regional plan for Lima and the plans for other cities in Peru, and after lunch took me for a drive through the Lima area and various residential sections to show me homes which were recently built under his direction as an architect.

In the United States, where the planning group is one profession and the architectural group another, few technicians practice both professions. There is too wide a gap of understanding between these two fields—which are in actuality so fundamentally related.

The third way in which Latin technicians whom I met differed from those of the United States was in their attitude toward their professional work. Latin technicians on the whole seemed to me to have a much more serious, scholarly, professional approach to the problem of city planning and city building, and a less commercial point of view than is found in the United States. They regard their work less as a venture for material gain or a means of security, and more as a grave social responsibility to the community and the country. It seemed to me that these men had worked harder toward establishing city planning as a science than we have in the United States, where too many planning technicians have been willing to carry the actual practice of the profession as far as zoning and no farther. Yet, with our mature technical and economic development, we should have been able to go a great deal farther in

159

city building—that is, in the sense of the very best that can be done —than any other country in the world. This we have not done. We have shown little of the imagination which Latin technicians have used to make parts of Rio de Janeiro, Buenos Aires, and Mexico City so attractive to North American tourists. We have not allowed our own technicians to use the imagination which could have given our cities that same charm. Where our technicians did show imagination, as in the case of Burnham's great plan for San Francisco, other forces worked against them. In that instance, the plan was completed and presented to the city fathers a month before the fire of 1906 laid waste the business and residential heart of the city, but the absence of a legalized planning commission, the opposition of property interests, and the haste to rebuild were barriers which prevented making the most of an unusual opportunity. Had the plan been carried out, San Francisco would today not only rival Rio de Janeiro in appearance, but would be provided with many badly needed traffic arteries. As early as 1906 the city fathers of Rio de Janeiro waited for no fire, but proceeded to plan and rebuild the magnificent waterfronts of Gloria, Flamengo, and Botafogo. Even today, the city fathers of most Latin American cities think differently about civic development than we do. They think: "This is *my city*"—not, "This is *my property*."

Practically every Latin planner I met has in his home a study from which he carries on both professional work and extracurricular activities. Juan Scasso, architect of Montevideo, showed me the separate studio building in the rear of his home where he has a completely equipped library on planning matters, his files, and drafting tables for spare-time work and study. Carlos della Paolera, Director of Planning in Buenos Aires, has a library and office in his home which includes a rare collection of books on cities of the entire world. Luis Migone of Buenos Aires, Rudolfo Oyarzún of Santiago, Emilio Harth-Terré of Lima, and many others have splendidly equipped studios where they spend a good deal of their spare time outside regular working hours in carrying on special studies, writing, and making public the problem of planning for people's needs.

They believe that city planning must be motivated by aggressively directed publicity or it will not succeed. Carlos della Paolera of Buenos Aires supplied me with a file of articles on *Urbanismo* (planners down there speak of *Urbanism*, rather than *planning*), which he had written for *La Nación*, one of Buenos Aires' leading daily papers, over a period of years since 1935. Luis Prieto Souza, graduate of the National University in Mexico City, edited a weekly newspaper column in Mexico City's *Universal* for twelve years in order to keep before the public and officials the idea of planning.

In many of the countries, the technical aspects of urban problems are made a living issue through professional organizations which carry on public relations work, and hold national and international conferences to discuss and promote the most recent trends and the highest standards.

In Chile the planning technicians have taken the lead in selling the planning idea by educational work carried on through several Institutes of Urbanism which have been established by planners in Santiago, Valparaiso, and other Chilean cities. The first of these was organized in Valparaiso by Hector Vigil, who, though one of Chile's most able, realistic men in planning, is not a planning "technician" at all, but a lawyer. This Institute has pioneered to bring the planning process into governmental activities. The Santiago Institute of Urbanism is headed by Rudolfo Oyarzún, who has done an aggressive job of putting over the planning idea, particularly in setting a higher standard for the earthquake reconstruction laws. Oyarzún is one of Chile's best trained, most capable men in the planning field.*

In Argentina, the Centro de Ingenieros, through Luis Migone, architect, has taken the lead in advocating planning legislation along the lines of that of the United States for the purpose of solving some of Buenos Aires' urban problems. Because of the similarity of these problems to those of our cities, many Argentine planners are looking to us for similar solutions.

Uruguay's progressive architectural school, the *Facultad de Arquitectura*, sponsors the *Instituto de Urbanismo*, a research and public education organization, made up of leading planning technicians. This group is educating the public toward an understanding of the democratic planning idea and the basic needs for an improved environment in Uruguay. Founded five years ago, it has carried on educational exhibitions, published a regular bulletin, and brought planning problems into the open. Presentation of these problems is always simple, graphic, and easily understood. One such study is for a regional plan for the Rio Negro region surrounding a great new dam and power plant. The Institute plans a baby TVA. Another study covers a proposed remodeling of the *Rambla*, the waterfront boulevard, along the bay-side of the city, while a third points out the need for an improved housing program for the entire republic. We need other active organizations like Montevideo's Institute for Urbanism, in all urban centers of both North and South America.

* In the architectural field Chile has taken steps to raise the level of public recognition: In 1942 the Chilean Congress passed a law forming a *Colegio* of architects, similar to the existing *Colegios* of lawyers and doctors of medicine. The *Colegio* regulates professional practices and acts as the official representative of the professions in any public activity. The law requires that all important construction be directed by architects. Since most Chilean city planners are also architects, they automatically become members of the *Colegio*.

The technical field of planning in Brazil has as yet very little professional standing, and is therefore without the organization necessary for the promotion and support of planning in practice. However, the architectural institute (under Nestor de Figuereido) and the engineering society have assisted considerably. It is unfortunate that professional planners in Brazil are not organized sufficiently to put planning on a more secure basis in the particular country which most needs the benefits of planned development.

If planning for a better environment is to be carried on effectively, technicians everywhere must be willing to contribute their energies and ideas, and to assume increased responsibility. North America, even more than South America, must learn how to use experts and expert knowledge in the public activities of our democracies. A new kind of democratic action can result from the close, working partnership of *technicians* who profit by the critical ability of informed citizens councils and *citizens* who profit by the objective leadership of technicians.

3. Outstanding Personalities

A few words about some of the technicians who are planning the cities of Latin America: Frequently I had letters of introduction to several individuals in a particular capital, but it was never very long before I was directed to one man who, I was told, was *the* man to speak with concerning the urban problems of that city. Thus some one person was generally found who has been for a long time the spearhead of planning activities, heading a cooperative, capable group of men, all of whom together have made sacrifices and fought hard to put over the planning idea.

Even before I reached Mexico, I had been informed that Carlos Contreras was recognized by his colleagues as the pioneer leader in the study of urbanism in Mexico. As we have seen, Mexico has to a certain extent based her planning on the practices of the United States. The reason for this is simply that Carlos Contreras has done more to push planning than any other single person, has been trained in the United States, knows our methods, and is in constant touch with us through the American Society of Planning Officials and other agencies. Contreras, after attending preparatory school in the United States, studied engineering at Massachusetts Institute of Technology in Cambridge, Massachusetts; and after spending several years in Mexico during the revolution, returned to the United States to take graduate work in architecture. He taught at M. I. T. for a number of years and in 1925 returned to Mexico, determined to organize planning. By 1931 Contreras had aroused enough support of the planning idea to make possible the formation of a National Planning Board, for which he wrote the legislation. This he followed with the Planning Enabling Act, which is the backbone of planning in Mexico and which follows in general outline the planning law in the United States. Contreras worked for the City of Mexico under the administration of Mayor Saenz, 1933-1935, during which period there was done the best planning and housing work Mexico has ever seen. In 1936 he assisted in the formation of the Master Plan Office, which is functioning today. Contreras has not been alone in his efforts. He has worked with able men like José Luis Cuevas, Luis Prieto Souza, and Carlos Tarditi, as well as others, and was the guiding force both in bringing the planners of Mexico together in the National Planning Association of Mexico and in bringing the International Planning and Housing Conference to Mexico in 1938.

During the last ten years, in Guatemala, President Jorge Ubico has done a remarkable, if somewhat superficial, job of putting that colorful country in order. His chief planner in this work has been Arturo Bickford, Mayor of Guatemala City, Chief Engineer, and Planning Commission all in one. Born in Guatemala of English parents, Bickford was educated in the United States and in Canada. Since 1926, he has devoted his efforts to making Guatemala City a better place in which to live.

In Bogotá, Colombia, Carl Brunner is the man who has done more to introduce the planning process than any other technician. He was brought to Bogotá in 1935 to organize a program for replanning the city, and to assist in preparing for the celebration of the fourth centenary of the founding of Bogotá. (Brunner had previously worked in Santiago, where he had been called from Vienna to direct a program of planning for the capital of Chile.) In cooperation with capable Bogotanos, Brunner has given impetus to the development of the Master Plan for Bogotá, has designed several of the city's low-cost housing projects, as well as an excellent middle-income housing group of some 500 units built by the Central Mortgage Bank. Brunner also instructs in City and Regional Planning in the University of Bogotá's recently organized School of Architecture, has published two volumes on the planning of cities throughout the world, and has under preparation a third.

In Lima, Peru, my colleagues directed me to Emilio Harth-Terré, whom I have already mentioned several times. He is unquestionably the leading Peruvian in planning matters. I found him to be an energetic, dynamic person with a brilliant, almost gymnastic mind, who heads the Section of Urban Studies in the Ministry of Development. As I have said, he is at once a planner and an architect, and bears more responsibility for planning work in the Lima region than anyone else. For twenty-two years he has been planning in Peru. His broad interest in the field is based on human values and his range of understanding includes the planning of the Incas as well as that of the New York Regional Plan Association.

The following, translated from some of Harth-Terré's writings, indicates his scientific yet human approach to city planning: "One art, as old as the cities themselves, is today transformed into a new science: *Urbanism*, or the art of developing cities scientifically. Urbanism is a science of observation which depends upon the appreciation of studied facts. To limit Urbanism to the art of drawing plans alone would be to confine the whole fate of cities to mere lineal concepts."

He continues: "To achieve the human city, ours must be cities *of* the people, *for* the people, and they must be governed *by* the people, in active cooperation and with general consent."

He writes also, of *La Ciudad Immortal*, The Immortal City, and expresses the belief that it is within the power of man to fashion enduring cities built upon new, human standards. He says, in an article written for the celebration of Lima's fourth centenary, in 1935, "The life of the city of today depends on human will: the city exists for man, it is his instrument for culture and progress. In using that instrument, general welfare and public health should be of first importance; beauty, order, and comfort will follow naturally. The city of today must be prepared *constantly* for the future by man himself. . . . It is in the hands of man to build *La Ciudad Immortal.*"

A very colorful person, and head man in the planning of Lima proper, is the Mayor, *Alcalde* Gallo Porras, whose office looks more like a planner's office than a mayor's. Maps and plans cover the walls. Gallo Porras keeps close watch over his large staff and has been responsible for many of the planning projects in Lima during the last ten years. He was at one time Mayor of Miraflores and became interested in planning when that area was first laid out as the garden suburb that it is today. He is largely responsible for the vision that was shown in its design. Gallo Porras became Alcalde of Lima in 1934; in 1935 he replanned the Plaza San Martín for the fourth centenary celebration.

In La Paz, Bolivia, the man who has been the spearhead of planning is Emilio Villanueva, Dean of the School of Architecture and Urbanism in the University of San Andres, and author of a book on planning, *Urbanismo—The Urban Evolution of Europe and America*. Among the younger planning technicians in La Paz there is Mario del Carpio, of the Section of Urban Studies in the city's Department of Urbanism, who studied at the University of Chile in Santiago and worked there in planning for three years before returning to La Paz. He has a scientific, informed approach.

In Chile I found not one, but a number, of technicians who shared the job of advancing knowledge and thought in the planning field. Of these Luis Muñoz Maluschka has the most responsible position as head of the Department of Urbanism in the Ministry of Development in Santiago. His basic training was gained from Europe, where he has studied and traveled; his is a comprehensive conception of planning based on a realistic understanding of the economic factors as well as the physical.

Another important Chilean planner is Rudolfo Oyarzún, who, as head of the Institute of Urbanism of Santiago for many years, has defended the interests of planning and has advanced planning legislation. Oyarzún also practices as a private architect and has built into his own home a well-equipped study. Here he works on planning assignments and architectural studies, and as a hobby, paints. One night at dinner at the home of another planner in Santiago, Oyarzún apologized for having to leave about one in the morning, just after having finished our late dinner. (Chileans always dine late, and never seem to go to bed.) When someone asked, "Why so early?", Oyarzún answered that he was rather tired: he had been up the morning before until three, painting in oils.

Perhaps the most internationally-minded planner in Chile is Ricardo Gonzáles Cortés of Santiago, who has done a great deal to bring planners of various countries in contact with each other through annual conferences. Other capable planners in Santiago are Federico Oerhens in the office of earthquake reconstruction and Roberto Humeres of the municipal planning office of the city of Santiago.

In Valparaiso there is Hector Vigil, who was instrumental in founding the Valparaiso Institute of Urbanism in 1933—an institute which has a large membership from all professions having an interest in planning better cities. A regular publication was put out by the Institute up to several years ago. This group initiated the first Chilean National Congress of Architecture and Planning. Vigil first developed an interest in urbanism when he was Secretary of the Municipality of Valparaiso, 1915-1917.

Argentina's leading planning enthusiast is Carlos della Paolera, head of the *Direccion del Plan de Urbanización*, or Master Plan Office, of the city of Buenos Aires. He is one of the most popular planners on the continent and has the largest private library of books on planning. Della Paolera's enthusiasm for planning, and his knowledge and love of this metropolitan region, were well displayed to me on frequent exploration trips, during which he systematically familiarized me with the whole Buenos Aires region from the city of La Plata to the Tigre River area.

Della Paolera is the author of the Symbol of Urbanism, which has been used effectively on an international scale in publicizing the objectives of planning. The symbol represents the three elements essential to human life: air, sunlight, and vegetation, which the application of urbanism can bring to city dwellers in larger quantities. The symbol is available in various forms: as lapel pins, as stamps to place on correspondence, and in banners used by della Paolera in planning conferences. Translated, portions of the statement which accompanies the Symbol of Urbanism read:

"In these human beehives, which we call our great cities, we have lost a rational balance between man-made construction and the basic elements of life offered us in such profusion by Mother Nature. Today, urbanists all over the world have come to the conclusion that it is essential to recover air and sun and vegetation for the inhabitants of the modern city. They agree on the ultimate objective, to insure an intimate union of the city and the living earth, allowing ample space for nature amidst massive blocks of urban buildings.

". . . That we have permitted the disorderly crowding together of dwellings for human beings in an atmosphere of impure air, smoke, and gases, producing conditions which are unhealthful and undesirable for the maintenance and improvement of the race, places us anachronistically in violent contrast with the degree of advancement which civilization has reached. . . .

"Urbanists desire that life may enter every home along with air and sunshine, and that the child may develop and grow strong in favorable circumstances, in close contact with the gifts and splendors of nature. . . . From the monumental urban project to the most modest garden city plan, green spaces must form an integral part of the urban pattern. Park systems, together with the thoroughfares for traffic, can comprise the structural framework of the modern city. Nature's reconquest of the city can be a promising offering of health and beauty for every city dweller. Future generations will be able to appreciate the results of the application of Urbanism to the regeneration of life in human society."

Another Argentine planner, who works closely with della Paolera, is Luis Migone, a private architect and engineer, who for a long time has been a friend of the United States. His book *Las Ciudades de los Estados Unidos* (The Cities of the United States) is the only one published in Spanish or English that completely covers planning, housing, and building practices and legislation in the United States. Migone is also a member of the American Society of Planning Officials, and in his position as president of the *Centro de Ingenieros* has long advocated application of our planning techniques in Argentina.

Nowhere in my travels did I find planners and architects as thoroughly trained and as completely welded into a forceful group as in Montevideo. The members of the group are too numerous to be listed here in full, but among them several are recognized by their fellow workers, not only in Montevideo, but in other countries as well, as leaders in their field. Montevidean planners deserve recognition in the United States. All the way down the West Coast and in Argentina, I had heard rumors of the excellence of the Montevideo group. When I met them, I was not in the least disappointed. In fact, if there were but one place to which I might return for the stimulus of working and studying with thinkers and doers in the planning field, that place would be Montevideo.

I have said that few Latin planners know the United States and that many know Europe far better; but Mauricio Cravotto of Montevideo is one man who has an exceptional knowledge of the cities of both parts of the world. He is placed in my mind as one of the most outstanding technicians and scholars in the planning field in our hemisphere. Cravotto directs the Institute of Urbanism, for a long time has been a leader in planning affairs, and is professor of planning at Montevideo's exceptionally fine *Facultad de Arquitectura*. He has studied European cities many times, both by travelling and through numerous books, and speaks of the plazas, streets, and districts of Paris, Rome, and Copenhagen with the same familiarity of a native of San Francisco speaking of the Embarcadero, Telegraph Hill, or Market Street. But I was astounded to find that he also knew well the Embarcadero, Telegraph Hill, and Market Street from a visit of twenty years ago to the United States. His memory of the San Francisco Bay region was so clear that he was able to draw for me a map of the whole area. Yet, he is anxious to come again to the United States, to see what we have done with our cities since his last visit and since the advent of the automobile. Cravotto is one of the four planners collaborating on the study of the Argentine city of Mendoza. His understanding of planning problems ranges from the basic subject of human geography to the social, economic, and political obstacles that stand in the way of man's rational use of land. Mauricio Cravotto knows thoroughly Lewis Mumford's *The Culture of Cities*, which he quotes frequently and wishes to translate into Spanish.

Another very capable man is Juan Scasso, who, with Cravotto, has been an active force in giving planning its impetus in Montevideo. Scasso, who is in charge of the Department of Parks and Gardens in Montevideo, has a functional approach to design and as a result the parks of the city are more usable than most in South America. He is also active in the Institute of Urbanism.

Among others is Julio Vilamajó, whom one person described to me as the South American Frank Floyd Wright because of his distinctive, individual approach to architectural design. His most outstanding building, a superb work of site planning and building location, is the yet unfinished *Facultad de Ingeniería*, the School of Engineering, set in a park on a slope overlooking the Rambla and the sea. Few, if any, examples of university building design in the United States can approach this work of Vilamajó for boldness of concept and relation of site plan to surrounding area.

The Montevideo list must also include Américo Ricaldoni and Luis Crespi of the City Planning Office, both products of the architecture and planning school, where both were pupils of Cravotto and Vilamajó. The reason for this large group of well-trained and exceptionally cooperative Montevideans is significant: the *Facultad de Arquitectura* is the best architectural and planning school in Latin America.

I have said that planning in Brazil lacks the professional organization of other Latin American countries. Nevertheless Brazil has some excellent and aggressive planning technicians. In Rio, the capital, there is Attilio Corrêa Lima, who did a large part of the planning of the new city of Goiania, and a complete plan for the northern coastal city of Recife. He has been engaged by the newly formed National Steel Company to plan the town for twenty thousand workers for the United States-financed plant under construction at Volta Redonda, and is also commissioned by the State of Rio de Janeiro to make studies for a regional plan for the entire eighteen-mile-long area affected by the new industrial development.

Another Carioca planner is Abelardo Coimbra Bueno, a young engineer who, with his brother, constructed the city of Goiania, and who has since established a well staffed planning office, with Alfredo Agache as consultant. They are engaged in planning for some seven cities and towns, including fast-growing Curityba in the south. Planning services offered by his firm are those ordinarily done in the United States by a planning commission.

Alfredo Agache, Coimbra Bueno's consultant, is the French city planner who was brought to Brazil some years ago to develop a plan for Rio de Janeiro, and has pioneered since then in planning many towns and cities of Brazil. He is particularly well known for the plan of Belo Horizonte, capital of the state of Minas Geraes, and for Interlagos, the planned community near São Paulo.

Prefeito Prestes Maia, mayor of São Paulo, is a fabulous figure in Brazilian planning. Twenty years ago, an engineer interested in planning, he worked to interest all of São Paulo in the idea of replanning the city, and in 1930 he published a Master Plan for São Paulo. Today, as Mayor, Planning Commission, City Planner, and City Engineer all in one he is carrying out that plan. I was told that his day begins at five in the morning and lasts until eleven at night; that, although he has never traveled outside Brazil, he knows several languages; and that his mind is a storehouse of knowledge of many varied subjects. He actually lives in the city hall, where he devotes all his time and energy to one interest: the rebuilding of São Paulo according to the Master Plan which is the dominant interest in his life.

I have already spoken of the work of Washington Azevedo and Lincoln Continentino, both of whom studied planning in the United

States at Harvard University, and who have done outstanding work in Brazil.

Although there is practically no profession of landscape architecture in Latin America, Brazil, with its wealth of flora and mild climate should offer new possibilities for landscape design. David Azambuja of Rio de Janeiro has worked in the United States and is now trying to establish the profession. He has a very complete file of photographs of gardens and parks in our country, and hopes to arouse more interest in the plant life of Brazil in order to establish an interest in gardens similar to that in the United States.

Roberto Burle Marx, well-known Brazilian painter, has gone into landscape work with the younger modern architects. His garden and park work is Brazilian and indigenous in the richest, most extravagant sense.

Before going on to discuss students and schools, I wish to speak of some of the younger practicing architects and planners. In each country I visited, I invariably found a group of technicians of the younger generation, men who had quite recently finished training, and who had a new point of view toward planning, housing, and architecture. These young men look toward the United States rather than to Europe to learn more about building the cities of the future, and they always asked of possibilities for traveling, studying, or working in our country. It is with this group particularly that the responsibility for better planning lies. Their zeal and their realistic point of view are the most promising sign on the horizon of Latin America.

Here are the names of a few: Among the Colombians there are Gabriel Serrano, José Gnecco Fallon, Luis Gomez Vargas, Alvaro Hermida, Jorge Arango, and others. In Ecuador, Guillermo ("Bill") Jones-Odriozola (from Uruguay) is undertaking studies for a Master Plan for Quito; in Peru, there are Luis Dorich (now studying at M. I. T.), Carlos Dunkelburg Weiss, and others. . . . In Bolivia, I have mentioned del Carpio and Castillo. Chile, Argentina, and Uruguay offer too many names to include here. Aguirre, Duhart, de la Barra, Collados, Roi, and Arredondo are among the Chileans; Sacriste and Hardoy among the Argentines; Martinez Serra, Lucchini, and Gatto, de los Campos, Puente, Tournier, and Barañano are a few of the Uruguayans. Space does not permit a complete list of the many talented young technicians to be found in all countries.

Brazil's young group is particularly significant. The work of Marcelo Roberto, Lucio Costa, Oscar Neimayer, Carlos Leão, Henrique Mindlin, and many others has a particularly contemporary significance which makes architecture and planning very much alive. The development of Brazil's resources lies with her young people. In both São Paulo and Rio de Janeiro these young

169

architects and planners are thinking in terms of social and economic needs of the forty million people of Brazil. In spite of political obstacles and the loose organization of technical people, they are expressing a new philosophy—have planned or built such outstanding modern works as the new Ministry of Education and Health, workers' housing projects, industrial trade schools, office buildings, and hospitals. The planning of the postwar future of all the American countries must fall to the younger generation.

4. Students, Schools, and Ideas

I have said that in the past Latin technicians have generally been trained abroad. However, that statement refers primarily to the older group, because most of the younger men, like those just described, have graduated from the schools of architecture and planning throughout Latin America. A few, but not enough of them, have been educated in the United States. Latin America's universities are well equipped to train students in architecture and frequently give courses in planning which are compulsory for all architectural students. The result is that architects have a broader understanding of building needs in terms of all-over planning, and planning technicians emerge who know architecture very well. This differs from training in the United States in that planning courses in our architectural schools are rarely considered an integral, necessary part of architectural training. However, certain elements are lacking in Latin American technical training; one is the need for specialized housing courses; another is a more realistic understanding of the legal aspects of planning; and a third is a greater range of specialized technical training in related fields of construction, public health, sanitation and social welfare. I was told many times by Chileans, Bolivians, Colombians, and others, that too many students go into law and medicine, that these are often considered the "right" subjects as the basis for a professional career, while subjects such as soil conservation, sanitary engineering, public health, sociology, structural and other kinds of engineering, so vital to the future of the countries, are considered socially somewhat tabu. But before such training can be accomplished more professors in these fields must be supplied. That is one way in which our assistance can be effective in Latin America. In this complicated twentieth century, the social and economic ills of our times will be closer to solution when there exists an abundance of specialists trained for technical fields related to the environment.

In spite of the broader base for technical education in the United States the oldest architectural school in the hemisphere is actually in Latin America. It is the *Escuela Nacional de Arquitectura* in Mexico City, founded in 1792 by Charles III. The school, now headed by Mauricio Campos, offers a five-year course with planning given in the fifth year. The student work which I saw was of a high standard.

The only university I saw in Latin America that was planned and built as a complete campus as universities are in the United States was the University of Bogotá. Most universities south of the border, like those of Europe, are a combination of many *Escuelas* or *Facultades,* each in a separate building and often with buildings located in different parts of the city. But in Bogotá, these have been brought together on one large campus in newly built facilities. The recently established architectural school includes planning courses given by Carl Brunner.

Although both Lima, Peru, and La Paz, Bolivia, have architectural schools of long standing, many students of these two countries travel to Chile to study in either of the two excellent schools in Santiago: the University of Chile and the Catholic University. Chile has a large, well trained group of planners for the important reason that thorough planning courses have been compulsory in the architectural schools for the past ten years.

The course in planning at the University of Chile is given as a part of the architectural curriculum and is required of all architectural students. It is directed by Rudolfo Oyarzún and Federico Oehrens. Typical city planning problems given by them call for solution, first within existing laws of the city, then according to the ideas and imagination of the students. Here are some of the typical problems which I had an opportunity to see:

1. A plan for a *Población* or small town including a community center, school, etc., for 3,000 workers on a site near Santiago.
2. A study for re-development of a typical "Spanish" block in Santiago, first as it would be possible under the municipal planning ordinance, second, as it could be replanned under new and broader laws.
3. A plan for rebuilding the Plaza Argentina and rail terminal area, including a new railroad station.
4. A *Población Veraniega* or summer colony for Algarrobo on the Pacific.
5. A study for replanning Plaza Italia, for improved traffic circulation and uniting of three parks.

Since 1931 the Catholic University, the other school offering architectural courses in Santiago, has had courses in planning compulsory for all architectural students. Because of the need for technicians, students go directly into responsible jobs in offices upon completion of university training. Alfredo Johnson, a progressive young architect who studied planning in Europe for several years, is in charge of the planning courses.

I found, invariably, that where courses in city and regional planning were well organized, these professions were proportionately advanced. Chile and Uruguay have the most effective, complete schools of architecture and planning, and it is there that the professions are most advanced and effectively used. The University of Buenos Aires does not have an adequately organized architectural and planning school, and Carlos della Paolera, who instructs there, must work within the limits of insufficient teaching facilities. But his approach to the teaching of planning is an interesting one, based upon steps followed in the medical school: first, a study of the anatomy and growth of the city; then, urban physiology and functioning of the city; and finally, urban surgery, or the operation required to give new health to blighted areas.

The excellence of the policy of the architectural and planning school in Uruguay, known as the *Facultad de Arquitectura*, and the thoroughness of the courses given in urbanism or planning, are primarily responsible for the progressive, effective work of the Montevideo group. For the last twenty years courses in urbanism and landscape architecture have been obligatory for all architectural students.

But before discussing the philosophy of the teaching in Montevideo I wish to introduce the reader to student life there, which I found to differ considerably from that in our schools. In general, Latin American youths are mature and self-assured at an earlier age than those of the United States. As students they take a deep, realistic, often active, interest in the political affairs of their own countries, and are well informed as to what goes on outside of their own country. They are frequently sceptics, and they tend to scoff at the unquenchable optimism of the typical "American" youth. They prefer to point to the future by realistically examining the past, rather than to drive ahead without thinking to a questionable, uncertain objective. The objective is of chief interest to the Latin American student and although he is not always free to attain it, he is at least generally well versed in the reasons why he may not. Latin American students frankly envy the opportunities of those of the United States and feel that we hold many of the instruments needed toward obtaining their desired objectives.

But to get back to the students of Montevideo, who in addition to working hard also play hard, as one memorable night taught me: My arrival in Montevideo with a young architect from Seattle was an excuse for play and overwhelming hospitality. This began in the drafting room of the *Facultad de Arquitectura* before dinner, and ended in the small hours of the morning in a remote corner of Montevideo. We North Americans were welcomed with a large colored poster of an Uruguayan gaucho shaking hands with *Tio Sam* (Uncle Sam) and saying ". . . 'allo, siñor!"—suggesting the worst North American accent. We were introduced to a pet

172

Paraguayan parrot, mascot of the architectural school; we tried *maté* from the *bombilla*, and after several rounds of *caña*, a powerful native brew, we feasted on Italian *faina* and *pizza* from one of the many nearby Italian restaurants. We were then marched off in serpentine, singing *La Marseillaise*, to an affair at the Student Center where the good señoras of Montevideo, mothers of the young ladies present, kept watchful, suspicious eyes on these young Bohemians. But the theme of the evening was not just Bohemianism; rather, it was a sincere spirit of *fraternidad inter-Americana*, which expressed itself throughout the evening in earnest, though interrupted, bull sessions, and during the weeks which followed, in less frivolous meetings.

Likewise unforgettable were the discussions among the students and their professors which continued during the remainder of my visit in Montevideo.

From them I learned something of the approach used in Montevideo in training architects and city planners, an approach based on human geography. For example, one of Juan Scasso's studies, a collaborative project done by the students of urbanism of the *Facultad de Arquitectura* and the members of the Institute of Urbanism, illustrates this point of view. Through a series of maps and charts, this project traced from earliest settlement the growth of four types of urban communities: one, a group of Greek cities; the other three, Italian cities—Rome, Milan, and Florence. Each study presented clearly the basic geography, land and water areas, movements of early settlers, the pattern of settlement and defense methods; it then analyzed the people, what they did to make a living, and why the city developed into the form it ultimately attained. Because it emphasizes the effect of man's activities on the land, such an approach has particular significance in the study of our changing cities in the twentieth-century New World.

Such studies as these were inspired by several interesting volumes on human geography in the library of Mauricio Cravotto and in that of the Institute of Urbanism. One series of volumes, *Geographie Humaine*, by Pierre Deffontaines (Libraire Gallimard, Paris), illustrates the variety and extent of man's influence on geography. The volume entitled *The Geographic Mark of Man* was particularly interesting for its emphasis on the permanence of man's effect on the land in colonization, settlement, and frontiers, and the later growth of larger cities.

Another significant work in human geography that has influenced the approach to city planning among the Montevideo students is Marcel Poéte's *Paris y son Evolution Créatrice* (Paris and her Creative Evolution). Illustrated with carefully drawn maps and diagrams, this book traces the development of Paris from its earliest times to the present, placing greatest emphasis on the human forces

which necessitated permanent physical marks upon the land—
roads, streets, boulevards, barricades, walls, parks. Such an approach transforms a static concept of the city, whether Paris or
Montevideo or East Orange, N.J., into a dynamic one which pictures the city as a living, organic thing, growing like man himself
—although at an enormously slower rate of speed. The product of
this almost biological growth becomes as subject to influence for
better or for worse as the human body. I saw how Poéte's study of
Paris had been applied in practice to the evolution of Montevideo
in a study under way by the city's Master Plan Office, whose personnel is composed of young technicians, all products of the *Facultad de Arquitectura*. This study traced significant forces influencing
the growth of Montevideo in twenty large maps dating from the
first chart made of the bay and city in colonial times to the most recent aerial photographs.

Another volume shown me was significant from a political as
well as an urban point of view. Prepared by a German named
Kreutsburg, this work indicated the wide knowledge of various
parts of the world which the Germans possess. Photos of land use
types from all over the world illustrated how similar land forms
and climate produce similar results in all parts of the world—similar cities, similar agricultural practices, similar road systems. For
example a photograph of an orange grove in southern Africa could
hardly be distinguished from an orange grove in southern California; modern highways in the Andes have the same contours as
those in the Alps.

The same idea was presented in another remarkable book in
Cravotto's library, a large volume of Italian origin, composed
chiefly of superb maps of Italian cities and villages. These showed,
first, various types of topography—the plain, the hill, the mountain,
the peninsula; then different kinds of agricultural practices on such
ground forms (agriculture taken as man's first mark on the landscape); then various methods of communication were shown as
they developed—the river, coastwise transportation, roads of the
mountain and the plain; and this was followed by the villages, the
towns, and the cities that developed through the centuries. The villages, towns and cities were then presented according to types, for
example, those which developed in the plain or on the hilltop, those
whose growth began on one side of a river and later spread to the
opposite bank, and those which grew as twin settlements on each
side of a river, and at some later date became single cities connected by bridges.

Thus, Cravotto and Scasso use the evolution of human settlement, the subject of human geography or the effect of man on the
land, as a basis for city planning study in Montevideo. Cravotto
lists as *Durables*: land forms, climate, and water movements, and

as *Variables*: roads, agriculture and man. These he applies with a broad, world-wide point of view, or what he calls *Mundividensis* in tackling the planning of city growth. Such a basis for the study of planning, such breadth of point of view on the part of students and teachers, has resulted in student work that is mature and comprehensive in understanding. This is furthered by the fact that many students work in architectural offices while attending school, continuing their period of training well over the four years generally allowed in the United States.

The instruction in planning at Montevideo's *Facultad de Arquitectura* has a consistently high standard. It is undoubtedly the best of the schools of *Urbanismo* in South America and compares well with our planning instruction in the United States. Its particular merit is that a year and a half of intensive work in city and regional planning is compulsory for all students of architecture. Any North American student of planning or architecture wishing to study further would do well to spend a year at this exceptional school, whose thorough courses are largely responsible for the progressive city planning work now being carried on in Montevideo. Since all Uruguayan architects pass through this school, there has been welded together a generation of architects who understand the whole problem of urbanism, and a group of urbanists who speak the language of the architects. Technicians of the United States might well learn by their example and attempt to bring into closer relationship the somewhat uncoordinated professions of planning and architecture. In order to effectively plan our cities, good planners—men who understand and constantly study the phenomena of present-day urban and regional growth—must be developed. This has been done, and done well, in Montevideo.

In Brazil the student situation is quite different from that in Uruguay, and, although the country is some thirty times the size of Uruguay, no organized center of study exists. Training in city and regional planning was started only a few years ago in Rio de Janeiro, where one course is given in the *Escuela Nacional de Belhas Artes* by Dr. Saboia Ribeira. There are few trained planners simply because there are few schools in which to train them. The younger men who really want to learn and to know have had to do so by study on their own or by travel in Europe. An important step toward the sound use of Brazil's rich resources could be made by founding at least one training center, employing the best of Brazil's thinkers and those from other countries, for the purpose of preparing men in all the necessary specialized technical fields.

The *Escola Livre de Sociologia e Política* in São Paulo, Brazil, is not a planning school, but has a broad, social purpose and is working close to housing needs. It cooperates closely with the municipal Division of Social Documentation and together they have made

175

a number of housing studies. One of the professors, Donald Pierson of the University of Chicago, pointed out to me that this is the only school of sociology in Brazil. It is certainly one to be depended on as a starting point for the kind of education which will promote social progress.

5. Señor Citizen

Now we turn to Señor Citizen and the role he plays in the growth of cities south of the border. One of the first facts I found to be true is that the average citizen in most of the Latin American countries hasn't nearly as much to say about the policies of his government as does Mr. Citizen in the United States. There is nothing like the galaxy of Women's Leagues for the promotion or prevention of this and that, the Parent-Teachers' Associations, Property Owners' Improvement Clubs, and many others, which in our country serve the purpose of making democratic action an actuality. Groups like these play an important role in making or breaking a particular civic program. The democratic basis of planning laws in the United States provides for and encourages such action and participation by an informed citizenry.

In Latin America, there is little citizen action to support planning and housing. But, on the other hand, there is little organized opposition. The reasons are significant: first, the middle class is too small to offer much support, and working class groups, excepting those of Mexico and Chile, seldom wield organized power; the result is that little pressure can be brought to bear on official groups by the citizenry. Second, hardly any provision for democratic action has been made in most of the countries in formulating laws concerning planning and housing. The education of the general public and the encouragement of its participation in government affairs must be established before planning can be carried on according to democratic principles.

I found exceptions, however, to this general rule. In fact, in Peru, Argentina, and Brazil, I came upon several examples of citizen action which might well serve as a a stimulus for greater effectiveness in the work of citizen groups in the United States.

I have said that Medellín, Colombia, is growing rapidly and doing so according to a plan. The outstanding planner there has been not a professional planner at all but a lay citizen, Ricardo Olano, a retired industrialist. Thirty-five years ago he was sufficiently impressed with the plan of Washington, D.C., which he saw in the Library of Congress, to return to Medellín to introduce the idea of planning for the future growth of the city. Ever since, he has worked to promote planning for Medellín and other cities and has been an active and effective leader in Colombia in this field. His accomplishments make an interesting story.

A unique citizen's group called the *Sociedad de Mejoras Públicas,* or Society for Public Improvement, has been Olano's chief instrument in the education of the public for forty-three years. Through it he has urged many towns to make master plans and form similar affiliated groups. In order to discuss the problems of the cities of Colombia he promoted the first national planning conference of that country. His work with S. M. P. has produced a community spirit that is making Medellín one of the best planned cities of the West Coast. This community endeavor has made possible the construction of Medellín's Art Building, financed with a $65,000 fund collected through public subscription. S. M. P. is also responsible for the opening, twenty-seven years ago, of the city park, the Bosque de Independencia, and today maintains a large nursery for growing trees, of which they have planted ten thousand throughout the city. S. M. P. has likewise shown public-spirited courage and vision is acquiring for the city, through private contribution, both sides of the Rio Medellín for parkway purposes. Nutibara Hill, rising above the city in the midst of the valley of Medellín, is being planted by S. M. P. under the personal direction of Olano, and a restaurant is planned for construction on the hilltop. Olano told me how his organization has shamed the public into cooperation by branding in the press anyone who resisted contributing his share to civic improvement as an *hombre estorbo*—a stubborn obstructionist. Since no one wants to be an *hombre estorbo,* property owners who oppose a particular project generally relent under the pressure of public opinion.

In 1917, Olano held S. M. P.'s first national Congress in Bogotá, and since then Congresses have been held every two or three years. Olano and the S. M. P. have worked with an interesting *Comisión de Cultura Aldeana* (Commission for Village Culture) to study the planning and improvement needs of small villages. Studies include sections on education, literature, health, agriculture, etc. Today Olano's ambition is to see a complete garden city built in the valley of Medellín according to highest planning standards. His studio, set in an orange grove on his small farm near the city, has walls covered with many maps—an airphoto-map of Washington, maps of old Mexican towns, and of modern European cities—but that of highest importance to Olano is the map of the tiny village where he was born, back in the Andes beyond Medellín.

Few citizen groups can be found in Latin American cities to compare with Medellín's *Sociedad de Mejoras Públicas* for effectiveness in meeting local problems, but I did find other examples of citizen action in Lima, Santiago, Buenos Aires, and São Paulo.

In Lima a large amount of unrestricted growth, typical of the twenties, led to widespread sale of small lots in newly subdivided areas without benefit of public control over lot sizes, location, and installation of utilities. Many purchasers found themselves with worthless, unusable property when the depression arrived in 1929, and a group of these property owners came together for the purpose of urging the government not only to provide proper protection for their interests, but also to protect other citizens against future exploitation by real estate groups. With the help of Emilio Harth-Terré, they were able to promote the idea of planned development of the Lima region, which resulted in the formation of the Section of Urban Studies in the Ministry of Development. Lima's newly subdivided areas now have the benefit of subdivision control, zoning protection, and minimum standards of design established by the government.

In Santiago, citizen action, through a group known as the *Sociedad Amigos del Arbol,* has been largely responsible for the beautifully maintained system of street tree planting throughout the city. This group, the Society of the Friends of the Tree, has worked for many years to establish standards for street planting in Santiago, and to increase the use of trees within the urban area. Santiago's system of irrigation of street trees is worthy of mention here as a suggestion for towns of California and our Southwest, where summer rainfall is scarce. A system of canals parallels the gutters of the streets, and at each tree a basin is maintained with an opening into the canal. At certain hours each day water is run through the canals, generously filling the basins and watering the street trees.

Unlike other South American cities, Buenos Aires' sense of property rights is strongly developed. The entrenched pattern of small property holdings stands in the way of solving many urban problems. One citizen organization, known as *Los Amigos de la Ciudad* (Friends of the City) which publishes *La Vida Urbana* (Urban Life) twice monthly, helps to draw the large middle and professional classes into the support of better planning practices. Jerónimo Rocca, the editor of *La Vida Urbana,* like Olano of Medellín, is a retired businessman. About eighteen years ago, Rocca went to Paris and, on seeing what had been done there in city planning, became intensely interested in the planning idea. On his return to Buenos Aires, he founded *Los Amigos de la Ciudad,* which has since publicized the need for planning in Buenos Aires. Rocca believes that first in importance among all urban problems is that of transportation. He would like to see a change from the tendency toward vertical transportation, provided by the elevators of modern buildings, to an ever-flowing system of horizontal travel. Thus, spreading the city over the land, says Rocca, we can revolutionize living habits, break down the pattern of congested housing, and return man not only to his earlier contact with nature, but to a sounder relationship with his fellow-man in smaller urban centers.

IDORT—the initials which make up the popular name for the

Instituto de Organização Racional do Trabalho of São Paulo, Brazil,— translated, becomes the Institute for the Rational Organization of Work, whose purpose it is to rationalize techniques of all kinds of production, to advance a more efficient organization in both public and private activities, and increase the application of scientific principle. This Institute, which is one of the results of the social changes which are taking place in progressive São Paulo, has proven to be an effective agent in promoting change, and does not confine its activities to São Paulo alone, but includes all of Brazil in its program of activities. Increasing membership indicates the growing strength of IDORT. In 1932, a year after the founding, there were 105 members; by 1941 there were 1621 members.

Each year a week-long conference or *Jornada* is held, based upon a theme of current importance. In 1941 the subject was low-cost housing; others have been food, nutrition, and transportation. The housing conference resulted in the formation of a permanent Citizen's Committee on Housing. For the *Jornada* IDORT, along with the city's Division of Social Documentation, prepared a remarkable documentary film on housing conditions in São Paulo. The broad boulevards and public works of that city are shown in dramatic contrast to the insanitary slum areas and *cortiços*. A solution to the problem is suggested by a few examples of planned housing for workers in or near the city.

São Paulo's citizens are leading in ideas of social change because of the basic changes taking place with the shifting from an agricultural to an industrial economy. As a result the people of São Paulo are seeing new objectives, thinking of new methods of achieving them, and are becoming the most advanced group in Brazil. That is why IDORT is possible.

If planning methods are to be effective in furthering social betterment in democracies, increased support and interest on the part of the citizen must be encouraged. The future of such planning in the United States and in Latin America alike depends primarily on its citizens and its technicians. This is a joint responsibility. Three kinds of action must be taken in order to make planning and housing the living, democratic issue it must be:

1. *Technicians* everywhere must agree upon a clear-cut set of objectives, assume an aggressive attitude and demonstrate a willingness to work together and accept their social responsibility.
2. *Training centers* must be established where a constant supply of technicians will be available to do the jobs which must be done.
3. An informed and educated *citizenry* must be developed, made aware of the possibilities of the planning process and just what it means to them as individuals.

When the free citizens of the twenty-one American democracies of the Western Hemisphere are given a fuller opportunity to express their needs and rights, and when the talents of the technicians are geared directly to meet those needs of the American environment—North as well as South—then we may begin to look forward to new cities in a truly New World.

Two radiophotos of the Graf Spee, German pocket battleship, in Uruguayan waters: top, in Montevideo harbor, getting ready to run the Allied blockade; bottom, scuttled, magazines exploding, within sight of land (photos: Acme.)

chapter 8

Latin America and the war

1. The Latins and the War

The effect of Pearl Harbor on the economic and political life of the cities of Latin America was nothing short of electric. The shock was felt from Mexico City to Santiago and Buenos Aires, as an outright attack on the security of the whole western hemisphere. Its effect was demonstrated immediately by the success of the Rio Conference in January, 1942, which achieved new agreements on Hemisphere solidarity, pledges to eliminate Axis activities and programs for wartime and postwar technical and economic cooperation. Shortly afterward, these agreements were carried further when relations with the Axis were broken by all but one of the republics of the Americas and war was declared by many of them. Pearl Harbor quickened past trends, gave new significance to routine activities, and focussed attention on the future. The cities of Latin America definitely embarked on a fifth and most promising period in their development when the Japanese attacked the hemisphere.

Far from complicating or obscuring my investigations of the past, present, and future of the cities of Latin America, the entrance of the western hemisphere into World War II actually heightened the importance of many of the trends I was observing. Moreover, our State Department representatives along the way felt that then, more than ever, was it essential to know thoroughly the people of Latin America, their specific problems, and their hopes for the future. It was pointed out to me that as Hitler became involved deeply in the war, he was sending more representatives of all kinds over to Latin America, rather than calling them home—that is, as long as the republics permitted him to maintain legal contact. This realization of the value of knowledge toward strengthening hemisphere solidarity quieted my natural impulse to return home at once. In that first confusion of news and rumors, my cab driver told me that San Francisco, my home town, was bombed by the Japanese and was in flames! I had him stop for a paper, and after struggling through two inches of the news column in Spanish in record time, I found this had been a vague story of a doubtful "attack." I suggested to the driver that he spread his news more conservatively.

And so with a more objective view of Latin America I went on my way. Some of my personal experiences, the direct result of war conditions, will bring to the reader a better understanding of the real feeling of Latin American people toward us in the crisis, of why they are in the war with us and what they want to win by winning the war.

As I left Lima several weeks after December 7, it was somewhat annoying, yet quite heartening, to have Peruvian authorities search our car for hidden Japanese, throughout the five-day trip from Lima to Cuzco. Immigration authorities in Bolivia, Chile, and all countries were likewise more cautious than usual. Credentials became more and more valuable as the months went by and Hitler's representatives were given the bum's rush. Although these conditions added endless complications to already inexplicably involved official procedure in Latin America, they also created incidents which gave me a better understanding of the people. As I entered Chile, the Rio Conference was being held in Brazil. Excitement was divided between two issues. One: *Would Chile break relations with the Axis, and if so, would she be attacked by the Japanese from Easter Island?* And two: *Would democratic Juan Antonio Rios win the current presidential election following the death of the beloved Popular Front leader, President Aguirre Cerda?* Over in Argentina, eighty-five percent of the people favored breaking with the Axis, but nevertheless in Buenos Aires two Nazi newsreel theaters were going full blast with propaganda films of Germany, Italy and Japan; and on the streamlined, stainless-steel train coming from Bariloche to Buenos Aires, I found myself sitting opposite two Argentine Germans, one of whom was reading El Pampero the Nazi-sympathetic newspaper, the other, a newspaper sympathetic to the United Nations.

But there was no such split opinion in Uruguay. There, the violent dislike for Nazi sympathizers expressed itself from the first, in particularly careful entrance examinations in Montevideo's customs. Uruguayans were anxious to demonstrate clearly their anti-Axis government action in contrast to the neutrality of Argentina, their rival. This strongly pro-United Nations feeling was demonstrated to me on my first day in Montevideo, when an architect

182

friend drove me out to the Rambla, the waterfront boulevard, to point out a mere sliver of black projecting above the water out on the horizon. "That," he said proudly, "is what is left of the Graf Spee"; and he proceeded to tell of its scuttling in 1939.

The next day a young student friend took me by the arm, into the new City Hall, up the elevator, and out on the roof. He pointed his finger to the horizon and told me to look. I looked and he said, "That speck out there—that, *mi amigo*, is the Graf Spee." I quizzed him innocently and he told me the whole lurid story of the sinking, flames and all.

And then a few days later, Ro Terry, my Seattle friend and I, were driven (this was before gas rationing began) around the little bay and to the top of the Cerro overlooking the sea. We stopped near the Fortaleza General Artigas, the historic fortress on top of the hill, and were told that "if we looked *derecho* (straight ahead) we could see . . ." I said, "Don't tell me that's the Graf Spee!"

Even after the fifth time this performance was repeated, I enjoyed the sincere expression of national pride and unity which always accompanied the telling. Uruguayos were proud to be able to let you know that they, unlike those Argentinos across the Rio de la Plata, were without question true friends of the U.S.A. and proven enemies of Hitler.

Brazilian expression of anti-Nazi feeling was even more active. Six times in one week on the long train trip from Uruguay through southern Brazil to São Paulo and Rio, I was addressed in German and asked to show my *salvo conducto*. This was a large document, heavily stamped and signed, that had been given us at the border town of Santa Anna do Livramento, after an endless wait from eight o'clock to ten, just before dinner our first night in Brazil.

On one of these six occasions, a waiter in the dining car of the train handed me a small note which read in Portuguese: "*Pedimos por especial de não falar o alemão, Agradecido.*" ("We ask you as a special favor not to speak in German. Thank you.") The note was signed by the dining room steward.

Our complaint was answered with a courteous apology—they were very sorry but English-speaking travelers were so rare in this southern state of Santa Catarina that they did not recognize our conversation as that of North Americans! Later, I found that a law had just been passed prohibiting the speaking of Italian, German, or Japanese in public. These Brazilians were doing their part in seeing that the law was obeyed. Whole German-speaking towns had to save their conversation for the privacy of their own home, since Portuguese is unknown to many of German blood in some of the southern sections.

I remember well my arrival in São Paulo at the end of that journey. After we had extracted as many of our suitcases out from under the chicken hutches in the baggage car as we could, we loaded our baggage and ourselves into a taxi. My exasperation reached new heights when one of the curious bystanders—there are always many bystanders in Latin America—said to me laughingly, "Sprechen sie Deutsch, nicht?" I said, not too laughingly, "Hell, no, and I don't want to speak any. I'm not a German! I'm a *Norte Americano,* and if one more Brazilian tries to make me into a German, I'll demand an apology from Getulio himself!" This brought good-natured laughter from the crowd and let off some of our own steam, and we rolled off with no hard feeling between us.

A few days later in Rio, where gas rationing had crowded the buses beyond believable capacity, we were on our way back into town from the immigration headquarters, where we had to go many times in order to secure a small red passbook for which we surrendered the temporary *salvo conducto* (as well as ten U.S. dollars). Standing in a jammed bus, I ranted on about the way the war had further entangled Latin American red tape, and how weary I was of being taken for anyone but a North American. At that moment, toward the rear of the bus appeared a vacant seat into which I immediately dropped, only to have the stout lady on my right say to me in German, "From which part of Germany do you come?" Using my meager Portuguese, I said, "Dusseldorf," and let it go at that.

2. Focus on the Home Front

But to return to the more lasting effects of the war: as I said, World War II has brought a fifth period of development to the cities of Latin America. This war has brought conditions which present new opportunities for revitalizing an economy which in the past has caused 126,000,000 citizens of the New World much social damage. For this reason World War II is the most significant event for our neighbors to the south since their own wars of independence; it has given a new, significant aspect to the technical and social possibilities of planning, housing, and architecture in both the cities and the rural areas of Latin America. The war, in cutting off contact with Europe and other parts of the world, is putting these countries to a series of new tests, which call upon their technicians to plan and produce in new ways. Unsolved problems are being spotlighted; basic weaknesses are now becoming obvious; and our own relations with Latin America are being tested. Enormous opportunities are opening for doing the job that has not yet been done in Latin America throughout the 400 years of European domination, not since the times of the Incas. That job consists of planning for the best development of her rich resources to supply the social needs of the Latin American people.

This new activity indicates a promising future, it is true. But what do these events actually add up to in terms of those 126,000,-000 people of the Latin American republics? How will victory affect their welfare? What are their objectives in the war?

The answers to these questions may not be clear in the minds of the people themselves; nevertheless, the issues for which we in North America are fighting are no less important to them than they are to us. If anything, our neighbors in the southern half of the New World have more to gain from the war than we have; for while we are highly concerned with *maintaining* a certain status quo within our borders, Latin America is faced with the task of *arriving at* a status quo which might be worth maintaining and defending. For the first time in their history, a way may be open for developing a twentieth-century environment and economy.

The reader should be aware by now that, far from having arrived at the twentieth century, the cities of Latin America today are patchwork quilts of Middle Age living and working facilities; Victorian, turn-of-the-century, useless splendor and wealth; and spots of advanced, but socially unrelated streamlining in the style of Le Corbusier which cannot even yet be matched in our own U.S.A. Low wages have been responsible for mass poverty and economic exploitation in Latin America, while a great degree of illiteracy prevents true democracy from operating. Together these two factors have stood as the chief obstacles in the way of the building of cities worthy of a "New World."

Up to now, we have had a picture of those cities in the light of their past and their present, with a glimpse at plans for the future. From now on we look beyond the turning point marked by the war. At this turning point, we find two new and significant trends of thought—trends which are taking place rapidly enough to be called shifts of focus. First, there is that shift to emphasis on local needs and resources, and the future of each individual country. Second, there is the amazingly sudden shift of focus from Europe to the U.S.A.

Focus Number One was bound to come eventually. The war merely brought it sooner and made the Latins realize that they can't be forever dependent on the outside world. Normal sources of supply outside the hemisphere have been cut off or sharply curtailed, and now each country has begun a search for ways and means of furthering economic independence—or at least getting as far in that direction as peculiarly unbalanced natural resources permit. I have shown earlier how these resources, unlike those of the United States, are often of the type that require the application of elaborate technical effort to put them to use. Development of roads, rail lines, power, and living facilities must precede development of resources. Since the Latin American countries can no longer secure many needed imports, they are now looking for methods of developing such facilities in order to get at, and make use of, the long-idle, rich resources of their own countries. They realize that by making the most of every usable resource available for local development, they can make themselves increasingly free of foreign influences and more nearly independent as to economy. This is one of the chief objectives of the Latin Americans in this war. A thorough examination of their resources and a close scrutiny of their possibilities for development would certainly indicate a greatly multiplied, more balanced agricultural production, and an increased industrial development geared to local needs rather than to foreign markets. The war has turned the spotlight on national resources, on long-standing local needs. This new self-interest, this new attention to home needs, this realisation of her potentialities, is the healthiest turn-of-events that could take place in Latin America.

New industrial and economic life had already begun to develop in many Latin American cities during the past decade. In the two or three years prior to Pearl Harbor some cities—for instance, Mexico City, Bogotá, and La Paz—had developed into boom towns whose expansion rivalled the growth of Los Angeles, California, or Houston, Texas, during the twenties. Let us trace the building booms up to the present in these three Latin American cities and see what has been the result of the war.

Since the beginning of the European phase of the war money formerly held abroad has been invested at home by Latin Americans who knew Paris, London, or Cannes better than Mexico City, Bogotá, or La Paz. I met Ecuadorians, Colombians and Chileans who spoke French and English with more facility than Spanish, and who were quite out of place in their new home—their native country. Now they have come home and with them have come millions of pesos, sucres, and bolivianos looking for safe investments.

Mexico City in particular has felt the effect of this new investment of capital. As we have seen, real estate development and new construction are changing the face of the great capital of Mexico. In addition to the war, a political factor entered the picture: during the Cardenas regime and earlier, money had been kept outside the country in the United States or in Europe because political conditions were unstable. Now, with the war abroad and confidence in President Avila Camacho's middle-of-the-road policy, Mexican capitalists are looking for safe and sound investments at home. According to the Latin tradition the safe place for money is investment in property rather than in business or industry. Thus, Mexico City is being practically rebuilt.

A similar situation existed, about the time of Pearl Harbor, in Bogotá, where not a single business street was without several eight- or ten-story buildings under construction. One authoritative

186

source gave fifty million dollars as the amount of construction of all kinds in Bogotá during the year 1941. As in Mexico, money which had been idle in foreign banks had come home to be put to work because of the war.

But unlike the effect on Mexico City, the war had caused a particular crisis in Bogotá: this building program was seriously imperiled because there was a shortage of steel and other building materials. During my visit, black-coated Bogotanos took their *tinta*, or small black coffee, in the cafes and talked about the threat of unemployment. North Americans said, "Let them go to work in industries important to the war." But the Bogotanos answered: "How can we, when construction has become the chief industry in industry-poor Bogotá?" Strongly pro-United States Bogotanos (and Bolivianos, too, in La Paz), worried that such unemployment might be an open door to underground Nazi agitation. They told me that a full bread-basket and a job are the best arguments for democracy, whether it's Bogotá, Colombia or Bogota, New Jersey. In this way Latin Americans are discovering by hard experience that a more balanced economy is essential to a stable future; that a building boom is meaningless without local industries as a basis for it.

Farther south, in La Paz, Bolivia, it was not alone the war which stimulated building. A realization of national needs and interests had resulted in legislation, passed about 1936, to hold some forty percent of the wealth due to tin exports in the banks of La Paz. This money, which formerly entered foreign channels of investment, has been going into modernization of the capital and other cities with new streets, boulevards, office buildings, worker's housing, and projects having to do with sanitation and health. As a result La Paz is becoming one of the strangest and most fascinating cities in the Americas, a modern skyscraper city, rising out of an immense hole in the top of the Medieval highlands of the Andes.

Thus, in Mexico City, Bogotá, and La Paz, and in other cities as well, the earlier stages of the war stimulated city building, and the period from Pearl Harbor on caused a shortage of building materials because most modern materials had to be imported. A basic weakness became obvious: most countries lack fully organized building industries. Without building materials—cement, wood, steel, hardware—labor has nothing to do in cities where construction itself is the chief source of employment. Such unemployment increases quickly as buying power decreases, and the result is a general weakening of all economic activity. Meanwhile, unemployment may also be a useful springboard for Axis-sympathetic parties (not by any means entirely stamped out) and political disturbance threatens. However, the very existence of this crisis is one of the reasons for the new focus on national life; and since we have come to understand the situation, the U.S.A. has been giving Latin

America a share in priorities as well as much economic assistance —all of which aids development of industries necessary to maintain the building program and normal employment. Necessity, the mother of invention, will in this case be the parent of new industries and new activities which can be guided toward opening the path to postwar economic independence for Latin America. The war has had other kinds of effects on the development of Latin America.

Ecuador, Peru, and Bolivia are aroused about agricultural needs. These countries want highways to make available new, rich, but undeveloped areas; dams to store water and provide cheap power and fuel; reforestation and soil conservation to re-enrich the Andes. They want the means of giving life to this potential source of plenty. Ecuador, particularly, wants modern agricultural and economic planning; like the other Andean countries, she needs a South American version of TVA.

Chile is looking for ways of developing a lumber industry with her rich timber resources in the south now that shipping conditions have cut off the supply of Oregon pine. A forestation program for Chile and a steady supply of low-priced lumber would act as a real threat to the *conventillo*. Argentina is jealously eyeing the strides that Brazil is making by virtue of her close cooperation with the United States. My young architect friend, Guillermo ("Bill") Jones from Uruguay, spent an hour telling me about the new power development at Rio Negro in his country—a dam so great that the resultant lake to be formed will require redrawing the maps of Uruguay. Begun by "helpful" German engineers and equipment, the project would have been abandoned had it not been for democratic Uruguay's breaking off with the Axis. The result is a credit of twelve million dollars from the Import-Export Bank and a crew of United States technicians to help the progressive, capable Uruguayans finish the job.

Brazil, of course, is going to town. Today she is as much a part of the future as was the United States fifty years ago. Her resources are enormous. Traveling north from Uruguay into Brazil, you first pass through the green *gaucho* land in the southernmost state of Rio Grande do Sul, and then enter the *pinheiro* forests of Paraná and Santa Catarina. Out of the lumber country, the rich, green, cultivated valleys of the State of São Paulo precede the vast sprawl of industry that is changing the city of São Paulo from an agricultural center to an industrial one, making this the fastest growing metropolis in the western hemisphere.

As you near Rio de Janeiro you see the new steel center at Volta Redonda, where United States loans are developing the plant for putting to work the great iron ore deposits of the State of Minas Geraes. At last, you roll out of the mountains into the extravagant, natural splendors of Rio de Janeiro. Beyond, to the west and north, there are the rich states of Goyaz, with its newly planned capital, Goiania; Matto Grosso; and the fabulous, enormous State of Amazonas. This growing Brazil displays the vigor and potentialities which the U.S.A. had when Chicago was a frontier.

Great things can be done with Brazil's green vegetation and rich earth. Hot and fertile, Brazil stretches on and on beyond the horizon. The southern states alone seem immense, but a look at the map tells you that this is but a corner of an entire territory larger than the United States. There is something exciting about Brazil that makes you feel it is geared to the future—that it has the push of a young growing thing. Brazil has an impossible-to-stop vigor, like a young sapling well on its way toward becoming a towering oak. Brazil's is really a *green* power, displayed in the chlorophyll of the grass and forests which cover the hills and mountains and in the deep green waters of her many rivers. The latent power turns out sleek, hump-backed cattle, plenty of corn, rice, beans and fruits, and platters of green spinach for growing dark-skinned boys and towheaded boys whose fathers work in the lumber mills of Rio Grande do Sul, in the machine shops of São Paulo, and the mines of the State of Minas Geraes. This green power has produced hectic, Chicago-like São Paulo, the rich seaport of Santos, luxuriant Rio, and thousands of growing cities sprinkled over a huge green area— the choice, not-quite-ripe kernel of the continent of South America. You don't have to be a prophet to say that Brazil is headed for top place in the economic lineup in the southern continent, or that her people will be rich contributors to a coming inter-American culture. A full use, now, of powers like these means a rich and prosperous land of plenty for Brazil's common man for centuries to come.

But to return to the effects of the war: I have spoken elsewhere of the first large, modern steel plant * "south of the border," which is under way at Volta Redonda near Rio, on United States war plant scale, and with the help of loans from the Import-Export Bank of the United States. Volta Redonda's industrial center will tap high-quality iron resources—one entire mountain of raw iron, near Belo Horizonte in the mineral state of Minas Geraes. Low-grade coal is to be brought by ship and rail from the State of Santa Catarina to be used as coke in the production of high grade steel. Preston James speaks of the importance of this new development: † "So pure are the Brazilian ores that the usual ratio of coal to iron can be reversed—making it possible to use more iron ore than coal in the steel-making process. The problem remains to bring the railroad lines up to the standard of effectiveness which will permit the

* Small plants already operate in the state of Minas Geraes, Brazil; in Corral, near Valdivia, Chile; and in Monterrey, Mexico.

† *Latin America*, by Preston James; Lothrop, Lee and Shepard, 1942.

uninterrupted shipments of raw materials and fuels. . . . The location proposed for the steel plant in the Paraiba Valley is an excellent one in terms of the domestic market for steel. About 45 percent of the steel will be used in São Paulo and about 30 percent in Rio de Janeiro; the remaining 25 percent will be consumed in other parts of Brazil which are most easily reached by steamer through Rio de Janeiro. The prospects are bright for the establishment of a stabilized industrial community in the Paraiba Valley and for the development of the surrounding rural areas for the production of food for the urban workers. Perhaps this marks the beginning of a new era for the Southeast, and for Brazil as a whole—an era of steel and heavy industries."

The ultimate production of steel in large quantities offers enormous opportunities for city building and for developing other related industries. For the first time in her history, a steady supply of steel will be produced in large quantities within the borders of the continent of South America. Although first production is intended for use primarily in Brazil, eventually portions of the supply of steel may be made available in other parts of South America. It can be used for rail lines which will extend to more distant rich resources in sections now inaccessible. Low-priced steel will make it possible to tap unused resources essential to building the modern physical environment needed by 126,000,000 Latin Americans.

Another development important to Brazil's future lies in the new search for rubber in the upper Amazon basin. Wild rubber trees by the millions stand deep in impenetrable jungles too costly to reach during normal times, but now, with our former supply in the hands of the Japanese, these trees must be reached in spite of cost. The Brazilian government, for a long time interested in intensifying the use of the Amazon region, is cooperating with our government and the United States Rubber Development Corporation in a program which will not only supply rubber for the war effort, but will also have postwar significance. Colonization is being pressed forward on a gold-rush scale, although instead of the covered wagon the airplane is being used.

Much of the region has been mapped photographically for the purpose of identifying rubber-bearing tree areas. Some sites are being cleared for distant airfields and for new settlements for workers. Manàos, the faded capital of the rubber empire of thirty years ago, is flourishing again as Brazil's biggest boom city. These activities—mapping, building, and penetration by airplane, and the experience derived from them—will all be of value after the war in Brazil's economic development and in furthering possible permanent colonization of sections of the potentially productive Amazon valley.

Brazil's other resources—the rich green grazing land of Rio

Grande do Sul, the dark green *pinheiro* forests of Paraná, the fertile agricultural land of São Paulo (the home state of my friend, Eddie), the vast State of Amazonas—all these are being put to work to develop Brazil's economic stature while she pitches in to work with the United States for the security of the hemisphere.

Many small Brazilian towns are spurting with new growth because new industrial development is spreading in Brazil. One planner, Lincoln Continentino, is working exclusively with small towns of from 5,000 to 30,000 population, like Curvelo, which has suddenly expanded because cotton production has increased, it is said, as much as 50 percent in all Brazil.

Pearl Harbor created a wave of defense plans in many of the cities I visited. Mexico City had a scheme for a combined shelter and garage under the Zocalo, the ancient plaza which has been the center of the city since the days of the Aztecs. Technicians in La Paz wanted information from the United States on construction of bomb shelters. Who the attacker would be they were not sure, but at the time of my visit, just after Pearl Harbor, anything seemed possible. They felt that an attack on Peru or Chile could be easily followed by one on La Paz, whose isolated position would render the city particularly vulnerable.

Lima, Peru, had not thought about the necessities of defense since its colonial walls were built, but after Pearl Harbor, Lima was concerned with plans for defense against aerial bombs, and even invasion. Chile's complete lack of an adequate road system down the length of the 2600-mile-long republic made her immediately aware of the defense needs of her long, unprotected coast. Remember that, although highways exist in most parts of Chile, out of a total of 27,900 miles only 212 are paved and graded to modern standards.

Buenos Aires was giving thought to bombing protection. Carlos della Paolera had written an article on the subject in *La Nación*. In it he pointed out that the aerial bombardment of London indicated the insufficient amount of open space in the city in normal peacetimes, to say nothing of such an emergency as this. And yet, he said, ". . . the center of London has two and one-half times as much open space as our capital, Buenos Aires." Then he adds, "we *porteños* (natives of Buenos Aires) could not resist very long if we were forced to feed ourselves on the vegetables that could be grown in the lawns of Palermo, the park of Chacabuco, and that of the Centenario!" Della Paolera pointed out the lack of green spaces to act as *cortafuegos* or firebreaks. He concluded: "The spirit of the city of peace is already beginning to triumph in this struggle in which will perish without doubt the spirit of destructive warfare. And when it does the urbanist will be able to plan cities for full living, not for needless death."

191

The war has brought thousands of refugees to the cities of Latin America. I found large colonies of French, Poles, Austrians, Germans, and other Europeans in all countries. The emigrés had not forgotten the twenty minutes they had had in which to leave Warsaw, Vienna, or Paris. Their tragic stories served to bring the war close to Latin America. The number of these newcomers was particularly startling in Ecuador, where it has been somewhat easier to gain entrance than into other countries. One was as likely to hear German spoken as Spanish on the streets of Quito or Guayaquil. One evening in Guayaquil I discovered myself to be the only person, out of some twelve or fifteen people sitting nearby in the park overlooking the river, who was not speaking German.

Bolivia probably holds second place in the number of refugees from Europe. The population of La Paz has been increased about 12,000 by this influx. In all countries, many are reported to be Nazis in the guise of refugees, but whatever their sympathies, these people are stimulating economic activity and accelerating war-born changes. Most are industrious and some have a good deal of money. They also have education, culture, and new ideas to offer, and as a result, Ecuadorians, Bolivians, and others who have never been outside their country are seeing new ways of living. In Quito, La Paz, and other cities, small night clubs, tea rooms, candy shops, and Viennese pastry shops have opened. New ideas in architecture, an enlivening of graphic arts, and a number of small industries have also begun to develop. Since Latins in general are more accustomed to Europeans than to North Americans these people fit into the pattern of living without attracting the attention they might in the United States.

Luis Quintanilla * sums up what victory in World War II means to the people of Latin America: "The triumph of democracy will prepare the day when the native populations of all America will be able to plow their own fields, weave their own clothes, and live in the houses they have built. These people have survived four hundred years of injustice. After victory, the forces of democracy in each country must release the full potentialities of their submerged population. That day, America will be a better place in which to live, and we shall speak with pride of our *American* standard of life."

3. Focus on the U.S.A.

One day in Montevideo an architect friend who had made many trips to Europe, but none to the United States, was talking about Uruguay's new interest in our nation. Talking with a pencil in his hand, like all architects, he sketched out a tiny map of the world. On it he laid out a shaft of light leading out from Uruguay to

---

*A Latin American Speaks, Macmillan Co., 1943.

192

Europe, and marked that "Stage No. 1" in the evolution of his country. Then he drew another shaft from Uruguay to the United States and marked that "Stage No. 2." With broad pencil strokes he completely blacked out the first shaft of light and said that the war had terminated that period for his country and all South America. From now on, he said, the focus is on the United States and a New World civilization which *North American technical skill and Latin American imagination can together make possible.*

This feeling is shared by many Latins with whom I spoke in different parts of the continent. These men think of the United States in no uncertain terms as the leaders in technical achievement; they recognize our technical ability as the best in the world, our standards of living as the highest, and they envy our many freedoms. Our good neighbor policy has done a great deal to assist this attitude, and to reassure Latin Americans that we may have begun to assume the responsibility of leadership that we have so long shunned.

But the Latins still realize that it will take considerably more than good neighborliness to put North and South America on an equal footing. They want the kind of technical assistance that will allow them to raise their standard of living and consequently achieve a democratic freedom like that of the United States. Our job during the war is to guide the newly needed development of resources in such a way that in the peace to come these will be Latin America's own plants, managed by her own people. Luis Quintanilla, in *A Latin American Speaks*, suggests the orientation needed for United States technicians and capital in Latin America: "The Latin American republics . . . have yet to win their vital struggle for economic emancipation. This does not mean that Latin America must fight United States capital; the intelligent cooperation of that capital is needed to build up the national economies of some twenty hemisphere republics. . . . We do need capital, but an entirely different type of capital.

"With its main sources of income virtually all under foreign ownership, and under the control of a very few people, Latin America is seriously handicapped in creating national wealth. For, contrary to the contention of the interested parties, foreign monopoly investments do not help the development of a country." Quintanilla continues, pointing out that such investments hinder development: ". . . by the very nature of their purpose, which is the artificial control of prices in order to insure high and steady returns to *distant speculators, for whom countries are not nations inhabited by human beings, but mere commodities.* The stockholders at home, not the native workers or the native population, thousands of miles away, are the principal concern of powerful foreign monopolies with large investments in Latin America." (The italics are my own.)

Of this job of orienting the development of resources, Luis Quintanilla says: "The United States *ought to be the first to take part in assisting that emancipation.*" (The italics are his.)

Before the war United States capital showed unforgivable stupidity in building up the industrial power of Japan by shipping that country steel, petroleum, and machinery—only to have these materials used to kill and capture our citizens. T. A. Bisson * says that the United States' share in preparing Japan for war was *54.54 percent in 1937* and *56 percent in 1938.* After the war, United States capital must show the wisdom of shipping our machinery and industrial supplies to those nations which have proven their intentions of democratic, peaceful use of those materials. Properly guided materials, capital, and technical aid mean greater national wealth, more economic independence to Latin America, and increased hemisphere democracy.

Where Latin America has profited in the past through close contact with Europe, today she looks toward an enriched future through new and stimulating contact with the United States. In 1942 we actually purchased more from Latin America than we sold her; this is a reversal of the usual trade relations. Working within this close economic relationship, it is of highest importance that we state our intentions clearly now during the war and that we go even further—putting into practice those intentions during our wartime cooperation in Latin America. Thus we could take steps toward the ultimate improvement of housing conditions for the Bolivian tin miners by not only paying a higher price for tin, but by following through and seeing that the increase actually reaches the miners in the form of real wages. International labor cooperation could be an effective force. High-sounding objectives such as hemispheric democracy and unity become pretty hollow words when you put them up against the 15-cent daily wage of Bolivian miners and their economic exploitation by tin companies whose chief customer is the U.S.A. Let's prove our high-spoken intentions by concerning ourselves with the well-being of each individual Latin American worker who is helping to supply the materials necessary to wage war against the Axis.†

The Latins also want us to prove our sincerity by demonstrating

*American Trade and Japanese Aggression, annals of the American Academy of Political and Social Science, Sept., 1940.

† A recent case in point is our failure to recognize progressive, pro-democratic elements among Axis sympathizers in the new Bolivian government which came into power December 20, 1943. We wisely rejected the new group because of pro-Axis influence, but we did the cause of democracy no good by abruptly closing the door upon those men of good will who had obviously used pro-Axis sympathizers in order to get the dictatorial President Peñaranda out of office. This former government with which we were cooperating closely had been known for such anti-labor action as the Catavi massacre in which 800 miners were fired upon under Army orders during a legal strike for a living wage.

194

now, within our own country, a practical democracy with reference to all racial minorities, particularly those of Latin American origins—the Mexicans, the Puerto Ricans. They would be more sure of us, too, were we to practice a clearer policy in our relations with European forces of questionable political character. I refer especially to Franco Spain, which in many sectors of Latin America is hardly considered synonymous with democracy. We have an almost purple record of appeasement there. That policy gains us, not the support of the right, the middle, or the left, but the distrust of all factions in Latin America. Without such a clear policy, demonstrated in events and action, we stand the chance of losing the hastily gained trust of the Latin Americans, and after the war they may once more look to Europe or other parts of the world.

These, then, are some of the changes which the war is causing in the cities of Latin America. The chief effects of these shifts of focus may be summed up chiefly as two-fold: the development of a new and sounder economic basis and a strengthened inter-continental unity.

4. New Inter-Continental Unity

Perhaps the most powerful effect of the war on the Latin American republics is that it has drawn them closer toward each other than ever before. The war is bringing the Americas together rapidly, through new highways and airports needed for the defense of the hemisphere.

The Pan-American Highway has received an enormous impetus from the war. The Nogales Highway to Mexico City is being completed and the extension from Mexico City to Oaxaca, thence to the Guatemalan border and beyond to Panama, will be a reality in 1944. Latin American countries think of the Pan-American Highway in somewhat different terms than our distorted concept of it as a means of rolling down to Rio in this year's newest car, snapping shots of the picturesque natives in their grass huts along the way. Latins think of the highway more as a means of advancing the economic integrity of their countries, and as a military aid. They are more concerned over the effect which the location might have on the economic development of resources than they are over the need for bringing the highway through—let us say—the picturesque Guatemalan highlands in order to attract tourists. Perhaps it would be better in the long run if North American tourists were not permitted to use the Pan-American Highway for a while, until the living standards and cultural self-reliance of the "natives" are strengthened beyond the level at which exploitation has held them.

Airlines and other air facilities have been completely taken away from European control and although the United States' commercial air companies now control air travel in most countries, many of the republics have developed their own subsidiaries and use their own personnel. These facilities have been extended and increased, bringing into close contact the countries of Latin America—not only with the United States, but with each other.

Other changes have resulted from this new feeling of inter-continental unity: The difficult situation which had kept Ecuador and Peru at loggerheads for a long time, and which was resulting in the draining of energy and resources so necessary to Ecuador, a country already too poor—this situation was brought to solution through the war itself, and, of course, through the Rio Conference. The resultant peace has made it possible for Ecuador to turn her attention to more important social and economic matters, and for richer Peru to employ military strength in the interest of hemispheric defense and security.

The long-range objectives of the Rio Conference, hub of inter-American wartime unity, stressed the need for economic and technical cooperation among the twenty-one republics in the interests of raising the standard of living. With such a basis for the future of the western hemisphere, opportunities for postwar action become enormous. When the war that is stimulating all of the Americas to a new understanding of the word *freedom* is over, let us hope that the fight will continue on any front necessary in order to combat and put down for all time poverty, undernourishment, illiteracy, bad housing, and twelfth century living.

Meanwhile, we need to direct these wartime changes with regard for home needs and the realization of postwar promises. The hotter becomes the fight in the outside world, the more the Latin American countries think about their own resources and how they can best be developed. They are thinking about the U.S.A. and the kind of help we have to offer. Latin technicians are a capable lot and are doing a good job on their own, in spite of the many limitations which confront them. To sum up the situation, here's what one hard-boiled engineer told me: "We Latins can't do the job alone. You people in the States have a chance to win us over forever if you show good sense and act constructively for the interests of the Latins. If you don't, the Germans will dominate here sooner or later, war or no war. We need technicians—people to show us how to organize. Train our young technicians in the states, send U.S. technicians down to show us how to do the job. . . ."

EXTENT OF AIRLINES - **1927**

-AND **1942**

chapter 9

Latin America and the U.S.A.

1. Shrinking Globe—Cause: The Airplane

The chief force causing the cities of Latin America and those of the United States to assume a new, mutual significance is the airplane. The airplane is shrinking the globe, and it is becoming an absolute necessity for us to revolutionize our conceptions of foreign policy. We in the United States, particularly, must catch up with this fast-moving world.

We have heard a lot about the shrinking globe from all who have taken to the air, but we have not yet heard nearly enough about it. To the person who has flown a great deal, the experience of flying, and thereby reducing days to hours and mountains to plains, is accepted, and the sharp importance of this single factor—the airplane—is no longer perceptible. But for me it was a new experience, one of great significance. I had never before flown, and in the comparatively small amount of flying I did in Latin America—only some 6600 miles in all out of the 22,000 I traveled—I came into first-hand contact with this shrinking process which the globe is undergoing.

My first experience with flying took me from Mexico City to Panama. North or South, air travel is the same, but one's first flight is always momentous. The plane taxies to the far end of Mexico City's airfield. The motors are turned up to a maximum and the grass on the field waves like the sea. The plane speeds the length of the field, and then with a rush of power goes twice as fast and you are flying. Trees and houses, animals and people, even mountains need new standards for identification.

Off at eye-level stand Popocatepetl and Ixtaccihuatl, white and glistening with snow against a clear blue sky. We edge along the

197

Pacific Coast over the Gulf of Tehauntepec. Below, rollers march in to a ribbon of white beach and deep blue water is streaked with patterns of reddish mud traced by strange birds as they cross from reef to reef. We fly into rain and on goes the lighted sign *Abroche su cinturon*—"Fasten your seat belt." We fly up and up and up and finally come out of the clouds into a fantastic place where the sky is infinitely bluer than in our world, and part of the time we look below at white hills and valleys composed of fresh cottage cheese. Other times we look across to towering hillsides which might be 20,000 feet high, or microscopic—none of the familiar standards remain. We follow the edge of a cliff of white clouds pierced with deep grey canyons. Later, the sun goes down and the vaporous world turns a ruddy pink. After darkness a lighted city appears to stand at a forty-five degree angle on your left as you bank to land in Guatemala City some five hours after leaving Mexico City, 800 miles away. At the risk of being called provincial, I describe my first flight as an afternoon's miracle that tossed out of the window all my former ideas of space, time, and geography.

After a few days, I continued. Flying from Guatemala to Panama is much like tracing your finger very, very slowly, all day long, over a very large map of Central America. Flying low over Lilliputian towns you see the colonial pattern of streets, parks, and plazas. At each capital, you have the feeling of descending with a magnifying glass until you are able to see buildings and people; and in this highly magnified world, you finally get off the plane and walk about the airport. When you return to the plane and fly away it all becomes a map again. Unlike maps, which are always pink, blue, and yellow, the color of all Central America is green—green and red. Green for the matted jungles, the open grazing fields, the banana plantations, and the dark mountains; red for the earth, exposed by heavy rains that keep the country green; red also for the house-tops, the tiled roofs of the towns, and the unpaved dirt roads which lie like ribbons between the green hills.

In those days, a month before Pearl Harbor, there was no blacking out of plane windows, and below at the end of the day appeared the Panama Canal. From the clear dry air of the upper levels you descend to the hot rain below; you pile into a taxi and head for a hotel in the drenched, sodden atmosphere. By contrast, the earth has become indeed earthy.

In Colombia I had a second opportunity to overcome time, space, and geography. The trip from Cali to Bogotá by train takes two days, if you make connections. The same trip by plane takes exactly one hour and a half! We first planned to leave Cali by train on Sunday and arrive in Bogotá on Tuesday. We decided to fly, left Cali late Sunday afternoon, and arrived in Bogotá in time for tea. Two more short flights of about an hour and a half each in Colombia saved a total of four days of train and bus travel—one from Bogotá to Medellín, and another from Medellín back to Cali.

But these small flights had none of the hemispheric significance of a four-day flight from Rio de Janeiro to Miami. I left Rio the morning of July 1, from Corrêa Lima's well-designed airport building at the airfield named for Santos Dumont, the Brazilian aviator who flew an airplane in public before the Wright brothers.

Looking back from the air, I see Sugar Loaf and Corcovado as islands in a sea of cotton fog. At noon we land 800 miles north at Barreiras where such twentieth-century comforts as ice water, hot coffee, and modern plumbing are contrasted with an eighteenth-century village on the lonely river's edge. Throughout the afternoon the silver, knife-edged wing of the plane slices through vague clouds and we arrive in a hot rain at Belém, just in time for a trial blackout.

Next morning, brown swimmers pull the Baby Clipper out to open water and we skim over the Amazon to the Guianas. This time no hills and valleys built of clouds are to be seen, but thousands of fluffy white kittens chase about the green below. Later, no kittens, but the blue-black mass of flooded tropic forest; sick shores, algae-infested, streaked and stained with odd, unpleasant colors. Crazy octopus arms of waterways come in from the sea. We roar down over the brown water at Cayenne, French Guiana, and pull up to a lone palm, lifeless in the heat. More brown swimmers pull us out to open water and we rise up high over Devil's Island. We stop at Paramaribo, in Dutch Guiana, Georgetown in British Guiana, and finally at Trinidad for the night.

The next is a day of stops at lovely islands—Martinique, Guadaloupe, Antigua, St. Thomas of the Virgin Islands, and at nightfall, San Juan, Puerto Rico. In the morning, the 4th of July, we make the easy, all-day flight from San Juan to Haiti, to Cuba, and over shallow turquoise water to Miami. After two minutes in the Immigration Headquarters, the health officer plunges a thermometer into our mouths while we meditate on the cleanliness, order, and wealth of the U.S.A. that come back to us with a rush after ten months' absence.

In the four days of that flight to Miami, I passed through places which for centuries had been separated by days of travel on wind-blown pirate vessels, were later drawn closer together by the invention of the steamship, and are now in the 20th century linked together as never before in history by a few hours of flight through the air. North and South America have suddenly moved together at a terrific rate of speed.

During the ten months I was away the luxury liner, symbol of our anaesthetized condition in the years between World Wars I and II, had been taken out of use, painted a dull gray, and mounted with guns. In its place eight planes a week fly from Rio to Miami where before there had been three; and, before that, one. These are the new facilities of wartime. When the war is over and new aviation facilities—airplane production, airfield and landing centers, pilots and technicians and planes—are all turned from war to peacetime use, the possibilities of increased air travel will become overwhelming. Latin Americans are today even more air-conscious than we. In a few hours' time they can get from one republic to another where before it took days of train and motor travel. Their mail and products can be moved faster. Most of the countries now have their own local air companies, which have not only replaced but improved the facilities which Italians and Germans operated until dangerously recent times within easy bombing range of the Panama Canal. Today, with the airplane an accepted fact in even the remotest sections, it takes no brave imagination to picture what tomorrow will bring. The ease and economy with which we will be able to fly north and south will indeed put Latin America in our front yard.

I saw the cities of North and South America as parts of two different worlds: for years, miles and centuries apart, today drawing together faster and faster. If we of the American hemisphere are to avoid a collision of interests it is obvious that, in a shrinking world, we must know and understand each other to the greatest possible degree. If through rapid air transportation we are brought together too quickly, without mutual understanding, friction may cause unnecessary fires. If we know the Latins well we can prevent this unnecessary type of difficulty from arising, and can successfully embark on a program of cooperation with them that will be mutually beneficial.

Wendell Willkie sums up what the airplane is doing to the globe in *One World*: * "There are no distant points in the world any longer. I learned . . . that the myriad millions of human beings of the Far East are as close to us as Los Angeles is to New York by the fastest trains. I cannot escape the conviction that in the future what concerns them must concern us, almost as much as the problems of the people of California concern the people of New York. Our thinking in the future must be world-wide." What Mr. Willkie has said of the globe is all the more true of the western hemisphere: we in the New World are naturally closer to each other than to the people of Asia, let us say. North and South America are swiftly becoming *One New World*.

2. Shrinking Globe—Effect: New Foreign Policy

If we take the airplane then as the chief cause of the shrinking of the globe, and grant the drawing together of the western hemi-

---

* *One World*, Wendell Willkie, Simon and Shuster, 1943.

sphere, then we must recognize the Number One effect to be the absolute necessity of revamping our former ideas of foreign policy. Our position in world affairs can no longer be side-stepped. Two factors—our technological advancement and World War II—have spotlighted our refusal in the past to assume leadership in freeing peoples from economic and political exploitation. Latin America, particularly, looks to us for leadership.

Economically, we cannot afford to continue our policy of taking much and giving little. A prosperous neighbor in South America is far more to our own interests than a poor one. Politically, we must spread our philosophy of freedom if we believe in it—the present war has shown us the cost of our failure to do so. We need to equip ourselves with new instruments to help us establish an effective foreign policy, based upon economic as well as political rights of man, and designed to compete with Fascist contributions, erase our own former blunders, and establish the principles of democracy we preach. Those instruments will require personnel trained for a new kind of leadership and representation not only in Latin America, but in all the world. To carry out an effective, socially-conscious foreign policy we need a new diplomacy—one that combines the best features of old-time diplomacy with the skills of the modern technician, planner, builder, organizer, cooperator, the thinker with long-range objectives. We need to rise above commercialism, even above well-meaning paternalism, and use our technical skill and economic experience to help raise the material well-being of the rest of the hemisphere.

A new foreign policy based on constructive assistance and the full use of technology can help us spread democracy faster than millions spent on good will. George Soule expresses what should be done: "Governments which are dedicated to raising standards of living everywhere can and should stimulate world production by an *international program* of road construction, housing, public health, and other projects."

Truly human objectives in hemisphere relations will be advantageous not to Latin America alone: benefits will accrue to both Latin America and the United States. We can learn as much from the Latin Americans as they can from us. Waldo Frank, in a public address given in San Francisco, spoke of the western hemisphere as two incomplete "half-worlds" that are essential to one another for complete maturity. Let us see what might be traded between the cities of North and South America to help raise standards of living.

3. What We Can Learn from Them

People have asked me many times, "But what can we learn from the Latin American cities? Where else in the world are there cities like New York or Chicago? Have we not the skyscrapers, the speed of the subway, the efficiency of new freeways, and homes for millions?" It is probably true that we have demonstrated the highest technical skill in the construction of our cities, but it is also true that we have shown disregard for the human being *in relation to the potentialities of that technical skill.* Daily, we ignore the costliness of built-in congestion, the permanent gloom of canyon-like streets, the inhumanity of profitable slums, the noise and unwholesomeness of crowded subways and street cars, the lack of trees, plants, and green spaces in large cities and small industrial towns. Our technical skill and our ability to provide facilities for living well have given us the greatest opportunity that any civilized group has ever had to build cities free of these urban fallacies. We haven't done so.

We have done the reverse. We have used our technical skill only to make habitable and sanitary to a tolerable degree—but no further—these intricate mazes which we call our great cities. Lewis Mumford, in "The Culture of Cities", says: * "Contrary to popular belief the growth of great cities preceded the decisive technical advances of the last two centuries. But the metropolitan phase became universal *only when the technical means of congestion had become adequate*—and their use profitable to those who manufactured or employed them. The modern metropolis is an outstanding example of a peculiar cultural lag within the realm of technics itself. . . ."

We have made the mistake of using our techniques to maintain congestion. We have defeated the very purpose of our political freedom by not making the most of our resources and technical ability. Now, this taken-for-granted technical skill which has made possible the building and operating of our gigantic cities, is far more sought after in Latin America, and is considered far more worthy of attainment there, than it is here in the U.S.A. Latin technicians feel that we haven't gone nearly far enough with our advanced technical development in building the kind of city that is possible for us to build. Many Latins think: "What *we* could do if we had the wealth and resources of the United States!"

But with nothing like the wealth and resources of the United States, Latin technicians have built, and are building, cities which outrank ours in the use of imagination and the provision of facilities for rich social living.

Thus we can learn from the Latins: to make our sterile cities more human, more habitable, more urbane. We can learn how satisfying are less material values, and we can give vigor to our still immature, newly-emerging culture. We can slow down our frantic pace,

* *The Culture of Cities*, by Lewis Mumford, Harcourt, Brace & Co., New York, 1938.

and reshape our cities for increased leisure and more pleasant living. We can use the cities of Latin America as a bridge to recapture some of those forgotten but coveted habits which our ancestors left behind in the cities of Europe. We can build into our own towns and our own lives those very things for which we travel thousands of miles on luxury liners, on which we spend thousands of dollars during the summer excursions we undertake in order to enjoy a brief escape from our technically "perfect" cities. We can treat ourselves to urban equipment essential to a way of life not unlike *The Latin American Way.*

Our own technical skill and advanced economic status can certainly make it possible to accomplish at least as many of these urban advantages as have the Latins. We certainly have it within our abilities to act with the boldness which motivates the Latins in opening new arteries like the Avenida 9 de Julio in Buenos Aires—there is no single recent work in the United States involving the tearing down of built-up areas that compares with this one alone. Among all of our cities built on bays or waterfronts, New York, Boston, Chicago, San Francisco or Seattle—not one can compare its waterfront treatment with that of Rio de Janeiro or Montevideo. And where is there one among all the cities of our West as boldly planned and built as Brazil's Goiania? The city planning attack on São Paulo exhibits a boldness of approach that no planner in any United States city has dared to show. São Paulo's program of modernization and reorganization of her civic facilities into an efficient, attractive scheme stands as an example of what may be gained by city planners and city builders in the United States out of closer contact and cooperation with South American technicians.

We can also learn from the Latins by studying their policies on the use of public resources, as public property, for the good of the people. Compare the community use of the beaches of Montevideo and Rio de Janeiro with privileged use at Miami Beach, Florida, or the beaches of the Los Angeles area. Too frequently we sell waterfront sites to individuals or clubs, for private use. At Miami Beach, only those who can afford to live in one of the hotels built on the beach side of the highway are entitled to easy access for swimming and an unbroken view of the sea. I once walked two blocks to find only a narrow opening to Miami Beach, because private hotels and apartments had been built so compactly along the beach side of the street. At Santa Monica Beach, near Los Angeles, one must belong to a special club or own a private home on the beach in order to swim and use what rightfully belongs to all people.

In Rio de Janeiro, in Montevideo, in every other Latin American seaside city which I visited, I found not a single case where private privilege had preference over public use of natural scenic areas. In Montevideo, not a single private building is allowed to break the crescent of beach and sand that lies along the Rambla, the seaside boulevard. In Rio de Janeiro, Avenida Atlantica and Copacabana Beach demonstrate a respect for nature quite lacking in similar developments in the United States. It is true that not all Rio's citizens can afford to rent apartments in the fifteen-story structures overlooking the crescent, but many can. Those who live elsewhere, even in the poorest *favella* or *vila* (not far distant!), have the view of an unbroken stretch of sea and the use of miles of sand and surf for absolutely nothing. In front of the Copacabana Palace Hotel, the lowliest worker, black, white, or tan, can sunbathe along with the highest diplomats. Yet we call ourselves democratic! On Copacabana Beach, blacks and whites mingle with absolute, unquestioned freedom. Since 1890 Brazil's census has made no distinctions as to Negro blood. This is democracy not in theory, but in practice.

In more specific ways, in the planning and housing field we can learn from Latin America. Their adaption of social security funds for housing purposes might well be applied in the United States as a means of making full use of those funds during the postwar period and at the same time providing necessary housing. Their *plus valia* system, which makes it possible for parks and boulevards to pay for themselves through increased values of adjoining properties, might well be adapted to financing postwar rehabilitation of blighted areas in the cities of the United States. In this urban redevelopment work we might also find useful Mexico City's system of Executive Committees made up of property owners from the area to be replanned. The aggressive work of the Montevideo planners in public education, research, and practical application can be a stimulus to similar groups in our cities. The Latins can help us in many ways to raise our own urban standard of living from a cultural, social, and even technical point of view.

4. What They Can Learn from Us

At the same time, closer cooperation on urban problems can make available to the Latins certain techniques in which we excel and for which they have a desperate need. Mutual benefits can result from the inter-American technical cooperation that exists now, during the war. These benefits can help greatly, after the war, to assist both North and South American technicians to replan and rebuild cities.

I must again emphasize how greatly Latin Americans envy the technical skill and industrial advancement that has made possible the building of our cities. The parts of their cities which have been built with imagination are a demonstration of what they might do with all parts of their cities when they have advanced to a higher degree of technical and industrial development.

Just how far behind us they are in this development is a difficult matter to put in black and white, but the following partial figures on technical proficiency and personnel of the United States compared with that of South America, taken from the National Roster of Scientific and Specialized Personnel, indicate their shortage of technical manpower.

NUMBERS OF PERSONS ENGAGED IN SCIENTIFIC AND PROFESSIONAL OCCUPATIONS, ARRANGED BY COUNTRIES

	U.S.A. (pop. about 130,000,000)	South America (Continent) (pop. about 90,000,000)	
Architecture	22,000	1,832	(excluding Paraguay)
Civil Engineering	102,000	1,827	(Argentina, Chile, Peru only)
Forestry	4,800	12	(Chile and Uruguay only)
Landscape Architecture	1,500	none	(*I found 3—F. V.*)
Social Welfare	31,000	40	(Chile only)

Although these figures are obviously incomplete, they do serve to indicate an acute shortage of technical personnel. With such a scarcity, full development of resources, both human and material, is impossible. Over and over again I was told by Latin technicians that the greatest thing the United States can offer is to show them how to organize, how to develop each particular country from a technological point of view. It is economic and technical assistance they want—cultural moves mean nothing to the man on the street, and only serve to demonstrate a defensive attitude on our part, as if we simply had to show them that we, too, are developed culturally. The advancement of their own industrial power through our assistance will be followed by a logical, spontaneous recognition of our own cultural achievements.

The first objective in our program of Latin American cooperation must be to make attainable a new standard of living based upon a broadened economy. Such an objective will provide opportunities for the exchange of ideas relating to city and regional planning and low-cost housing. I emphasize again the demand I found on the part of Latin Americans for material and data on our experience in these matters, and their pleas for more widespread technical training in engineering, construction, and sanitation, particularly in Ecuador and Bolivia, parts of Colombia, Peru, and even Brazil.

A well-rounded program of city and regional planning in Latin America cannot be achieved on the existing undeveloped background of limited planning legislation. It is true that in the United States laws enabling planning to be practiced by cities and states and supported by citizens are often more advanced than is the actual practice, but at least the basis is provided. Without that legislative basis at all levels of government there is no backbone for a long-range planning program. Legislation at the national level might permit or even *require* planning in towns and natural geograpic or social regions. Within these smaller units more detailed legislation could provide the democratic framework for increased zoning control of private property, better standards of land subdivision, building construction, and all other aspects of a master plan. The application of our democratic planning processes, the use of effective planning commissions which in reality represent the citizens, and the proper administration of land use plans, zoning laws, and housing and building codes, would not only serve a purpose in bringing up to date the cities of Latin America, but would also increase the practical application of democracy and further citizen participation in municipal and government affairs. The Latin republics could use well the application of more decentralized, initiative-giving housing laws—particularly in the larger countries, Brazil and Argentina.

Latin Americans need and want assistance in developing their resources to meet their own essential needs, but they also need and want the kind of *planned development* of resources that will make them economically and politically independent. We have experience to offer them in the technical and industrial fields, as we offered Russia during her post-revolutionary years, but we as well as they lack the experience in the *planning* of such development to meet real needs. We have many tools with which to plan, many of them not fully used. We are learning much during the war about scheduling production to meet certain objectives. We may also learn from Russia about the importance of thinking ahead in order to avoid wastes and losses. In the matter of future use of resources, future building of the equipment for our environment, all of us must learn *together* how to best plan to meet our needs.

Our own resources in the United States are no longer so plentiful that we can afford to develop them without planning of some sort; the resources which rightfully belong to Latin Americans have sometimes been as wantonly wasted as ours; other times they have gone undeveloped—in either case planning is essential to their effective use.

5. Let the Latins Speak

But let the Latin technicians speak for themselves as they spoke to me about typical urban problem with which they are confronted, and about the kind of assistance and cooperation they want from us, to help solve those problems. The Latins were always more anxious to talk over their problems with me than to boast of their achievements. They unfolded their ideas on the special kind of help they needed, as though I were some omnipotent representative of miraculous technical power, symbolizing the inventive and organizing ability of the United States. They look upon this intangible power of ours as capable of solving any problem whatever—once we set out to do so. From a technological point of view, they have put us on the spot! That is why they have such faith in our ability to combine planning and production for the purpose of defeating the Axis. Their faith in our initiative seemed such that they would have believed me if I had told them that we had under construction in the midst of Oklahoma, an inverted skyscraper resting on a single column two feet in diameter. Anything is possible in the U.S.A.!

Here is a cross-section of ideas suggested, in the interest of building better cities throughout the Americas, by those with whom I came in contact. Carlos Contreras of Mexico City contributed the idea of studying the problems of slum clearance and housing in his capital. He proposed to use semi-student personnel, young men half of whom would come from the United States and half from Mexico, and in this way bring into direct contact both groups on a working research basis. Mexicans and Americans would learn together the techniques of low-cost housing and at the same time reach a better mutual understanding. This principle could be applied in other republics—Chile, Argentina, or Brazil—and in other fields—soil conservation, forestry, or social welfare—as a practical experiment in cementing bonds of inter-Americanism in the technical fields. Young North Americans would gain perspective on their own country and learn new methods of working as well. Such a program could be carried out through joint cooperation of universities, research groups, and governments, both here and in Latin America.

Several Colombians with whom I spoke said that Colombia needs technicians to help her industrialize resources; they wanted that rather than the abstract good will of pre-Pearl Harbor days. They complained that we too frequently send them people who have too shallow an understanding of such basic needs.

One architect-engineer in Bogotá told me of an incident which illustrates the kind of understanding which not only Colombians but all Latin Americans expect from us. My friend had gone to our embassy to see what could be done about getting priority help on certain construction materials urgently needed to maintain employment in the building industry. One of our representatives, who had resided in Bogotá for a long time, said to him: "Why worry? Your workers can be employed in other industries around town." The Colombian builder asked, "What other industries?" The point was that, like many Latin American capitals, Bogotá had no other major industry than building and construction, and although this builder was a good friend of the United States and understood our intentions, he was annoyed at the fundamental misunderstanding which our representative showed of his country's real needs.

Since that incident took place, however, adjustments have been made; but the story does point out our weakness and their need for planned industrial development in the interests of economic independence. Because Colombia is growing up, economically and socially, faster than any other West Coast country, and because her people know and like the United States, they want technical help from us rather than from any European source.

Ecuador's builders stressed the need for trained workmen, carpenters—skilled technicians of all kinds—and schools in which to train them. One architect spoke of a non-constructive, standoff-ish attitude on our part while Germany has been constructively cooperative in the interests of the Ecuadorians and to her own interests as well. All Ecuadorians spoke of the need to equalize the monetary exchange: high prices in the United States and the low value of the sucre make it impossible for them to buy our products, building materials, or machinery for industrialization. This problem, they said, must be faced if the internal economy of Ecuador is to be brought up to 20th-century level. Miguel Albornoz, a young lawyer and writer, sums up Ecuador's needs as threefold: trained technicians of all kinds, assistance from the United States in the form of money and men, and adjustment of the international exchange.

Peruvian technicians stressed the desire for closer contact with the architectural, housing, and planning groups in the United States. They wanted to know more about our working methods, what kind of low-cost housing we were building in California, how structural practices differed from ours, and what we had done about the problem of maintenance and client education in our public housing projects. The planners of Lima wanted to know more about regional planning methods in Los Angeles and New York and what we had done by way of zoning that could be applied to their problems. They felt that closer contact with members of their profession in the United States would bring them in touch with the answers to these questions.

In Bolivia, Victor Paz Estenssoro,* a young Representative in Congress, summed up the needs of his country. First, a program for the planned development of agriculture in order that Bolivia may eat properly: 40 percent of the 19-year-old young men examined for army training in 1941 were found to be undernourished. Many people in Bolivia live on one meal a day—yet there is plenty of good land for crops if water were supplied. Second, development of dams to supply cheap electric power and water in large quantities for irrigation of dry, unused areas. Scarcity of fuel in Bolivia —coal and oil are not to be had cheaply—goes hand in hand with scarcity of water, but construction of dams would provide electric power, the cheapest of all, and at the same time store the needed water. Third, improvement of transportation. Roads need to be

---

* Victor Paz Estenssoro was one of the progressive, pro-democratic leaders in the December 20, 1943, *coup d'etat;* he was made Minister of Finance in the new government.

built into potentially productive areas to link them with existing growing and consuming areas, so as to provide more food at lower cost. Bolivia also needs easier access to the sea at Arica, the Chilean port which exists chiefly because of La Paz. Paz Estenssoro emphasized that, most of all, Bolivia must have an economic plan which will develop its agriculture and provide an economic base for the people rather than for the mines. To fulfill these needs, he said, Bolivia needs technical assistance and carefully placed loans from the United States.

Graciela Mandujano of Chile knows her country's housing problems well, and has travelled in the United States enough to know how we can best aid her country. She says that one of the best contributions we can make is in the form of technicians and technical information to show the Chileans how to do the job themselves. However, she told me we must remember that the United States is very much farther advanced socially than Chile and therefore technical material designed for our use might be too advanced for Chile. Such material must be elementary. For example, agricultural booklets sent to Chile on types of fertilizers used in the United States were useless because Chilean farmers first had to be convinced of the worth of using fertilizers at all. Miss Mandujano drew an analogy between our public works and slum clearance program during the New Deal and Latin America's need for bettering living conditions today. I felt that she exaggerated our achievements, but nevertheless she recognized the principle that when the United States found conditions in the cities were dragging down the whole national economic life, there was an effort to rehouse, rebuild, and create a new economic life for healthy citizens who would no longer be a drain on the community. Today, she said, Latin America is a poor relation who is more a burden than an asset. Encouraging the development of industry and construction of public works projects in Latin America will lead to a new economic life, and the well-being of the United States will advance because we will be assured both a market and a prosperous neighbor with whom to trade. Improved living conditions and increased consuming power in South America is far more than a mere philosophical need for us; it will give us better foreign markets for the many things we will still be able to make best. The United States cannot have a lasting prosperity with a poor, dependent South America. However, Miss Mandujano told me, the Latins would rather have independence and poverty than prosperity as an economic colony of the United States. Rather, we must use our technicians to raise the standard of living of South America in order to fulfil the meaning of democracy in the U.S.A. The war has put our democracy under scrutiny. Many in Chile told me that the war has brought the sympathy of the working classes closer toward the United States. For example, Chilean labor groups, which had been pro-Russian but unsympathetic toward the United States, have now changed their attitude and favor us as well. However, they want proof of our democracy.

Hector Vigil of Valparaiso voiced the opinion that the greatest help the United States can give Chile is economic aid. He would like to see loans made directly to cities in Chile for specific work to be done in accordance with stated technical standards, and under supervision by United States technicians. He also feels that mutual benefits are to be had through a program of cooperation in the planning field between North and South American technicians, and looks forward to some kind of permanent organization for that purpose.

Luis Migone of Argentina is a good friend of the United States, an architect and engineer, and is also a member of the American Society of Planning Officials. He states that Argentina needs to centralize and coordinate various planning and housing agencies. He told me, "Such centers could coordinate physical planning with industrial development. For example: standard plans and specifications for housing types could be developed in a single agency for use in various parts of the country. In the same way, population decentralization could be guided along with industrial development. Social needs like housing could be met by promoting forestry development and the wood industry. A program of reforestation is needed to stop the loss of our timber through over-cutting. In fact, what Argentina needs is a national planning agency. In the past our country has developed industrially, but in a wasteful, inefficient way."

In answer to my question: "What kind of a housing and planning program would you like to see in Argentina?" Migone said, "I would like to see a program like that of the United States; the establishment of a national planning board—similar to your National Resources Planning Board—as proposed by the *Centro de Ingenieros*. In housing I would like to see a national housing agency with government control of building standards as in the United States. Our excess funds in the banks need to be circulated. The United States has gone through many economic struggles, made many mistakes, and evolved a great deal by experience. Argentina must likewise develop, but we have the chance to profit by the errors of the United States.

"Send down material printed in Spanish to educate the people to understand the meaning of planning as a solution to problems, *and thus foster democratic planning*. We have a good middle-class to work with, but the people don't realize the need for a plan. They expect complications rather than simplifications because of past experience with government reforms and improvements. Show our people what you have actually done and let's develop an organized,

210

informed citizenry in order to get democratic action. We have practically no informed citizenry as yet in South America."

Migone says, in *Las Ciudades de los Estados Unidos*: "About a quarter of a century ago the great capitals of the United States were in worse condition from the point of view of planning than are in actuality Argentina's principal cities today." He indicates how our cities have been improved by the use of building and planning legislation, and how backward are the cities of Argentina in this respect, pointing out that codes mean nothing if the location of buildings as to use is not also taken into consideration.

Migone tells of the need in Argentina for the use of advanced technical legislation concerning zoning and building, as applied in the United States. Buenos Aires he says, with its many young *rascacielos* (skyscrapers) needs enforced legislation controlling volume as New York controls her tall buildings. The practical result of Migone's trip in the United States, his study of our legislation and publication of his above-mentioned book, has been a new zoning code, brought out in the spring of 1942—the only zoning and building laws in any South American city patterned directly after those of the United States.

And likewise in Brazil I was told of the need for technicians, for good schools in which to train them, and especially of the need for planning technicians. Many Brazilian technicians lamented the lack of a coordinated national policy on planning and housing practices. They would like to see legal steps taken to advance a consistent program of city and regional, state and national planning. Also, they voiced the need for a coordinated national policy on housing. The general feeling among them was that Brazil's future is potentially too great to jeopardize through wasteful, unguided progress. In this respect Brazil may well learn by our own past errors in building urban environment. She has that opportunity through the broad program of technical and economic cooperation which Brazil and the U.S.A. are carrying out together. But Brazil's needs would require a volume to list.

This is no more than a cross-section of many suggestions made to me by the Latins themselves, but it may indicate the kind of help technical groups expect of us. Such a truly constructive attitude as this is the only one that we, as a civilized democratic nation, fighting a war against the medieval minds of the Axis, can afford to take. No other is possible. The effort, the wealth, the energy that goes into this kind of cooperation during and after the war will help tremendously in making the cities of the entire western hemisphere the kind we Americans want them to be. The effort necessary to do this job, when geared to a new world-wide foreign policy, will be colossal, but actually small compared to that which would be required to put down future wars.

I repeat, Latin Americans recognize our technical ability as the best in the world, our standard of living as the highest, and they envy our many freedoms. They want technical assistance in order to raise their standard of living so that they may achieve democratic freedom. I emphasize again that low standards of living remain a threat to their democracy and to ours. As long as unhealthful, insanitary living conditions remain in the *conventillos* of Santiago and the *favellas* of Rio de Janeiro—slums, wherever they may exist in the Americas—real democracy can never gain a secure foothold. These are outposts of Nazi infiltration, the strongest arguments against the good neighbor policy. Our job is to see that Latin America gets out of the social and economic doldrums in which four centuries of exploitation have left her.

I summarize below specific objectives needed in bettering the urban environment, objectives which Latin American technicians with whom I spoke would like to see furthered by our program of inter-American cooperation:

1. An improved general standard of living reached through a program of urban and rural rehabilitation and establishment of wages at human levels.
2. A balanced development of resources owned by the Latins and planned specifically to meet the needs of the people.
3. Expanded facilities for training technical personnel.
4. The development of more complete building industries as part of an independent, industrialized economy.
5. Slum clearance—both urban and rural—and construction of housing to meet the needs of all income groups.
6. Construction of dams to develop cheap power and fuel, conserve water, and provide for irrigation.
7. Soil conservation through improved methods of farming.
8. Reforestation on a large scale, and development of a more usable, extensive lumber supply.
9. Highway and road construction; improvement of communications in undeveloped interior regions.
10. Equalization of monetary exchange to permit purchase of machinery and other needed equipment from the United States.

6. What We Can Do About It

How can we achieve these objectives in Latin America and at the same time benefit ourselves? What role can the technician play within our existing inter-American program?

I list below ten ways in which technical service and knowledge may be interchanged between the twenty-one American republics, in order to accomplish our objectives. They are predicated on the belief that such a program requires two-way cooperation, based upon the principle that we have as much to learn from Latin America as that part of the New World has to learn from us. These ideas are also predicated on the belief that private, group action in matters of inter-Americanism count for more than official, governmental action.

Briefly stated below, and expanded later, are some of the things we can do:

1. Encourage many more technical fellowships for students in universities, and provide similar methods for interchange of professors for teaching and study.
2. Establish a tourist dollar after the war, to make possible travel in the United States on a large scale by Latin Americans, technicians and others.
3. Create exchange positions in both public and private organizations which will permit technical personnel in the United States and Latin America to be traded for limited periods of time.
4. Interchange professional services through special consultation assignments and inter-American competitions for planners, architects, engineers, and other technicians.
5. Augment the technical missions on economics, road building, agriculture, etc., already operating in our embassies in Latin America.
6. Form special commissions composed of Latin American and North American personnel on housing, resources, and urban planning methods, to prepare for postwar action.
7. Establish committees on inter-American cooperation in technical organizations for the purpose of maintaining closer professional ties throughout the hemisphere.
8. Encourage exchange of published technical data and the translation of some of that data.
9. Provide loans to Latin American cities for public works programs.
10. Activate citizens' groups and labor organizations to take a greater part in inter-American affairs relating to increased effectiveness of technical services.

It is true that such a program as this cannot be carried out by any one group alone, but requires the support of all of those now working and gaining valuable experience in the field of Latin American affairs. These include the Office of the Coordinator of inter-American Affairs, the State Department, Pan-American Union, other public and semi-public agencies, and many technical organizations, citizens' groups, and universities. Many of these types of activities are already being practiced now, during the war; many of them are not new; most of them have been suggested by Latin Americans themselves.

1. EDUCATIONAL INTERCHANGE. The younger people in the technical fields are anxious to come to the United States to study at Harvard University, Columbia, or M.I.T., where years ago the schools of Paris and other European centers were their Meccas. I was constantly asked for information about technical training in the United States. We technicians have an excellent opportunity to strengthen our future bonds with southern neighbors by assisting these young men and women to study in our universities in large numbers. At the same time, our students should realize the benefits to be derived from studying in South American schools such as the University of Chile in Santiago, the *Facultad de Arquitectura* in Montevideo, and others. A year of such foreign study will give the North American student an opportunity to know conditions of living in Latin America, learn another language, and best of all, to become thoroughly acquainted with our *simpáticos* neighbors.

Arrangements should also be made in universities, both here and in Latin America, for a wider exchange of professors and teachers. Professional people in architecture, planning, and related fields should be invited to teach in our universities, and we should send more of ours to Latin America.

2. TOURIST DOLLAR. It will be most important to make it possible for the Latin Americans, particularly technicians and professional people, to travel in the United States in large numbers. This could be done after the war by the establishing a "tourist dollar," on which the visitor to our country could travel here with the buying power of his own country. At present the average Latin American visitor generally finds living costs two to three times as high in this country as in his own, because of the difference in monetary exchange.

The advantages of actual travel in our country were pointed out to me by many with whom I talked. Those who had toured the United States were always stimulated by our methods of urban planning and wanted to make use of them in their countries. Ricardo Olano, who came to Washington thirty-five years ago, on his return sold planning to his city of Medellín, Colombia, and has worked ever since to make Medellín a city planned like our capital. Luis Gomez Vargas, a young planning engineer in Bogotá, traveled in the United States for three or four months and gathered enough ideas to keep him busy for years in Bogotá. But he wants to take time out for a second visit to the States. David Azambuja, landscape architect of Rio de Janeiro, has a complete file of photos and plans of parks, subdivisions, and gardens which he collected while traveling in the United States. As a result of his visit, he is trying to establish in Brazil a landscape profession patterned after ours.

We, ourselves, shall undoubtedly travel a great deal more in Latin America after the war, but we must do so with a higher purpose and with sharper objectivity than we did before World War II, if we are to profit by our past errors.

3. INTERCHANGE OF PERSONNEL. A program of technical exchange positions could be developed in public agencies connected with soils, planning, housing, and other subjects. For example, an expert on agricultural housing might go from one of the government agencies in the United States to take the place of a man doing similar work for the government in Chile. Each would work in the other's position for a limited length of time and in this way come into contact with actual practice and methods of work. I believe this type of program has already been put into practice, among industrial firms, by the Office of the Coordinator of Inter-American Affairs.

Technicians who have worked in the United States and know our methods generally return to their own country to introduce similar practices. Carlos Mathews of Santiago, Chile, had been at the University of California in the College of Agriculture, where he worked with Walter Weir, the soil expert. During my visits to the office of the *Caja de Colonización Agricola,* where Mathews is now employed, I saw charts and maps upon which Weir's methods of soil classification were actually being applied.

4. PROFESSIONAL INTERCHANGE. There is no reason why we should not overcome the barriers of lingual difficulties and nationalist tendencies to make more international use of professional services in technical fields. Planning consultants of Latin American cities might indeed contribute much to postwar plans for—say—Chicago, San Francisco, or Syracuse; and at the same time our architectural, planning, and engineering technicians might be called upon for assignments in Latin American cities like Rio de Janeiro, Santiago, or Medellín. In fact, the new Nutibara Hotel in Medellín has been designed by architect Paul Williams of Los Angeles. Why should not cities in Florida or California call upon the imaginative designers of Brazil for hotels, theaters, or public buildings? Harland Bartholemew of St. Louis was once invited to Bogotá, Colombia, to act in the capacity of planning consultant. But I know of no instance where a Latin American planner has been called to a city in the U.S.A. for a similar reason.

5. EXPANDED TECHNICAL MISSIONS. Most of our embassies in Latin American cities have established technical missions during the last few years, for the purpose of studying economic, agricultural, military, and other problems. The opportunities for furthering technical cooperation through these channels are becoming larger as the Latin American governments come into closer contact with our technicians. These missions should be expanded in

those technical fields bearing upon housing, resources development, and urban planning.

6. COMMISSIONS ON POSTWAR PROBLEMS. Special commissions composed chiefly of Latin American technicians might be formed in each country, for the purpose of research and action on problems of housing, resources, and urban planning. Through our embassies the United States might contribute consultant advice and technical aid to such commissions, which should be empowered to make plans now, during the war, for immediate postwar action. For example, a commission on the housing problem in Brazil could survey the extent of conditions, determine how many dwellings are needed, where and for what income groups. It could determine what industries and what building materials are needed, and lay out the successive steps to be taken in solving that country's housing problem on a truly comprehensive scale.

Such commissions might use Contreras' idea, outlined earlier, which would bring together young Mexican and North American student-technicians to study housing problems in Mexico City, and to make plans for their solution. Commissions may also be established to provide *international* planning procedures, in such areas as the Caribbean, or in Central America, where common problems need joint solutions.

7. INTER-AMERICAN PROFESSIONAL COOPERATION. Committees on inter-American cooperation within our professional organizations could be particularly effective in maintaining contact, because such activities would be unofficial in nature. Some of these organizations have already taken steps in that direction; the American Institute of Architects and the American Society of Planning Officials are two that I happen to know about. Others which might take similar action, if they have not yet done so, are the National Association of Housing Officials, the American Society of Civil Engineers, the National Planning Association, and others. These committees could accomplish much through closer contact with professional people throughout the Americas. They could invite and encourage Latin Americans to take membership in their organizations; act as centers for distribution of technical data; assist in providing technical fellowships or exchange positions. Many opportunities present themselves for promoting closer professional relations between North and South American technicians through the activities of such committees. Hector Vigil of Valparaiso, Chile, suggested the establishment in Chile of a permanent committee of the American Society of Planning Officials, to be made up of men from each important city in that country for the purpose of forming a nucleus and instrument for technical cooperation. Similar groups could be formed in other countries to work closely with organizations in the United States.

Philip Goodwin's recent study of modern architecture in Brazil *
is a typical example of the kind of thing that goes a long way toward providing understanding in a technical field. A recognition by
the United States of the best works of capable Brazilian architects
has gone far to bring closer together the members of that profession in Brazil and in the U.S.A.

Such committees could also perform an important service in
promoting inter-American technical conferences like those which
have already been successful in introducing professional men.
Among those already held have been the two Inter-American Congresses on Municipalities—one in Havana, Cuba, the other in Santiago, Chile, in 1941. These did a great deal to introduce North and
South American technicians to one another and to stimulate sustained programs of contact by exchange of ideas, manpower, and
students. Immediately after the war, a third such congress on
urban problems should be held in the United States. The first Pan-
American Congress on Popular Housing was held in Buenos Aires
in 1939. It was agreed at that Congress to hold a second, in Washington, D.C., and many times I was asked why the United States
had not taken further action in making necessary preparations for
another meeting.

Following is a detailed outline of the type of inter-American
activity which an association of technicians might adopt:

A. Prepare a directory of Latin American technicians (in the
   particular field) to be published in the U.S.A.
B. Compile a directory of agencies and offices in Latin America.
C. Circulate bibliographies of books, reports, etc., published in
   the field.
D. Translate important books, reports, etc., on the subject into
   Spanish, Portuguese, or English.
E. Send out monthly bulletins in Spanish and Portuguese on
   activities in the particular fields in the U.S.A.
F. Promote fellowships for study in technical schools.
G. Procure professorships for lecturing in universities.
H. Arrange exchange positions.
I. Assist employment of technicians on a consulting basis.

I have shown how South American technicians look to the United
States as the leader in technical matters and how they want that
kind of help and cooperation. Mr. Jacob Crane of the National
Housing Agency stated upon his return from Santiago's Congress
of Municipalities in 1941 that "South Americans are very eager
to interchange information and to learn from our experience."

* *Brazil Builds,* by Philip L. Goodwin, Museum of Modern Art, New York,
N.Y., 1943.

This statement can be backed by the similar experience of the author, gained in visiting housing officials throughout Latin America. I cannot overemphasize how consistent were the requests for data and information, nor how frequent were the suggestions for establishing some means of permanent contact between North and South Americans in the housing and planning fields. Dr. Raul Migone of Argentina's Ministry of Foreign Relations, who has been active in housing on an international basis, suggested the establishment of an Inter-American Commission on Planning and Housing—a sort of clearing house for bringing together technicians for interchange of ideas and techniques.

A committee on planning could assist in the formation of such a clearing house on planning, housing, and other aspects of urbanism, from the national level on down to the village—in all of the Americas. The organization could be useful in the dissemination of published material from the U.S.A. into the offices, libraries, and schools of Latin America. Traveling exhibits could be prepared showing the work of technicians and students of both Latin America and the U.S.A. Inter-American Congresses could be held.

8. INTERCHANGE OF TECHNICAL DATA. An important activity of our program must be the exchange of technical data and the translation of such data into the three chief languages of the Americas, English, Spanish, and Portuguese. I was constantly asked for assistance in obtaining specific technical data on some special phase of planning, housing, or city development in the United States. Salvador Arroyo of Mexico City's Master Plan office requested copies of planning reports of New York and Los Angeles. Ignacio Angel of Medellín's planning office was anxious to obtain material on master plan techniques in our cities. Antonio Russo of the housing department of Ecuador's social security agency wanted material on low-cost dwelling construction in the United States. Fermín Bereterbide of Buenos Aires asked for data on methods of financing the Kansas City parkways, and for data on the Los Angeles Regional Plan. These were only a few of the many requests which came to me along the way.

Here in the United States, we may also profit by obtaining information about the public works and city planning projects of the Latins. Postwar planning developments should be extensive in the United States and we may well be stimulated by the imagination of the Latin Americans in such work.

There is a need for translating some urban planning laws of the United States for use in Latin America and their writing on urbanism should be available in English. We need to disseminate all kinds of printed information having to do with planning, housing, health, and sanitation in all the schools, libraries, and technical offices in both North and South America.

9. CAREFULLY PLACED LOANS. An older method of assistance, used many times in the past by the United States, has been that of providing loans to governments for public improvements in Latin America. I have stated before how Hector Vigil, of Valparaiso, Chile, suggested that loans might be made directly to municipalities, but with the stipulation that the development be carried out under standards laid down by United States technicians. This sort of thing has already been done by us, in relation to the construction of sections of the Pan-American Highway in Central America and Ecuador; and in numerous projects of international importance.

10. CITIZENS' GROUPS—LABOR ORGANIZATIONS. A program of co-operation which springs from the people themselves is bound to be more effective than one receiving artificial stimulation from government and commercial circles. For this reason citizens' groups such as the Pan-American League, Pan-American Society, and others in both the United States and Latin America can play an important part in our program of technical cooperation.

Another potential group representing large sections of the citizenry are labor organizations, which could be particularly effective in working with similar trade groups in Latin America to see that technical schools and training are provided, and that more extensive use is made of technicians' services which affect the public welfare. Our own CIO and AFL leaders at present maintain contact with the CTAL (*Confederación de Trabajadores de América Latina*) Latin America's most progressive body representing labor, through the President, Vicente Lombardo Toledano. In the postwar period these hemisphere labor groups can achieve much, by working even more closely together, toward improving housing and other conditions discussed in earlier chapters.

Some of these suggestions, if carried out within our program, would serve to give Latin America freedom from foreign influences and act as the beginning of a democracy that will make possible the kind of environment worthy of the New World and the twentieth century. An enormous gap, between rich resources on the one hand and social needs on the other, must be overcome before we can expect South America to be free of foreign influence and economically independent. She must be freed of her slums—the *conventillos, favellas*, and *cortiços* of Santiago, Rio de Janeiro, and São Paulo.

In the ten years of its existence, the good neighbor policy has already accomplished a great deal in the directions of many of these activities discussed above, but little has yet been done in the fields of housing and planning. It would be to the interest of that policy to encourage a widespread program of low-cost housing in Latin America. This alone would give a tremendous boost to economic development, particularly to the building industries. We could assist hemisphere security through establishing democratic standards for development—whether of resources or of cities—according to a rational plan. A good neighbor policy more closely tied to the principle of *planning* to meet social needs of all kinds will go far toward proving our intentions in Latin America to the 85,000,000 good neighbors who live without houses.

7. More Than Win the War

Our cooperation with Latin America during the war has matured. We long ago discarded movie stars and swing bands as ambassadors, and replaced them with practical economic, military, and technical representatives. Collaboration along these lines was furthered by the Rio Conference, and as a result our embassies in Latin American capitals have many economic and technical missions which, of course, are now primarily concerned with winning the war. Latin America, herself, is doing a huge share of work in the prosecution of the war, and most of our inter-American agencies and organizations are concentrating chiefly on that phase of Latin American affairs. Never before have we been in such close contact with our neighbors as now, during World War II, and never before have we sent North Americans in such large groups, or for such a varied number of reasons, to Latin America. And, as we have seen, we are now offering the kind of cooperation the Latins want of us.

But we will not win them merely by winning the war. We must remember that two-thirds of Latin America is ill-clothed, ill-housed, ill-fed. They know this themselves; and so did the Germans, who, in Chile and Brazil developed agriculture and small industries, built whole cities like Joinville, Brazil, and Valdivia, Chile, which take the lead in demonstrating higher standards of living. We must make the most of our wartime cooperation, and *after* the war coordinate our present activities into a long-range hemisphere plan for an all-out attack on the bad housing, the undernourishment, and the poverty of the two-thirds of Latin America. That hemisphere plan must be based on attaining in living reality true freedom for all the Americas. But the plan cannot be carried out overnight, nor without preparation. Stuart Chase (in the "Wake Up America" debates) has said that although "Freedom from Want" *is* possible in the United States today, and that it *would be* possible in Europe under a federation of commonwealths, it *is not yet* possible "for Asia, Africa, South America—not in 1940. Maybe in 1980. Freedom from want is possible only where the big machines and the high-powered tranmission lines hum."

Big machines and high-powered tranmission lines are only attainable through economic and technical advancement; herein lies the technician's responsibility in Latin America. The practical application of such a policy on an intensive, comprehensive scale would

220

result in a new development of agriculture made possible by a combined program of water and soil conservation, power and road development. The snow and rainfall of the Andes, if stored in dams to supply fuel and power, would also irrigate land that is now dry though fertile. Ecuador and Peru could once again be as rich and productive as they were during the times of the Incas; the Indian of today would be restored to his former noble state; and the feudal pattern of agricultural life could be replaced by one that is more human, efficient, and productive. The Andes could be reforested with trees adapted to conditions, for the use of generations to come. The wealth of the copper and tin mines of the Andes, if invested in dams, power lines, and roads to dot the West Coast with a whole chain of TVAs, would open up a new life for the millions of inhabitants of those resourceful mountains.

In the past, we have in many ways been followers rather than leaders. We believed that we could set the example of democracy and let the rest of the world follow, but that, we found, was not leadership. Instead, Hitler took the lead in spreading the reverse of democracy in Spain, in Finland, and especially in Latin America. In the future, if we believe in the democracy we preach at home, we must not be afraid to take leadership boldly away from our enemies even during peacetime, and to fight not only for democracy but *with* it. This is what Latin Americans expect of us. They look to us for leadership in the peace to follow World War II.

Henry Wallace speaks of this peace in his famous "Century of the Common Man" address delivered to the Free World Association, May 8, 1942: (The italics are my own.) "The peace must mean a better standard of living for the common man, not merely in the United States and England, but also in India, Russia, China, and *Latin America.* . . . Older nations will have the privilege to help younger nations get started on the path to industrialism but there must be *neither military nor economic imperialism.*

"The methods of the nineteenth century will not work in the people's century which is now about to begin. India, China, and *Latin America* have a tremendous stake in the people's century. As their masses learn to read and write, and as they become productive mechanics, their standard of living will double and treble. Modern science, when devoted wholeheartedly to the general welfare, has in it potentialities of which we do not yet dream. . . ."

8. A Good Neighborhood for Good Neighbors

Today, at the beginning of another great period in the history of the Americas, we have it in our power to look ahead and build cities worthy of free men. Complex factors have today made it possible to produce food, dwellings, clothing, and all environmental necessities in such quantity that *our* potentialities, in contrast to the labored methods of the Middle Ages, seem nothing short of miraculous. Our efforts in the task of removing from the face of the earth the barbarism which runs loose from Berlin to Tokyo have demonstrated our ability to produce and to cooperate. After the war, we have only to turn this ability to peacetime needs.

In doing so, there will be benefits to be gained by all. Both North and South America can achieve a greater security based on a mutually strengthened democracy and a renewed faith in our common heritage in the New World. Today, joined together by the threat against that heritage, we have it in our power to achieve a fuller security providing higher degrees of racial, economic, and political democracy. We will then have no more wars of nerves with any Hitler; and the security promised in the Atlantic Charter will be a reality for the common man, whether he lives in Alabama, Peru, or Puerto Rico.

We who live in the United States will gain cities equipped for a richer culture. Close contact with the imagination and the sensitivity of the Latins will encourage us to rebuild our cities at a more human and rational scale, better equipped for our people's life, work, and play.

Those who live in Latin America will gain more healthful and efficient cities and a higher general standard of living, based upon a more independent economy. There will be less differentiation of social and economic levels, and a more intensive use of resources.

The vital forces that can make possible these new cities are modern technology and science, the application of rational democratic planning, plus the drive and vitality of youth. The full use of all resources—human as well as physical—in the reconstruction of the cities of the Americas can produce a new economic life that would surpass even that of wartime and bring a more stable, constructive prosperity, a new vigor, to our cities and their urban populations.

In turning this power toward the objectives of peace, we cannot afford to restrain ourselves by a fear that advancement of higher material standards of living means the end of spiritual life for man. In fact, it can mean the beginning. Spiritual life and religion were, in less advanced ages—and are even today, in parts of the hemisphere—mere opiates to make bearable the misery of an existence on earth marked by mass poverty, disease, and ignorance. We must have the courage to move ahead to a new period, in which elevated material standards of living in all parts of the hemisphere, even of the globe, may be accepted as normal; and religion may be released to fulfill its higher function. Society will then be free to progress toward a spiritual life and true civilization based on a positive, scientific understanding rather than on the negative, fearful superstitions of the past.

But the raising of material standards of living need not mean the spreading to all corners of the hemisphere the cultural mediocrity of a middleclass whose aims are no higher than the electric refrigerator, the streamlined bathroom, or the first television instrument. Some ask, why raise the standard of living of people in backward sections of Mexico or Peru? Are they not happy with their quaint songs, their native arts and crafts? Why not leave them alone? Why worry about the carefree Chilean *roto* and Mexican *pelado*? I have only to call attention to the disease and dirt, the ignorance and exploitation which take an unnecessary toll of lives each year. Tile bathrooms and high standards of health and cleanliness *can* go hand in hand with the folk songs and traditions of cultural and spiritual life, if we act intelligently, with those objectives in mind. Some countries have done this. Norway and Sweden have accomplished a higher general distribution of material standards than has the United States, and while doing so have maintained in reality a high level of popular art and culture.

The raising of standards of living is in itself, to a certain extent, a spiritual endeavor expressing, in a practical way, an awareness of the other fellow. Where the past has been an age of colonization, invention, and exploitation, we may now embark upon a period of intensification, stabilization, and cooperative understanding. Our technological ability today makes possible, even imperative, the actual practice—rather than the preaching—of consideration for one's fellow man, for we can achieve the realization of our objectives on a large scale in a brief period of time. Through our cooperative, understanding efforts we can see sordid slums torn down and new homes built in spacious settings of green lawns and trees. We can watch entire cities being rebuilt and follow the consequent rehabilitation of young people as they grow up in a truly New World, which will offer opportunities for new forms of pioneering, and fresh fields for adventure.

Appendix A: Principal Latin American Cities

Following are population figures for one hundred Latin American cities. These include all those with populations over 1,000,000; all, over 500,000 and a selection of other principal cities. (Statistics from the Inter-American Statistical Yearbook, edited by Raul C. Migone; Macmillan Co., New York, 1942)

City	Country	Population
Buenos Aires	Argentina	2,542,000
Rio de Janeiro	Brazil	1,711,000
Mexico City	Mexico	1,456,000
Sao Paulo	Brazil	1,120,000
Montevideo	Uruguay	770,000
Santiago	Chile	696,000
La Havana	Cuba	569,000
Lima	Peru	521,000
Rosario	Argentina	517,000
Recife	Brazil	473,000
Bahia	Brazil	364,000
Bogota	Colombia	330,000
Porto Alegre	Brazil	322,000
Belem	Brazil	293,000
Cordoba	Argentina	274,000
Guadalajara	Mexico	228,000
Caracas	Venezuela	203,000
La Paz	Bolivia	200,000
Valparaiso	Chile	193,000
Monterrey	Mexico	181,000
Guayaquil	Ecuador	180,000
Guatemala	Guatemala	177,000
Asuncion	Paraguay	177,000
San Juan	Puerto Rico	169,000
Medellin	Colombia	168,000
Belo Horizonte	Brazil	168,000
Barranquilla	Colombia	152,000
Quito	Ecuador	150,000
Sante Fe	Argentina	149,000
Tucuman	Argentina	149,000
Fortaleza	Brazil	143,000
Puebla	Mexico	137,000
Maceio	Brazil	129,000
Panama	Panama	127,000
Niteroi	Brazil	125,000
Managua	Nicaragua	118,000
Curitiba	Brazil	117,000
Port-au-Prince	Haiti	115,000
Mendoza	Argentina	111,000
Maracaibo	Venezuela	110,000
San Salvador	El Salvador	108,000
Santiago	Cuba	107,000

City	Country	Population
Ponce	Puerto Rico	105,000
Cali	Colombia	102,000
Joao Pessoa	Brazil	101,000
Santa Clara	Cuba	100,000
Merida	Mexico	98,000
Port of Spain	Trinidad	93,000
Sancti Spiritus	Cuba	92,000
Santa Ana	El Salvador	89,000
Manaos	Brazil	89,000
Leon	Mexico	86,000
Manizales	Colombia	86,000
Cartagena	Colombia	85,000
Tampico	Mexico	81,000
San Luis Potosi	Mexico	78,000
Concepcion	Chile	78,000
Torreon	Mexico	77,000
San Jose	Costa Rica	76,000
Parana	Argentina	76,000
Callao	Peru	75,000
Ciudad Trujillo	Dominican Republic	71,000
Vera Cruz	Mexico	71,000
Colon	Panama	66,000
Kingston	Jamaica	63,000
Ibague	Colombia	61,000
Chihuahua	Mexico	57,000
Antofagasta	Chile	54,000
Cochabamba	Bolivia	52,000
Pachuca	Mexico	52,000
Bucuramanga	Colombia	51,000
Saltillo	Mexico	50,000
Pasto	Colombia	50,000
Vina del Mar	Chile	49,000
Tegucigalpa	Honduras	47,000
Iquique	Chile	46,000
Arequipa	Peru	46,000
Oruro	Bolivia	45,000
Talca	Chile	45,000
Iquitos	Peru	40,000
Cuzco	Peru	40,000
Villa Rica	Paraguay	40,000
Potosi	Bolivia	36,000
Temuco	Chile	36,000
Chiclayo	Peru	35,000
Valdivia	Chile	34,000
Paysandu	Uruguay	31,000
Salto	Uruguay	30,000
Talcahuano	Chile	28,000
Sucre	Bolivia	28,000
Ambato	Guatemala	25,000
Magallanes	Chile	24,000
Granada	Nicaragua	22,000
Ayacucho	Peru	20,000
Rio Bamba	Ecuador	19,000
San Pedro	Honduras	18,000
Latacunga	Ecuador	18,000
Limon	Costa Rica	17,000
Chinandega	Nicaragua	16,000
Los Cayos	Haiti	12,000

Appendix B: Bibliography

The following publications are included here to augment the information given in this book; these are grouped under two separate headings: (1) *Books*, and (2) *Reports, Pamphlets and other publications*. Most of the *Books* are of a general character and the author has included only those which relate especially, either in whole or in part, to the cities of the Latin-American countries. Most of them have been published in the United States, but there are undoubtedly many more pertinent works published in Latin America which should be included. The list of *Reports, Pamphlets and other Publications* was prepared for the most part from technical material gathered in Latin America by the author. Both lists should be considered as only partially representative of the published material relating to planning, housing and architecture in Latin America, but it is hoped that this Bibliography may serve as a nucleus for the formation of a larger, more complete one.

In preparing the *Bibliography*, the author found an abundance of general information on Latin America, but a scarcity of data of a more detailed nature, thus suggesting the need for a larger number of works dealing with specific regions, the particular problems and specialized characteristics of the Latin-American countries.

Books

Carleton Beals, *America South*, J. B. Lippincott Co., New York, 1937.

———, *Rio Grande to Cape Horn*, Houghton Mifflin, Boston, 1943.

R. H. Bonnycastle, *Spanish America* or a Descriptive, Historical and Geographical Account of the Dominions of Spain in the Western Hemisphere, Philadelphia, 1819.

Carl Brunner, *Manual de Urbanismo*, Volumes I and II, Imprenta Municipal, Bogotá, Colombia, 1939.

Alejandro E. Bunge, *Una Nueva Argentina*, Guillermo Kraft, Buenos Aires, 1940.

Stuart Chase, *Mexico: A Study of Two Americas*, Macmillan Co., New York, 1933.

Stephen Duggan, *The Two Americas: An Interpretation*, Charles Scribner's Sons, New York, 1934.

Erna Fergusson, *Chile*, Alfred A. Knopf, New York, 1943.

Waldo Frank, *America Hispana: A Portrait and a Prospect*, Charles Scribner's Sons, New York, 1931. (Re-issued in 1939 as *South of Us*.)

———, *South American Journey*, Duell, Sloan and Pearce, New York, 1943.

Philip L. Goodwin, *Brazil Builds; Architecture New and Old, 1652-1942*, Museum of Modern Art, New York, 1943.

Philip Leonard Green, *Our Latin American Neighbors*, Hastings House, New York, 1941.

———, *Pan American Progress*, Hastings House, New York, 1942.

Earl P. Hanson, *Chile: Land of Progress*, Reynal and Hitchcock, New York, 1943.

Frank Henius, *The ABC of Latin America*, David McKay, Philadelphia, 1942.

Samuel Guy Inman, *Latin America, Its Place in World Life*, Willett, Clark and Co., New York, 1937.

Preston James, *Latin America*, Lothrop Lee and Shepard, New York, 1942.

Vera Kelsey, *Brazil in Capitals*, Harper and Bros., New York, 1942.
P. A. Means, *The Ancient Civilizations of the Andes*, Charles Scribner's Sons, New York, 1931.
Luis V. Migone, *Las Ciudades de los Estados Unidos*, Editorial El Ateneo, Buenos Aires, Argentina, 1940.
Raúl C. Migone and others, *Inter-American Statistical Year Book*, Macmillan Co., New York, 1942.
Nicolas Besio Moreno, *Buenos Aires, Estudio Critico de Su Poblacion*, 1536-1936, Buenos Aires, 1939.
Dana Gardner Munro, *The Latin American Republics: A History*, D. Appleton-Century Co., New York, 1942.
Robert S. Platt, *Latin America: Countrysides and United Regions*, Whittlesey House, New York, 1943.
William H. Prescott, *The Conquest of Mexico* and *The Conquest of Peru*.
Luis Quintanilla, *A Latin American Speaks*, Macmillan Co., New York, 1943.
John Lyon Rich, *The Face of South America: An Aerial Traverse*, American Geographical Society, New York, 1942.
Juan A. Scasso, *Espacios Verdes*, Facultad de Arquitectura, Montevideo, Uruguay, 1941.
John Steinbeck, *The Forgotten Village*, Viking Press, New York, 1941.
John Reese Stevenson, *The Chilean Popular Front*, University of Pennsylvania Press, Philadelphia, 1942.
Watt Stewart and Harold F. Peterson, *Builders of Latin America*, Harper and Bros., New York, 1942.
Benjamín Subercaseaux, *Chile: A Geographic Extravaganza*, Macmillan Co., New York, 1943.
Emilio Villanueva, *Urbanismo*, José Gitschtaler, La Paz, Bolivia, 1939.

Pamphlets, Reports and other Publications

GENERAL

"Publications and Reports of the First Inter-American Congress of Municipalities, La Havana, Cuba, November 14 to 19, 1938."
"Publications and Reports of the Second Inter-American Congress of Municipalities, Santiago, Chile, September 15 to 21, 1941."
"Publications and Reports of the First Pan-American Congress on Low Cost Housing, Buenos Aires, Argentina, October 2 to 7, 1939."
"Actas y Trabajos," Volumes I and II, First Pan-American Congress on Low Cost Housing, Ministerio de Relaciones Exteriores y Culto, Buenos Aires, 1940.
"Bibliography and Guide to Literature on Housing in Latin America," Division of Foreign Housing Studies, New York City Housing Authority, 1939.
"Housing Agencies in Chile and Argentina: Functions and Organization," Division of Foreign Housing Studies, New York City Housing Authority, 1940.
"Bulletin of the Pan American Union," issued monthly, Washington, D.C.
"International Glossary of Technical Terms Used in Housing and Town Planning," 16th International Congress on Planning and Housing, Mexico, 1938.
Lewis L. Lorwin, "National Planning in Selected Countries," National Resources Planning Board, Washington, D.C., August, 1941.

ARGENTINA

"La Vivienda Popular," Publications Nos. 1 and 2, First Pan-American Congress on Low Cost Housing, Buenos Aires, 1939.
"Record of Proceedings, Volumes I and II," First Pan-American Congress on Low Cost Housing, Ministerio de Relaciones Exteriores y Culto, Buenos Aires, 1940.
"Publications and Reports of the Comisión Nacional de Casas Baratas" (National Housing Commission), Buenos Aires.

Raúl C. Migone, "Politica de la Vivienda Popular," Buenos Aires, 1941.
"El Momento Actual de la Construcción," Unión Argentina de Asociaciones de Ingenieros, Buenos Aires, 1941.
Carlos M. della Paolera, "Proposals of the City Planning Department of the City of Buenos Aires," Instituto Cultural Argentino-Norteamericano, Buenos Aires, 1938.
Carlos M. della Paolera, "La Avenida Nueve de Julio," Buenos Aires, 1937.
Carlos M. della Paolera, "Algunos Aspectos de Buenos Aires a Visto de Pájaro," Buenos Aires, 1939.
"Segunda Exposición Municipal de Urbanismo," Dirección del Plan de Urbanización, Buenos Aires, 1939.
Pascual Palazzo, "El Tráfico en Buenos Aires—Red de Vias a Bajo Nivel," Talleres Graficos A. Baiocco y Cia., Buenos Aires, 1933.
Pascual Palazzo, "Trazado y Diseño de la Avenida General Paz, "Dirección Nacional de Vialidad, Buenos Aires, 1940.
"Bulletins and Bibliographies of the Dirección Nacional de Vialidad," (National Highway Department), Buenos Aires.
F. H. Bereterbide, A. B. Blanco, M. Cravotto, J. A. Scasso, "Plan Regulador de la Ciudad de Mendoza—Primera Etapa: Pre-Plan," Editorial Hiperion, Montevideo, Uruguay, 1941.
"Publications of the Dirección de Parques Nacionales" (National Park Department), Buenos Aires.

BOLIVIA

Remberto Capriles R. and Gastón Arduz Eguía, "El Problema Social en Bolivia, "Editorial Fenix, La Paz, Bolivia, 1941.

BRAZIL

"Revista Municipal de Engenharia," Vol. 7, No. 2, March, 1940 and Vol. 8, No. 4, July, 1941, Rio de Janeiro.
Washington Azevedo, "Urbanismo no Brazil," Casa Editora Henrique Velho, Rio de Janeiro, 1934.
Washington Azevedo, "A Organisação Technica dos Municipios," Irmãos Pongetti, Editores, 1935.
Lincoln Continentino, "Saneamento e Urbanismo," Livraria Medica Editora, Rio de Janeiro, 1937.
Oscar Egídio de Araújo, "Uma Pesquisa de Padrão de Vida," Departamento de Cultura, São Paulo, 1941.
J. Marianno, A. Pires Amarante, A. Campello, "O Problema das Favellas no Rio de Janeiro," Rotary Club of Rio de Janeiro, 1941.

CHILE

"Principales Acuerdos y Conclusiones Habidas en el Primer Congreso Nacional de Arquitectura y Urbanismo," Asociación de Arquitectos, Santiago, 1934.
"Bulletins of the Instituto de Urbanismo de Valparaiso."
"Plan Urbanistica para Valparaiso," Instituto de Urbanismo de Valparaiso, May, 1938.
"Memorias: Primer Congreso Chileno de Urbanismo," Instituto de Urbanismo de Valparaiso, 1938.
"Urbanismo y Arquitectura," Official publication of the Asociación de Arquitectos de Chile, Santiago, Chile.
"Bulletins Nos. 2, 3, and 4, Caja de Habitacion Popular," Santiago.

COLOMBIA

Manuel Monsalve, "Medellin, Su Presente y Su Futuro," Medellín, 1941.
"Progreso," Publication of the Sociedad de Mejoras Públicas, Medellín.

MEXICO

Carlos Contreras, "National Planning Project for the Republic of Mexico," Reprinted from "City Planning," July, 1925.

Carlos Contreras, "La Planificación de la Ciudad de Mexico, 1918 to 1938," 16th International Congress on Planning and Housing, Mexico, 1938.

"National Planning Law for Mexico," Ministry of Communications and Public Works, Mexico, D.F., 1930.

"La Legislación Sobre Planificación en la República Mexicana," Departamento del Distrito Federal, Mexico, D.F., 1938.

Luis Prieto Souza and Armando Santacruz, Jr., "Planificación de Nuevo Laredo, Tamaulipas," Dirección General de Bienes Nacionales, Mexico, D.F., 1938.

Edmundo O'Gorman, "Reflecciones Sobre la Distribución Urbana Colonial de la Ciudad de Mexico," 16th International Congress on Housing and Planning, Mexico, 1938.

M. Toussaint, F. Gómez de Orozco, and J. Fernández, "Planos de la Ciudad de Mexico," 16th International Congress on Planning and Housing, 1938.

Unión de Arquitectos Socialistas, "Proyecto de la Ciudad Obrera en Mexico, D.F.," 16th International Congress on Planning and Housing, Mexico, 1938.

"Other publications of the 16th International Congress on Planning and Housing," Mexico, 1938.

Aaron Saenz, "Las Casas Para Obreros y el Departamento del Distrito Federal," Government Printing Office, Mexico, D.F., 1934.

PERU

"El Gobierno Peruano y la Vivienda Obrera," Ministerio de Fomento, Lima.

URUGUAY

"Bulletins Nos. 1 to 7, of the Instituto de Urbanismo, Facultad de Arquitectura," Montevideo, 1937 to 1942.

"Anales de la Facultad de Arquitectura," Montevideo, March, 1941.

Appendix C: Latin American Planning Technicians

ARGENTINA

Srta. Elisa Bachofen, Ingeniera Civil
Córdoba 543
Buenos Aires, Argentina

Fermin Bereterbide
Segurola 3525
Villa De Voto
Buenos Aires, Argentina

Alberto B. Blanco, Arquitecto
Depto. de Arquitectura
Ministerio de Obras Publicas
Avenida 9 de Julio 1925
Buenos Aires, Argentina

Carlos A. Loza Colomer
Facultad de Ingeniería
Universidad de La Plata
La Plata, Argentina

Jorge Kalnay, Arquitecto
San Martín 244
Buenos Aires, Argentina

Luis V. Migone, Ingeniero
Arenales 2428
Buenos Aires, Argentina

Raúl Migone
Ministerio de Relaciones Exteriores y
Culto
Palacio San Martín
Arenales 761
Buenos Aires, Argentina

Benjamín F. Nazar Archorena, Presidente
Comisión de Casas Baratas
San Juan 250
Buenos Aires, Argentina

Pascual Palazzo, Ingeniero
Bartolome Mitre 2977
Buenos Aires, Argentina

Carlos della Paolera, Ingeniero Urbanista
Director del Plan de Urbanización
1427 Calle Pelegrini
Buenos Aires, Argentina

Srta. Carmen Renard, Arquitecto
Estomba 1830
Buenos Aires, Argentina

Julio Rinaldini
Sec. del Plan de Urbanización
1427 Calle Pelegrini
Buenos Aires, Argentina

Jerónimo Rocca
Los Amigos de la Ciudad
651 Diagonal Norte
Buenos Aires, Argentina

Eduardo Sacriste, Jr., Arquitecto
Morelas 38
Buenos Aires, Argentina

Dr. José Lo Valvo
Prof. de Derecho Civil
Universidad Nacional del Litoral
Santa Fé, Argentina

BOLIVIA

Victor Andrade, Gerente
Caja de Seguro Obrero
La Paz, Bolivia

Gastón Arduz
Ministerio de Previsión Social
La Paz, Bolivia

Roberto Azcui, Ingeniero
Avenida Perú 246
La Paz, Bolivia

Jorge Rodriguez Balanza, Arquitecto
Universidad de San Andrés
La Paz, Bolivia

Mario del Carpio G., Arquitecto
Depto. de Urbanismo
Municipio
La Paz, Bolivia

Federico Castillo
Jefe de la Sección Zonificación
Municipalidad
La Paz, Bolivia

Victor Paz Estensoro
Edificio Iglezia
La Paz, Bolivia

Lucio P. Velasco
Depto. de Urbanismo
Municipio
La Paz, Bolivia

Emilio Villanueva, Arquitecto
Casilla 179
La Paz, Bolivia

BRAZIL

Alfredo Agache
Edificio Rex—s/1508
Rua Alvaro Alvim
Rio de Janeiro, Brasil

Dr. Jesuino de Albuquerque
Secretario Geral de Saude e Assistencia
Prefeitura
Rio de Janeiro, Brasil

Moacyr E. Alvaro
IDORT
Rua da Libertade, 470
São Paulo, Brasil

Oscar Araujo
Sub-Divisão de Documentação Social
Depto. de Cultura
Rua Cantareira 216—1°. andar
São Paulo, Brasil

Herminio de Andrade e Silva, Arquiteto
Comissão do Plano da Cidade
Prefeitura
Rio de Janeiro, Brasil

David Azambuja
Av. Nilo Pecanha 151—s/105
Rio de Janeiro, Brasil

Washington Azevedo
Rio de Janeiro, Brasil

Abelardo Coimbra Bueno
Edificio Rex—s/1508
Rua Alvaro Alvim
Rio de Janeiro, Brasil

Americo R. Campello, Arquiteto
Edificio Rex—5°. andar—s/509
Rua Alvaro Alvim
Rio de Janeiro, Brasil

Paulo Candiota, Arquiteto
Instituto dos Maritimos
Edificio Concordia
Av. Rio Branco, 10—9°. andar
Rio de Janeiro, Brasil

Lincoln Continentino
Rua General Camara, 8—2°. andar
Rio de Janeiro, Brasil

Carlos F. Ferreira, Arquiteto
Instituto dos Industriarios—(IAPI)
Castello
Rio de Janeiro, Brasil

Dr. Nestor E. Fiegueiredo
Rua Copacabana 92, Apt. 19
Rio de Janeiro, Brasil

Ulysses Rodriques Hellmeister
Divisão de Engenharia
Instituto dos Comerciarios—(IAPC)
Av. Rio Branco 120—4°. andar
Rio de Janeiro, Brasil

Carlos Leão, Arquiteto
Instituto dos Bancarios—(IAPB)
Castello
Rio de Janeiro, Brasil

Atilio Correa Lima, Arquiteto e Urbanista
Avenida Rio Branco, 181
Rio de Janeiro, Brasil

F. Prestes Maia
Prefeitura
São Paulo, Brasil

Henrique Mindlin, Arquiteto
% Marcelo Roberto
Rua Rodrigo Silva, 11—2°. andar
Rio de Janeiro, Brasil

Oscar Niemayer, Arquiteto
% Ministerio de Educacão
Rio de Janeiro, Brasil

Dr. Edison J. Passos
Secretaria da Viação
Prefeitura
Praça da Republica
Rio de Janeiro, Brasil

Donald Pierson
Depto. de Cultura
Rua Cantareira 216—1°. andar
São Paulo, Brasil

Srta. Carmen Portinho
Distrito de Penha
Rua Graça Aranha 39A—4° andar—
s/304
Rio de Janeiro, Brasil

José Oliveira Reis
Comissão do Plano da Cidade
Rua Benjamin Constant, 123A
Rio de Janeiro, Brasil

Marcelo Roberto, Arquiteto
Rua Rodrigo Silva 11—2°. andar
Rio de Janeiro, Brasil

Mario Torres, Arquiteto
Praia do Botafogo, 48—Apt. 14
Rio de Janeiro, Brasil

CHILE

Largio Arredondo, Arquitecto
Caja de Colonización Agrícola
Casilla 137—D
Santiago, Chile

Tomás de la Barra, Arquitecto
Caja de Habitación Popular
Santiago, Chile

Alberto Bustos, Arquitecto
Dept. de Arquitectura
Caja de Seguro Obrero Obligatorio
Edificio La Nación
Calle Augustinas
Santiago, Chile

Ricardo Gonzáles Cortés, Arquitecto
Morande 322, Of. 606
Santiago, Chile

Emile Duhart H., Arquitecto
Ahumado 236, Of. 610
Santiago, Chile

Roberto Humeres, Jefe
Depto. de Urbanismo
Palacio Municipal
Santiago, Chile

Luis Harding, Arquitecto
Chillan, Chile

Alfredo Johnson, Prof. de Urbanismo
Escuela de Arquitectura
Universidad Católica
Santiago, Chile

Srta. Graciela Mandujano
% Mr. James Wilson, U.S. Embassy
Santiago, Chile (Please forward)

Claudio Muñoz C., Arquitecto
Calle Nueva Orleans 438
Santiago, Chile

Luis Muñoz-Maluschka, Jefe
Depto. de Urbanismo
Ministerio de Fomento
Santiago, Chile

Federico Oehrens, Arquitecto
Calle Claudio Arrau 0230
Santiago, Chile

Rodolfo Oyarsún, Prof. de Urbanismo
Escuela de Arquitectura
Universidad de Chile
Santiago, Chile

Srta. Alice Riedel
Casilla 2621
Santiago, Chile

Santiago Roi, Arquitecto
Oficina 14, Piso 3
Amunategui 73
Santiago, Chile

Theodor Smith-Miller, Arquitecto
Bandera 75, Of. 330
Santiago, Chile

Hector Vigil
Instituto de Urbanismo
Calle Blanco 653
Valparaiso, Chile

COLOMBIA

Ignacio Angel B.
Sección de Planeamiento
Depto. Técnico del Municipio
Medellín, Colombia

Prof. Carlos H. Brunner
Consultante de Planificación
Apartado 143
Bogotá, Colombia

Gabriel Congote M., Jefe
Asuntos Sociales del Municipio de
   Medellín
Palacio Municipal
Medellín, Colombia

Joaquin Martínez
Depto. de Urbanismo
Municipio de Bogotá
Bogotá, Colombia

J. V. Garces Navas, Gerente
Instituto de Credito Territorial
Bogotá, Colombia

Ricardo Olano
64-12 Carrera Balboa
Medellín, Colombia

Julio Ortiz
Administrador de Casas para Traba-
   jordes
Palacio Municipal
Medellín, Colombia

Carlos Uribe Gaviria
Instituto de Acción Social
Carrera 6-11-17
Bogotá, Colombia

Luis Gomez Vargas
Depto. de Urbanismo
Municipio de Bogotá
Bogotá, Colombia

ECUADOR

Miguel Albornoz
Apartado 776
Quito, Ecuador

Jose Benitez, Ingeniero
Chimborazo No. 128
Quito, Ecuador

Eduardo Meno C., Arquitecto
Quito, Ecuador

Prof. Antonino Russo, Arquitecto
Casilla 352
Quito, Ecuador

GUATEMALA

Arturo Bickford, Ingeneiro
Municipalidad de Guatemala
Guatemala, C. A.

MEXICO

Eduardo Arochi, Ingeniero
Comité Ejecutivo de la Comisión
Nacional de la Habitación
Calle Lopez 12
México, D. F.

Salvador Arroyo
Oficina Controladora de Crecimiento
de la Ciudad
Palacio Municipal
México, D. F.

Mauricio Campos
Escuela Nacional de Arquitectura
Academia 22
México, D. F.

Luis D. Cervantes, Ingeniero
Apartado Postal 1662
México, D. F.

Carlos Contreras, Arquitecto
Edificio "La Nacional"
Despacho 1004
Avenida Juarez 4
México, D. F.

Jose A. Cuevas, Ingeniero
Consejero Técnico
Comité Ejecutive de la Plaza de la
República
Ramos Arizpe No. 1
México, D. F.

Jose Luis Cuevas, Arquitecto
Avenida del 5 de Mayo 23, Of. 13
México, D. F.

Enrique Aragón Echeagaray, Arqui-
tecto
Avenida Popocatepetl 9
Hipódromo—Condesa
México, D. F.

Federico E. Mariscal
Presidente del Instituto de Arqui-
tectos
México, D. F.

Juan Palomar, Ingeniero Civil
Calle México 140
Guadalajara, México

Luis Prieto Souza
Dirección General de Bienes Na-
cionales
Secretaría de Hacienda y Credito Pub-
lico
Palacio Nacional
México, D. F.

Vicente Urquiaga, Arquitecto
Consultante de Planificación
Isabel La Católica 24
México, D. F.

PERU

Alberto Alexander R., Ingeniero
Sociedad de Ingenieros
Av. Piérola
Lima, Perú

Lizandro Velasco Astete, Ingeniero
Municipio
Cuzco, Perú

Salvador Boza, Jefe
Depto. de Urbanización
Ministerio de Fomento
Lima, Perú

Rafael Marquina y Bueno, Arquitecto
General La Fuente 521
Lima, Perú

Luis Dorich
Casilla 2326
Lima, Perú

Roberto Haaker Fort, Arquitecto
Servicio Técnico de Arquitectura
Ministerio de Fomento
Lima, Perú

Carlos Montero
Municipalidad
Lima, Perú

Luis Gallo Porras, Alcalde de Lima
Av. Benavides 290
Miraflores
Lima, Perú

Emilio Harth Terre, Arquitecto
Casilla 625
Lima, Perú

URUGUAY

Raul Lerena Acevedo
Depto. de Censo y Inventario
Municipalidad de Montevideo
Montevideo, Uruguay

Mauricio Cravotto, Arquitecto
Director del Instituto de Urbanismo
Sarmiento 2360
Montevideo, Uruguay

Luis Crespi
Dirección de Plan Regulador
Palacio Municipio
Montevideo, Uruguay

233

Juan Giuria, Arquitecto
Instituto de Viviendas Económicas
Paysandu 896
Montevideo, Uruguay

Horacio Acosta y Lara
Intendente Municipal
Montevideo, Uruguay

Carlos Perez Montero, Arquitecto
Cuareim 1471
Montevideo, Uruguay

Ricardo A. Munz
Instituto de Urbanismo,
Facultad de Arquitectura
Cerrito 73
Montevideo, Uruguay

Américo Ricaldoni, Arquitecto
Director del Plan Regulador
Palacio Municipio
Montevideo, Uruguay

Juan Scasso, Arquitecto
Director de Parques y Jardines
Avenida J. M. Ferrai 1301
Carrasco
Montevideo, Uruguay

Cesar Martínez Serra, Arquitecto
25 de Mayo 544
Montevideo, Uruguay

Julio Vilamajó, Arquitecto
Facultad de Arquitectura
Cerrito 73
Montevideo, Uruguay

VENEZUELA

Carlos Raúl Villanueva
Caracas Comisión de Planificación
27 Avenida de los Javillos
La Florida, Caracas, Venezuela

INDEX

A

Acapulco, Mexico, city planning commission, 91

Acevedo, Raul Lerena, 100

Agache, Alfredo, 168

Agriculture, industry vs., 12-14

Air transportation, development of intercontinental, 195-196; shrinking globe, 197-200

Airports, development for intercontinental defense, 195-196; Goiania, Brazil, 123; Santos Dumont Airfield, Rio de Janeiro, 37, 130, 159; São Paulo, 112

Albornoz, Miguel, 208

Andrews, Oscar Alvarez, 72

Angel, Ignacio, 218

Arango, Jorge, 169

Architecture, modern, master plans, 127-130

Argentina, city and regional planning, 94; financial situation in, 53-54; highways, 49; illiteracy in, 56; land use planning, 102; middle class conditions, 73; modern architecture, 129; national planning program, 99; national resources planning, 131; needs of, 210-211; parks, 119; rural housing problems, 85; slum conditions, 73-75; technicians, 161, 165-166; wage level, 54-55; zoning law, 102

Arroyo, Salvador, 218

Assimilation vs. heterogeneity, 8-11

Azambuja, David, 169, 214

Azevedo, Washington, 115, 168-169

B

Bahia, Brazil, founding of, 30-31

Banks, building by, 152

Barra Mansa, Brazil, 103

Bartholomew, Harland, 101, 215

Basic data, collection of, master plans, 100

Bereterbide, Fermin, 218

Bickford, Arturo, 96, 147, 163

Bisson, T. A., 194

Bogotá, Colombia, antiquity of, 20; building boom, 51-52; city housing projects, 146-147; city planning development, 93; founding of, 29; location, effect of, 7; modern architecture, 128; new capital investment, 186-187; school of architecture, 171; slum conditions, 65-66; streets, master plan, 106; subdivision control, 114; technicians, 163; wage level, 55; zoning law, 101-102

Bolívar, Simón, 31, 32

Bolivia, city planning development, 93-94; development of resources, 188; illiteracy in, 56; national planning agency, 98; needs of, 208-209; refugees, influx of, 192; slum conditions, 67-68; social security housing, 145-146

Brazil, anti-Axis reactions, 183-184; building industry, lack of, 80-81; citizen influence, 178-179; city planning development, 95-96; development of resources, 188-191; illiteracy in, 56; landscape architecture, 169, 214; modern architecture, 129-

235

239

Traffic, master plans, 104-113; problems, 48-49
Transportation problems, 48-49
Tschopik, Harry and Marian, 26

U

Ubico, Jorge, 96, 163
University of Bogotá, 171
University of Buenos Aires, 172
University of Chile, 171
Urban development, beginning of, 36; Colombia, 44
Urban planning, circulation, streets, traffic, 104-113; collection of basic data and background information, 100; earthquake replanning, 124-127; land use planning and zoning, 101-104; modern architecture, 127-130; new cities, 123-124; parks and recreation, 115-121; public buildings, 121-123; subdivision control and neighborhoods, 113-115
Urquiaga, Vicente, 105
Uruguay, economic problems, 54; government housing, 136-137; illiteracy in, 56; modern architecture, 129; national planning program, 99; national resources planning, 131-132; recreation program, 121; schools of architecture, 172; slum conditions, 75-76; technicians, 161; wage level, 54-55

V

Vargas, Luis Gomez, 169, 214
Vera Cruz, Mexico, city planning commission, 91; founding of, 29
Vigil, Hector, 161, 165, 210, 219
Vilamajó, Julio, 121, 129, 167
Vilar, Antonio, 129
Villanueva, Emilio, 164
Volta Redonda, Brazil, 103

W

Wages, low level of, 54-55; rural, 84
Wallace, Henry, 221
Warchavcik, Gregory, 129
Waterfront treatment, 203
Weir, Walter, 215
Weiss, Carlos Dunkelburg, 169
Williams, Paul, 215
Willkie, Wendell, 200
World War II, focus on the home front, 184-192; focus on U.S., 192-195; Latins and, 181-184; new inter-continental unity, 195-196

Y

Yumbel, Chile, earthquake replanning, 126

Z

Zoning, master plans, 101-104